THE COMMAND BOOK

ISBN 0-940296-58-6

Written by
Stephen Mark Silvers

Edited by James J. Asher

**Published by
Sky Oaks Productions, Inc.
P.O. Box 1102
Los Gatos, California 95031**

Copyright 1988
All Rights Reserved. No part of this publication may be reproduced, stored in a retrieval system or transmitted in any form or by any means: electronic, magnetic tape, mechanical, photocopying, recording or otherwise, without permission in writing from an executive officer of **Sky Oaks Productions, Inc.**

Acknowledgements

I would like to acknowledge with gratitude the administration of the University of Amazonas and my Department (Foreign Language), for the opportunity to work on this book. I would also like to thank Dr. James J. Asher for his encouragement throughout the project.

Dedicated to

my wife Neusa

my children Paula, Sergio and David

my mother and the memory of my father

CONTENTS

                                                               Page

Preface 4

Introduction 6

The Commands .... 22—259

Appendixes .... 260—293

    A — Cardboard Cutouts 260

    B — Picture Cards 265

    C — Cue Cards 278

    D — Operatives 287

    E — Races and Contests 292

Other TPR Materials   293

PREFACE

There are two motives that led to the development of this book. In the first place, I felt a personal need for a data bank of commands which would facilitate my work in the design and production of Total Physical Response (TPR) courses and teaching materials. In the second place, I wished to provide ESL/EFL teachers with a handy reference book that would permit them to select commands for supplementary exercises based on the specific vocabulary of whatever textbook he or she is teaching. Thus **The Command Book** is intended as a reference book, not only for teachers who are using Total Physical Response as the principal method but also for those who are using other methods or approaches, such as Audio-Lingual, Communicative, Notional-Functional, etc., and would like to include a TPR component.

To this end, three sources were used for the selection of the commands: (a) numerous EFL textbooks, (b) the **New Horizon Ladder Dictionary,** and (c) the **Cambridge English Lexicon.**

Although TPR is generally associated with beginners, our experience has been that, when used as supplementary exercises, intermediate and even relatively advanced students enjoy and benefit from this approach, which accounts for the inclusion of some vocabulary items normally not presented in the beginning stages. One of the reasons for using TPR with post-beginners is, I believe, the fact that vocabulary learned using the muscular-motor system tends to be retained much longer.

With a view towards improving this and future works, I would welcome and appreciate comments and suggestions on the materials presented. I can be contacted at the following addresses and phone numbers:

Home
Stephen Mark Silvers ("Gil")
Rua Silva Ramos, 665
69.000 Manaus, AM —
BRAZIL

tel. (092) 2323637

Work
Dept. de Linguas Estrangeiras
Universidade do Amazonas
Campus Universitario
Estrada do Aleixo
69.000 Manaus, AM
—BRAZIL

tel. (092) 2378875

INTRODUCTION

The Command Book is a resource book of TPR commands for ESL/EFL teachers. It presumes that the teacher is familiar with both the rationale and the techniques of the TPR approach to language instruction. For detailed information on the theory and the practice of this method, please refer to James Asher's **Learning Another Language Through Actions: the Complete Teacher's Guidebook,** and Ramiro Garcia's **Instructor's Notebook: How to Apply TPR for Best Results,** both published by Sky Oaks Productions. I would also recommend viewing the films produced by Dr. Asher (see pages 294 to 304).

The Command Book presents over 2000 entry forms. Since each entry consists of 1-5 commands, each one itself frequently having several variations, **The Command Book** offers literally thousands of commands that can be used to introduce, practice, and reinforce the vocabulary and the grammatical structures found in most beginning and intermediate ESL/EFL textbooks.

For each entry form an attempt has been made, as far as possible, to present commands representing its various meanings and grammatical functions. For example, for the entry *back* you will find commands in which it functions as (a) a noun (Touch your back); (b) an adjective (Touch the back wall); (c) an adverb (Throw the ball back); and (d) a verb (Back the car to the door).

The entry forms are printed in bold type and the commands are separated by numbers in italics. In most of the commands you will find other words in parentheses that can be substituted into the original command, thereby greatly increasing the number of commands you can make. For example, in the command

Hold a book (magazine, notebook) against
your chest,

7

you could replace the word *book* with *magazine* or *notebook*.

Since nearly all of the words used in the commands are also included as entry forms, you can find other related commands by looking these words up. Thus for the above example, you will find other commands listed under *hold, book, magazine, notebook, against,* and *chest.* By this system of cross-reference you can "spin a web" of links between commands.

Frequently the commands presented consist of a series of two or more short commands:

Pick up the circle, show it to the class, and put it down.

Depending on your objectives and on the stage of listening comprehension your students have reached, you could present the series as one long command or you could break it up into short commands, pausing after each one for the students to perform the actions.

Some of the commands require a prior preparation of the command situation; that is, in some cases you will first have to give the students one or more commands to "set the stage" before they will be able to perform the command as given in the book:

Jump to the student who can't see because her glasses are on the table.

Before giving this command, you would first have to command a student to take off her glasses and put them on the table.

Often the Total Physical Response takes the form of a simple drawing. As you can see from the example below, no artistic talent is needed or expected.

Draw a man at the bottom of a stairs.

Frequently the commands require the students to pretend or to use pantomime:

> Pour yourself a cup of coffee.

If you can actually have coffee in your classroom, so much the better, but normally this will not be the case. The use of pantomime and imaginative "make believe" permits the students to perform a great number of commands that would otherwise be impossible.

Many of the commands can be performed without anything other than the objects you normally find in a classroom, including the students' objects of personal use:

> Erase the chalkboard.
> Take off your watch.

Other commands use simple, easily obtainable props. These props, along with explanatory comments, are listed on pages 11 to 18.

With the exception of the commands that use picture cards or cue cards (explained later), the commands do not specify the props to be used. What you will need will be apparent from the commands themselves:

> Put the thin book under the thick book.

Evidently for this command you will need both a thin book and a thick one.

Still other commands use (a) cardboard cutouts, (b) picture cards, (c) teacher-made cue cards, and (d) student-made cue cards.

a. cardboard cutouts. Various commands make use of cardboard cutouts of cars, fish, ties, geometric figures, etc.:

> Drive the red car to the door.
> Put on the narrow tie.

These easy-to-make cutouts are described in **Appendix A**.

b. picture cards. Many commands are coordinated to picture cards representing occupations or places:

Shake hands with the mechanic *(pc)*.

Wave to the student who's at church *(pc)*.

The symbol *(pc)* indicates that these commands use picture cards. **Appendix B** presents 75 simple drawings of occupations and places that you can copy to make your own set of picture cards for these commands.

c. teacher-made cue cards. These are similar to the picture cards except that they have written rather than pictorial cues:

Hop to the student who speaks French *(cc-5)*.

The parenthetical information *(cc-5)* tells you that for this command you would use Cue Card Set No. 5. **Appendix C** presents thirteen sets of cue cards for you to make, dealing with numbers, money, languages, etc.

d. student-made cue cards. These are similar to the teacher-made cue cards, except that the students make them themselves using information from their own lives. For example, to use the command

Swim to the student who gets up at 7:30 *(student-made cc)*,

you would distribute strips of paper or light cardboard (so that all of the cards are of a uniform size) and instruct the students to write the time they get up, preferably with a marking pen or a dark crayon.

In addition to the three appendixes described above, there are two other appendixes to facilitate your use of TPR in the classroom. **Appendix D** presents a set of operatives, that is, commands that one student can perform on or in relation to another student, thereby creating situations of student interaction. And **Appendix E** presents thirty classroom races and contests.

Assembling the Props

Below you will find a list of all of the props used in the commands. Although the list is somewhat extensive, the objects are not difficult to find, and the effort spent in obtaining them will certainly prove to be worthwhile. Ideally you would make a TPR "kit" by assembling these props and storing them at your school, preferably in your classroom. If this is not possible, you may wish to make and use cardboard cutouts.

To make the cutouts, either glue magazine pictures to light cardboard, or if you are artistically inclined, draw your own pictures of the objects you wish to represent. Then cut them out and have them laminated or covered with a clear adhesive plastic.

The items marked with an asterisk should be obtained as empty containers (see Notes on the Props). As you obtain each object, or make a cardboard cutout, check it off on the list below.

List of Props

__ airplane
__ almanac
__ aluminum foil
__ ambulance
__ anniversary card
__ apple
__ apron
__ ashtray
__ aspirin
__ baby bottle
__ baby food *(jar)**
__ badge
__ ball

__ balloons
__ banana
__ Band-Aids
__ bar of soap
__ baseball bat *(plastic)*
__ basket
__ batteries
__ beads *(about 10)*
__ beans *(can)**
__ beard
__ beer *(can)**
__ bell
__ bib

11

- binoculars
- birthday card
- blindfold
- blocks
- board
- boat
- bolt *(for nut)*
- bone *(rubber)*
- books
- bottle
- bottle caps *(about 15)*
- bottle opener
- bow tie
- bowl
- box
- bracelet
- Brillo pad
- brooch
- broom
- bubble gum
- bus
- butter dish
- buttons
- calculator
- camera
- can
- can opener
- candle
- candy
- candy bar
- canoe
- cap *(hat)*
- cape
- car
- carbon paper
- carrot

- catalogue
- cereal *(box)**
- chain
- chalk
- checkbook
- cheese *(rubber)*
- Christmas card
- cigar
- cigarette lighter
- clock
- clothespin
- coffee *(jar)**
- coffee pot
- coins (about 10)
- cold cream *(jar)**
- comb
- comic book
- compass *(directions)*
- compass *(drawing)*
- cookies
- cork
- corn *(can)**
- corn cob
- cotton balls
- cough medicine*
- crackers
- crayons
- cream *(packet)**
- creamer
- crown
- cucumber
- cup
- cylinders
- deck of cards
- dice
- dictionary

__ doll
__ drum
__ duster
__ earring
__ envelopes
__ eraser
__ extension cord
__ eyedropper
__ fan *(manual)*
__ feather
__ firetruck
__ fish cards
__ flag
__ flashlight
__ flower *(plastic)*
__ flute
__ fork
__ fried egg *(rubber)*
__ fruit drink*
__ frying pan
__ funnel
__ furniture polish*
__ geometric figures
__ get-well card
__ glass
__ glove
__ glue
__ graduation card
__ grapes
__ guitar
__ gun
__ hairbrush
__ hairpins
__ hammer
__ handkerchief
__ hanger

__ harp
__ hat
__ horn
__ ice-cream cone
__ iron
__ jacks
__ jar
__ jeep
__ jigsaw puzzle
__ jug
__ kettle
__ key
__ key chain
__ knife
__ knitting needles
__ lemon
__ lipstick
__ lock
__ magazine
__ magnifying glass
__ mask
__ match boxes
__ matches
__ menu
__ milk bottle
__ milk carton
__ mints
__ mirror
__ modeling clay
__ motorcycle
__ mouse
__ mustache
__ nail clippers
__ nail file
__ nail polish*
__ nails

13

___ napkins
___ necklace
___ needle
___ newspaper
___ notebook
___ nut *(for bolt)*
___ nutcracker
___ nuts *(food)*
___ oil can*
___ onion
___ orange
___ orange peel
___ pack of cigarettes
___ package
___ pail
___ paintbrush *(artist)*
___ paintbrush *(house)*
___ pamphlet
___ pan
___ paper bag
___ paper clips
___ paper cups
___ paper plates
___ paper towels
___ peach
___ pear
___ peas *(can)**
___ pebbles *(about 10)*
___ peeler
___ pen
___ pencil
___ pencil sharpener
___ pepper shaker
___ perfume *(bottle)**
___ piano
___ pillow

___ pineapple
___ pipe *(smoking)*
___ pipe *(tube)*
___ pitcher
___ plate
___ play money
___ pliers
___ postage stamps
___ postcard
___ pot
___ potato
___ protractor
___ purse
___ radio
___ rag
___ raisins
___ rake
___ rattle
___ razor
___ record
___ ribbons
___ rice *(box)**
___ rifle
___ ring
___ rock
___ rods
___ rope
___ rubber bands
___ rubber stamp set
___ ruler
___ sack
___ safety pin
___ salt
___ salt shaker
___ sandpaper
___ saucer

- __ saw
- __ scarf
- __ scissors
- __ screw
- __ screwdriver
- __ scrub brush
- __ seeds
- __ shampoo *(tube)**
- __ shaving cream*
- __ shaving lotion*
- __ ship
- __ shoe polish*
- __ shotgun
- __ shovel
- __ soap dish
- __ soap powder *(box)**
- __ sock
- __ soda pop *(can)**
- __ soup *(can)**
- __ soup *(package)**
- __ spade
- __ spider
- __ sponge
- __ spools
- __ spoon
- __ squirt gun
- __ stamp pad
- __ stapler
- __ stethoscope
- __ sticks
- __ stone
- __ stove
- __ straws
- __ string
- __ sugar bowl
- __ suitcase

- __ sunglasses
- __ sword
- __ syringe
- __ tank *(army)*
- __ tape
- __ tape measure
- __ tape recorder
- __ tea bags
- __ telephone
- __ telescope
- __ television
- __ tennis ball
- __ test tube
- __ thermometer
- __ thread
- __ thumbtacks
- __ tie
- __ tissue
- __ tomato
- __ toothbrush
- __ toothpaste *(tube)**
- __ toothpicks
- __ top *(toy)*
- __ towel
- __ tractor
- __ tray
- __ trophy
- __ truck
- __ tuna *(can)**
- __ twine
- __ umbrella *(toy)*
- __ vase
- __ veil
- __ wall calendar
- __ wallet
- __ wallet calendar

15

__ watch
__ watering pot
__ whistle
__ wig
__ wire *(metal)*

__ world map
__ wrapping paper
__ wrench
__ writing tablet
__ yarn

Notes on the Props

The props used in the commands are all inexpensive objects, many of which can be found in your own home. Others can be obtained at a supermarket, a hardware store, a department store, or a toy store. Still others you can make yourself (see **Appendix A**).

As you go about obtaining the props, keep in mind the following four characteristics: they should be **small, light, unbreakable,** and **safe.** You want props that are big enough to be easily manipulated, yet small and light enough to permit them to be easily stored and transported. For items that are naturally very small, for example, the dice or the beads, you will want to use a fairly large size. Whenever possible, use objects that are unbreakable. Finally, pay attention to the safety factor: the scissors and the knife should have rounded tips; the syringe shouldn't have a needle; the razor shouldn't have a blade.

Toys that imitate real objects make particularly good props; in fact, many of the items on the list, such as the stove, ambulance, guitar, stethoscope, mouse, etc., only make sense when considered as toys. Even when you theoretically could use the real object, common sense will often dictate that you use a toy: bringing a real broom, suitcase, or milk bottle to class would normally prove to be highly impractical, if not clearly impossible.

In many cases an empty container, that is, an empty can, bottle, box, tube, or jar, with its label, makes an effective prop. Those items which could be obtained as empty containers have been marked with an asterisk (some of them can also be found as toys).

I have included several food items that can be used as real objects: candy, cookies, crackers, raisins. These items will keep for quite some time without spoiling and make nice rewards for the races and contests suggested in **Appendix E.**

Several of the props are quite small, e.g., the beads, pebbles, nails, seeds, etc., and should be stored in small plastic containers.

Some of the props need a little explanation:

aspirin — small bottle of aspirin tablets
batteries — for flashlight, tape recorder
blocks — about 5, child's toy
board — thick enough to pound a nail into
bottle — plastic, liquid detergent or similar
box — small, with a lid
buttons — several square and round ones
can — powdered milk or similar. Use with the lid.
cape — from child's Superman costume
checkbook — Mimeograph the checks and make the cover from construction paper.
clock — educational toy or made from pasteboard
cylinders — 6 cylinders from toilet paper rolls, each painted a different color
food cutouts — magazine cutouts of dishes such as fried chicken, roast beef, etc.
jar — small jar with a lid
jigsaw puzzle — not more than 10 large pieces
match boxes — about 8 small ones
nails — short nails to pound into the board
orange peel — dried out orange peel
package — small box wrapped up as a package
radio — small, battery operated
ribbons — several of different colors and lengths

rods — several rods of different lengths and colors
rope — should be fairly long
rubber stamp set — child's toy
seeds — dried watermelon seeds or similar
spools — 6 thread spools, each painted a different color
sticks — 3 of different lengths and thicknesses
stove — child's toy with oven door that opens and closes
string — ball of kite string
tape — Scotch tape or masking tape
test tube — from child's chemistry set
wire — several short pieces of stiff wire that can be bent into different shapes
yarn — several small balls of different colors

a few *1.* Draw a few (many, several) circles (squares, triangles, clouds, flowers). *2.* Touch (shake hands with, point to, say hello to) a few (many) students. *3.* Jump (hop, blink, clap) a few times.

a lot of *1.* Draw a lot of (a few) hearts (diamonds, triangles, stars). *2.* Give a lot of (some, several) bottle caps (clips, small paper balls) to Maria. *3.* Swim (run, jump) to a student who has a lot of (much, very little) money *(cc-9)*.

abbreviate Abbreviate these words: *mister, December, New York, company.*

able Shake hands with the student who was able to walk to the door balancing a book on his head (touch his toes without bending his knees).

about *1.* Stick your hand into the bag and take out about eight bottle caps (clips). *2.* Without counting, quickly draw about twenty circles (triangles). *3.* Show the class a book about history (math). *4.* Look (run, walk) about the room.

about to Touch (kick, pinch) the student who's about to open the door (close the window, erase the chalkboard, turn on the lights, draw a circle, shake hands with Pedro).

above *1.* Write a number above ten but below fifteen. *2.* Draw an airplane (a butterfly) flying above (below) some clouds.

abrupt *1.* Run (jump, swim) around the class and come to an abrupt stop. *2.* Smile at the students in the class and then abruptly become angry (sad, nervous, afraid).

absent *1.* Shout (whisper, sing, write) the name of a student who's absent (present) today. *2.* Pull the hair (nose, left ear) of a student who was (wasn't) absent yesterday.

absorb Pick up an object that will (won't) absorb water *(e.g., the sponge, pencil).*

accent Speak your native language with an American accent.

accept Maria, Pedro is going to give you a present. Accept it with a smile (frown, grin).

accident When Pedro crashes his car into the wall (door, desk), Maria will drive the ambulance to the scene of the accident and take him to the hospital *(pc).*

accompany *1.* Accompany me to the door (window, desk, chalkboard). *2.* Maria is going to sing for us. Accompany her on the guitar.

accuse Pedro, go out of the room. While you're out, one of your classmates will take your pen. When the class calls you back, accuse the student that you think did it.

across *1.* Wave to (pinch) the student (person) who's sitting across from (opposite) Pedro. *2.* Jump (walk) across the class. *3.* Draw a street on the floor in chalk and then walk across the street. *4.* Draw a bridge across the river you just drew.

act *1.* Act like a clown (drunk, cowboy). *2.* Act as if you were drunk (crazy). *3.* You're sick. Take some medicine *(empty container).* The medicine has acted quickly and now you feel better, so smile.

action *1.* You will perform some actions and the class will try to guess what you're doing. *2.* Perform an action that begins with the letter that I call out. *(If the teacher says "r," the student could run or read.)*

actor *1.* Make a list of five famous actors and a movie they acted (starred) in. *2.* Write the name of your favorite actor on a slip of paper and put it in Pedro's pocket. *3.* Scratch the back of the actor *(pc).*

actress 1. Propose to (give the flower to, touch the nose of) the actress *(pc). 2.* Write the name of an actress whose name begins with the letter "m."

add *1.* Add the numbers seven and three. *2.* Pick up the coffee pot and pour yourself a cup of coffee. Take a sip and make a face. The coffee is bitter. Add some more sugar.

address *1.* Write your address and draw a rectangle (circle) around it. *2.* Jump (throw the ball) to the student whose address is 2330 Elm Street *(student-made cc). 3.* Address the envelope.

adjust Adjust the volume on the tape recorder (television, radio). *(One student pretends she's the radio and her voice goes up or down as another student pretends he's adjusting the volume.)*

admit Pedro, go out of the room. When he knocks (bangs,

pounds) on the door, Maria will go and admit him (let him in).

adult Draw a picture that has two adults and three children in it.

advance Advance (move, walk, go) forward three big (small) steps.

advertisement Find (cut out) an advertisement for cigarettes (cars, clothing, furniture, food) and show it to the class.

afford Hop (walk, point) to the student who can (can't) afford to buy a new car (house, watch, radio) *(cc-9)*.

afraid When Pedro makes an angry face (pretends he's a monster, aims the gun at you), you will become afraid and run away (hide behind the desk).

after *1.* Stand in line after (before, behind) Maria. *2.* Write the number that comes after (before) ten. *3.* After you clap (stamp your feet, shake your head), point to the ceiling (cry, laugh). *4.* Go out of the room and come back after two minutes.

afternoon Write the name of a program that's on television in the afternoon (morning, evening).

again *1.* Count to ten (touch your nose, hop around the desk). Now do it again. *2.* Pull Maria's hair, laugh and pull her hair again. *3.* Shake hands with Pedro and go back (return) to your seat. Now stand up and shake hands with him again.

against *1* Lean against the wall (door, desk, teacher). *2.*

Hold a book (magazine, notebook) against your chest. 3. Pretend you're swimming against a strong current. 4. Write the names of two teams that are going to play against each other tonight.

age *1.* Write your age on the chalkboard and draw a circle around (under, over, next to) it. *2.* Hop to a student who's twice Pedro's age *(cc-1)*.

ago Jump (walk, run) to the event that happened (occurred, took place) twenty years ago *(cc-7)*.

agree *1.* If you agree with what I say, nod. *2.* Copy the sentences I wrote on the chalkboard and check off the ones you agree with.

ahead *1.* Stand (get) in line ahead of (behind) Maria. *2.* We're going to walk to the door (window, desk) together. Walk ahead of (next to, behind) me.

aim *1.* Aim the rifle (gun) at Pedro and shoot him. *2.* Aim the camera at Maria and take her picture. *3.* Blindfold Pedro, spin him around three times, and aim him at the door.

air *1.* Blow some air into the balloon and then let it out. *2.* Throw the ball (block, comb, eraser) into the air and catch it. *3.* Draw two birds, one in the air and the other on the ground.

airplane *1.* Extend your arms, pretend you're an airplane, and fly around the class. *2.* Draw an upside-down airplane (an airplane taking off, landing). *3.* Make a paper airplane and fly it.

airport Fly the plane (drive the car, push Pedro) to the airport *(pc)*.

alike *1.* Write two words that sound alike (similar). *2.* Draw a picture of two men (women, boys, girls, cars) that look alike (that are very different).

alive Write (print, whisper, shout) the name of a famous author (actor, singer, actress, statesman, scientist, composer) who is (isn't) alive today.

all *1.* Put all of the bottle caps in Pedro's pocket. *2.* Touch all (some, most, a few) of the objects that are on the desk. *3.* Hit all of the students in the last row. *4.* Point to all six students who are behind the desk. *5.* Smile at the girl who's sitting all alone.

allow *1.* Draw a sign showing (indicating) that smoking isn't allowed (permitted). *2.* Pedro, Carlos, and Ricardo, go out of the class. Maria, when they knock on the door, allow (don't allow) them to come back in.

almanac Open the almanac and find the population of France (Spain, Brazil).

almost *1.* Find a student who's almost as tall as Pedro. *2.* When it's almost 2:15, stand up and clap (cry). *3.* Draw a line that's almost (nearly) as long as the line that Maria drew. *4.* Cut off a piece of string that's almost (not quite) ten inches long.

alone *1.* Throw (toss, roll) the ball to the student who's sitting alone. *2.* Hop (jump) to the chalkboard (door, fan, window, desk) alone (with a friend).

along *1.* Draw some trees (houses, flowers) along a river. *2.* Draw a road on the chalkboard and then drive the toy car along the road. *3.* Come along with me to the window (door, fan). *4.* Take a booklet (card, answer sheet) and pass along the rest.

alongside Stand alongside of someone who's wearing a watch (beard, bracelet, necklace; something red).

aloud Read the sentences in your book aloud (silently to yourself).

alphabet *1.* Write the first (second, last, next to the last) letter of the alphabet and give it to Maria. *2.* Write (say) the alphabet backwards as fast as you can.

alphabetical Put the words you see on the chalkboard in alphabetical order.

alphabetize Alphabetize the list of words you see on the chalkboard.

already Shove (stand on the feet of, cut the hair of) the student who has already finished (is about to finish) her drawing (the exercises).

also *1.* Maria has a number under twenty *(cc-12).* Pedro, if your number is also under twenty, point to your nose. If not, jump up and down. *2.* Hop (swim, run) to a student who speaks Spanish *(cc- 5).* Now skip to another student who also speaks Spanish.

aluminum foil *1.* Wrap the potato (carrot) in aluminum foil. *2.* Crumple a piece of aluminum foil into a ball and throw it to a student who's wearing a tie (watch, necklace; glasses).

always *1.* Write the name of a television program that you always (never) watch. 2. If you always have a big breakfast (get up early, go to bed late), raise your left hand (right foot).

ambulance Drive (speed, rush) the ambulance to the hospital *(pc)* (door, chalkboard, window, teacher, student lying on the desk).

among *1.* Draw a kite (bird, butterfly) among some clouds. *2.* Draw a circle among some stars (hearts, triangles, squares). *3.* Write three names that are among the most common in your country. *4.* Divide these cards among the students in your group.

amount *1.* Pour a small (large) amount of water into the cup (glass, bowl). *2.* Pick up the play money and give a small (large, generous) amount to the student who has a beard. *3.* Give some money to Maria and then give a greater amount to Pedro.

amuse Maria, pretend you're sad. Pedro, pretend you're a clown and try to amuse her (make her smile).

anchor Draw a ship with an anchor resting on the bottom of the sea (hanging over its side).

angel Stand in front of the angel *(pc)* and pray (light the candle, sing a song).

angle *1.* Draw a geometric figure with three angles. *2.* Use your protractor to draw a forty-degree angle. *3.* Pretend you're a photographer and take a picture of Maria from different angles.

angry *1.* You're angry. Shake your fist (pound on your desk, slam your book shut). *2.* Make (draw) an angry face. *3.* Give the teacher an angry look.

animal *1.* Draw (imitate) an animal that lives in the ocean (lives in a tree, crawls, flys, eats plants, eats other animals). *2.* Write the name of an animal that begins with the letter "d."

ankle *1.* Touch (point to) one (both) of your ankles. *2.* Jump to the door (window, teacher) holding the ball between your ankles (knees). *3.* Tie the rope (ribbon, string) around your ankle (wrist). *4.* Tie (bind) Pedro's ankles together.

anniversary Today's Pedro's wedding anniversary. Give him the wedding anniversary card.

announce *1.* Maria, go out of the class. Pedro, pretend you're a butler. When Maria knocks on the door, go see who's at the door and then announce her name to the class. *2.* Announce the winner of the election to the class.

announcement Please give me your attention. I'm going to make an announcement.

another *1.* Draw a circle (heart, star). Now draw another one. *2.* Hit (kick, touch, point to, wink at, smile at) a student. Now hit another student. *3.* Brazil is a country in South America. Write the name of another South American country.

answer *1.* Answer my questions by nodding for "yes" and shaking your head for "no." *2.* Add the numbers five and four, and then draw a circle around your answer. *3.* Check your answers to see if they're correct. *4.* Count the students who answered correctly.

ant Draw an ant and pretend you're crushing it with your thumb.

any *1.* Hop (jump, swim, run) to a student who doesn't have any money *(cc-9)*. *2.* If there aren't any books (papers, notebooks, bottle caps) on the teacher's desk, scratch your nose (arm, chin). But if there are, then sneeze (cough, hum).

anybody *1.* Shake hands with all the students in the class, but don't shake hands with anybody wearing glasses (a beard, something green). *2.* Throw (toss, roll, hand) the ball to a friend. Choose anybody you wish.

anyone Stand in front of someone, but don't stand in front of anyone whose name begins with the letter "m" (ends with the letter "o," has seven letters).

anything Walk to a student who doesn't have anything on her desk and pull her nose (cut her hair, draw a picture of her).

anywhere Sit (stand) anywhere you wish.

apart *1.* Sit (stand) apart from the rest of the class. *2.* Take the flashlight apart and put it back together.

apartment *1.* Make a list of (count) the students in the class who live in an apartment. *2.* Comb (cut, brush) the hair of a student who lives in an apartment. *3.* Drive the car (bus, jeep, truck) to the apartment *(pc)*.

apologize Bump into a student (step on a student's toes) and apologize by saying, "I'm sorry."

appear *1.* Walk around a student who appears (looks,

seems) sad (happy, angry, upset). 2. Pedro, go out of the room. When he appears in the doorway (window), I want everybody to stand up and clap (wave to him, make a face at him).

applaud *1.* After Maria and Pedro dance a tango (sing a duet), everybody will stand up and applaud. *2.* Applaud the student who could (was able to) throw a raisin in the air and catch it in his mouth.

applause After Maria finishes (gets done) singing (erasing the chalkboard, pretending she's a cat), give her a big round of applause.

apple *1.* Slice (peel, bite into) the apple. *2.* Put the apple on your head and walk around the class.

apply Gently squeeze Pedro's hand. Now apply some pressure.

appointment Pick up the phone, call the doctor (dentist) *(pc's),* and make an appointment for tomorrow.

approach *1.* Approach the teacher from behind (the rear, a side). *2.* Draw a castle on top of a mountain whose only approach is a long winding path.

approximately *1.* Write the name of a city (town) that is approximately fifty kilometers from here. *2.* Stick your hand into the bag and take out approximately ten bottle caps. *3.* Jump (hop, clap) for approximately (exactly) twenty seconds.

apron *1.* You're a maid. Put on the apron, pick up the broom, and sweep the floor. *2.* Draw a woman wearing an apron.

architect Take a sheet of paper to the architect *(pc)* and have him design (draw) a house (bridge, church, castle).

area *1.* Calculate the area of the square (rectangle) that I drew on the chalkboard. *2.* On a map of your country locate an area where many (few) people live.

argue Pedro and Carlos, you are arguing. Shake your fist at each other.

arm *1.* Hit (tap, slap) Pedro on the arm two times. *2.* Tie the ribbon (rope, string) around my (your) arm. *3.* Draw a man with long (short) arms. *4.* Draw a woman. Make one arm longer (shorter) than the other. *5.* Measure your teacher's left arm.

army *1.* I want this group (row) of students to pretend they're soldiers in the army. Stand up, form a single (double) column, and march around the class. *2.* You're in the army and I'm an officer. Salute me.

around *1.* Run around the desk. *2.* Turn (spin) around two times. *3.* Turn the teacher around. *4.* Everybody, stand (form a square) around Maria. *5.* Tie the string around my wrist. *6.* Shake hands with around half of the class. *7.* Draw a circle (diamond) around the sum of the numbers you added.

arrange *1.* Arrange the bottle caps (toothpicks, coins, matches, students) into a square (triangle, circle). *2.* Look at the papers scattered on my desk. Please arrange them for me.

arrest You're a policeman. Put on the badge, arrest the

student who's wearing the mask, and take him to the jail *(pc)*.

arrive *1.* Wave to (smile at, shake hands with) the student who just arrived. *2.* Stand up and slowly walk around the class. When you arrive at your seat, clap (sneeze, cough, sigh) twice and then sit down.

arrow *1.* Draw an arrow through (pointing to) a heart (tree, fat man, hat). *2.* Draw a circle with three curved arrows.

article Pick up the newspaper and cut out an article about sports (politics, food, crime, television).

artist *1.* Give the artist *(pc)* a pencil (pen, crayon) and have her draw your picture. *2.* Write (whisper, shout, print) the name of a famous artist.

as *1.* Do as I do. *2.* Run (swim) to a student who was born in the same month as Maria *(student-made cc)*. *3.* Touch a student whose name has the same number of letters (begins with the same letter) as yours. *4.* As Pedro walks around the class, everybody will clap (sing). *5.* As it's almost time for the bell, close your books.

as ... as *1.* Find a student who's as tall as the teacher. *2.* Throw the paper ball as far as you can.

as if *1.* Walk as if you were drunk (dizzy, injured). *2.* Hold your head as if you had a headache.

as soon as As soon as Maria walks in the door (arrives, sits down), raise your right hand (shake your head, applaud, lay your head on your desk).

ashtray *1.* Empty the ashes from the ashtray into the wastebasket. *2.* Make a few tiny paper balls and put them in the ashtray. *3.* Tap some ashes from your cigarette (pipe) into the ashtray.

aside *1.* Draw a flower (heart, happy face, fat man; your teacher) on the chalkboard. Now stand aside so that everybody can see what you drew. *2.* Pull Maria aside and whisper something in her ear.

ask *1.* Ask Pedro what time it is. *2.* Ask Maria to stand up (close the door, open the window, erase the chalkboard). *3.* If there's any word you don't know (recognize; aren't familiar with), please ask me.

asleep *1.* Pretend you're asleep (sleeping) and suddenly wake up. *2.* Pretend you're asleep. Smile, you're having a pleasant dream.

aspirin Hold your head as if you had a terrible headache. Now take two aspirin tablets and smile because you feel better.

assemble *1.* Mix up the pieces of the jigsaw puzzle. Now assemble the puzzle. *2.* I want the boys to assemble in the front of the class and the girls to assemble in the back.

assignment *1.* Turn (hand) in your homework assignment. *2.* Sing a song to (throw a piece of chalk at) the student who left (forgot) his homework assignment at home.

assist Maria's going to erase the chalkboard (pass out the papers, move the desk, collect the tests). Please assist (help) her.

associate Draw a picture of something that you associate with the words I say. For example, if I say "coffee," you could draw a cup.

at *1.* Stand at the desk (chalkboard, door, window). *2.* Touch the student who's at church *(pc)*. *3.* Throw the paper ball at me. *4.* Laugh at the student who's jumping. *5.* Swim to the student who gets up (has dinner, goes to sleep) at 7:30 *(student-made cc)*.

at once Close the door (open the window, stoop in front of the desk, draw a tall man). Do (don't do) it at once.

attach Draw a picture of your teacher and attach (fasten) it to the wall (door) with a thumbtack (some tape).

attack *1.* Attack me with the sword (gun). *2.* Pretend you're Indians attacking.

attempt *1.* Attempt to write your name with your left hand. *2.* Make (set up) a tower with the blocks (coins, spools) and attempt to knock it over by rolling the ball. *3.* Smile at the student who knocked over the tower on his third attempt.

attend *1.* Shout (whisper, sing) the name of a student who is (isn't) attending class today. *2.* Shake hands with (pull the nose of) a student who attended (didn't attend) class yesterday.

attendance *1.* Maria, it's your turn to take attendance. Please come to the desk. *2.* Stand next to (in front of, behind, beside, in back of) the student who took (who's taking) attendance today.

attention *1.* Stand at attention. *2.* Give Pedro your full

33

attention. *3.* The next command is a long one, so pay attention.

attract *1.* Pretend you're in a restaurant and are trying to attract (get) the waiter's attention. *2.* Draw a picture of something that's used to attract fish *(e.g., a worm).*

author *1.* Write the name of a famous American (French) author. *2.* I'm going to write some well-known authors on the chalkboard. Copy the list and next to each one write one of his or her famous works. *3.* Hop (run, swim, jump) to a famous author *(cc-8).*

average Average (find the average of) the numbers I wrote on the chalkboard.

avoid *1.* Pedro, hop. Maria, hop and chase him. Let's see how long he can avoid getting caught. *2.* Pedro, walk towards Maria. Maria, you don't want to talk to him. Avoid him by turning around and walking (running) away.

award *1.* Pedro and Carlos are going to race to the door. Award the winner a cookie (raisin, trophy cut out of paper). *2.* Give the winner of the race her award.

away *1.* Walk (run, jump, swim) away from the student who's wearing a mask. *2.* Face the chalkboard (teacher, window) and then turn away. *3.* Stand away from (next to) the door (desk).

awkward *1.* Walk around the class with awkward (graceful) movements. *2.* Pick up (draw) an object that's awkward (easy) to carry.

ax *1.* Draw a man with an ax in his hand cutting down a tree. *2.* Pretend the pencil is an ax and Pedro is a tree. Cut down the tree *(Pedro would then fall down).*

baby *1.* Cry like a baby. *2.* Pretend Pedro is your baby and burp him (give him his bottle). *3.* Pick up the jar of baby food *(empty container),* put the bib on Maria, pretend she's your baby, and feed her.

baby bottle Pretend Maria is a baby and you are her mother. She's hungry, so give (feed) her her bottle.

bachelor Count the men in the class who are bachelors (married, engaged, still single).

back *1.* Touch your back. *2.* Hang the towel on the back of the chair. *3.* Stand in the back of the class. *4.* Attach the picture you drew to the back wall. *5.* Remove something from my desk and then put it back. *6.* Catch the ball and throw it back. *7.* Back the car to the door.

back up Back up (go back) five big (small, tiny, huge) steps.

backwards *1.* Jump to the door (window, teacher) backwards. *2.* Walk (hop, swim) around the desk (teacher, class) backwards. *3.* Write your (my, a friend's) name backwards. *4.* Let's see who will be the first one to write the alphabet backwards.

bad *1.* Taste the medicine (empty container) and make a face because it tastes very bad. *2.* Pretend you got a bad grade on the test and cry. *3.* Pretend you have a bad cold (cough).

badge *1.* Pin the badge on the policeman *(pc).* *2.* Give the flower (candle, cookie, cracker) to the student who's wearing the badge.

bag *1.* Fill the bag with crumpled newspaper. *2.* Put the pen in the bag. *3.* Drop the coin into the bag. *4.* Close your eyes, stick your hand into the bag, take out an object, feel it, say what it is, and then open your eyes. *5.* Stick the bag over your head.

bake Draw (cut out) a small picture of a cake (pie), put it in the toy oven, and bake it.

bakery Go to the bakery *(pc),* buy a cookie, put it in your mouth, chew it slowly, and then swallow it.

balance *1.* Balance the pencil (candle, ruler) on your finger (thumb). *2.* Walk around the class balancing a book (notebook, ruler, paper cup, sponge) on your head.

bald Draw a bald man next to a man with long (short, curly, wavy) hair.

ball *1.* Throw (hand, kick, toss, roll) the ball to Maria. *2.* Sit on (jump over) the ball. *3.* Hold the ball between your knees (ankles) and jump to the door. *4.* Bounce (dribble) the ball several (many) times. *5.* Throw the ball into the air and catch it with your left hand.

ballet Pretend you're a ballet dancer and dance with graceful movements.

balloon *1.* Blow up (inflate, sit on, kick, hit) the balloon. *2.* Stretch the balloon and snap it. *3.* Balance the balloon on your nose. *4.* Draw a happy (sad, crazy, funny) face on the balloon. *5.* Stick a pin (needle) in the balloon and pop it. *6.* Let out the air and watch the balloon shrink (fly away).

banana *1.* Peel the banana. *2.* Cut a slice of the banana, put it on the plate, and serve it to Maria. *3.* Imitate (write the name of) an animal that likes to eat bananas.

band *1.* We're going to form a band. Maria will play the guitar; Pedro, the drums; and Carlos, the piano. *2.* Draw a man wearing a hat with a feather in the band. *3.* Band some matches (pencils, pens) together with the string (rubber band).

Band-Aid Pretend you're peeling the potato (orange, cucumber) and the knife slips and cuts your finger. Say "ouch" and put a Band-Aid on the cut.

bang *1.* Bang (pound) on the door (wall, teacher's desk). *2.* Aim the rifle (gun) at Maria, pull the trigger, and say "bang."

bank *1.* Run to the bank *(pc)* and deposit some money. *2.* Put on the mask, pick up the gun, and rob the bank. *3.* Write the name of the bank where you have an account. *4.* Draw a river with some trees (flowers, people standing) on one of its banks.

bank clerk Pick up the checkbook, hop (swim) to the bank clerk *(pc)*, and cash a check.

bar *1.* Smell (stick the pin into) the bar of soap. *2.* Offer a chocolate bar (candy bar) to the student wearing the red dress. *3.* Draw a window with bars. *4.* Pedro, go out of the class. Carlos and Eduardo, bar (stop, keep) him from coming back in.

37

barber *1.* Carry (take) the scissors and the comb to the barber *(pc)*. *2.* You're a barber. Pick up the scissors and cut my hair. *3.* Touch (draw) an object that you associate with a barber.

barber shop Go to the barber shop *(pc)* and get a haircut (have the barber cut your hair).

bare *1.* Draw a boy walking with bare feet. *2.* Draw a man who is bare except for a pair of shorts.

bark *1.* Bark (howl, growl) like a dog. *2.* Bark some commands to Pedro. *3.* Go outside and touch the bark of a tree.

barrel *1.* Draw a man carrying a barrel. *2.* Touch the barrel of the rifle (gun).

base Draw a lamp with an arrow pointing to the base (shade).

baseball Pick up the bat and pretend you're playing baseball.

basket *1.* Put the banana (orange, apple, scissors, candle, can) in the basket. *2.* Draw a woman carrying a picnic basket.

basketball Pretend you're playing basketball and toss a paper ball into the wastebasket (dribble the ball to the door).

bat *1.* Pick up the plastic baseball bat and hit (bat) the paper ball. *2.* Toss the paper ball into the air and bat it with the ruler (book, notebook, palm of your hand). *3.*

Draw a bat hanging from a branch of a tree (flying near the moon).

bath Pick up the bar of soap and pretend you're in a bathtub taking a bath.

bathroom Go to the bathroom *(pc)* and pretend you're shaving (taking a shower, brushing your teeth).

battery *1.* Draw (pick up) an object that uses batteries. *2.* Put the batteries in the flashlight. *3.* Roll (toss, hand) a battery to Maria.

beach *1.* Run (jump, hop) to the beach *(pc)* and pretend you're swimming (surfing). *2.* Pretend you're walking barefoot on some hot sand on a beach. *3.* Draw a beach scene. *4.* Write (sing, whisper) the name of a famous beach.

bead *1.* Count the beads on the necklace. *2.* Thread the beads onto the string and tie the ends of the string together to make a necklace.

beans Pick up the can opener, open the can of beans *(empty container),* pour some beans into the pan, heat the beans on the stove, and serve them to me.

beard *1.* Put on (take off) the beard. *2.* Pinch (hit, smile at, laugh at) a student who has (uses, is wearing) a beard. *3.* Draw a man with a long (short, bushy) beard.

beat *1.* Beat me on the arm (head, shoulder, back) with the plastic bottle (bat). *2.* Put your head against Pedro's chest and listen to his heart beat. *3.* Shake hands with the student who beat (defeated) you in the race.

beautiful Write the name of a beautiful (pretty) actress (singer, movie star).

beauty salon Go to the beauty salon *(pc)* and have your hair done (combed, brushed, cut).

because *1.* Smile at the student who's dizzy because he was spinning around. *2.* Touch the student who's tired because she was running (jumping). *3.* Give the flower to the student who can't see because his glasses are on the teacher's desk.

become Smile, you're happy. Now become sad (angry, nervous, silent, noisy, calm).

bed *1.* Draw a bed. *2.* Pretend your desk is a bed and lay (put) your head down.

bedroom *1.* Swim (hop, run) to the bedroom *(pc)* and pretend you're going to sleep. *2.* Yawn, say good night to the class, and walk (jump, skip) to the bedroom *(pc)*.

bee *1.* Buzz like a bee. *2.* Draw some flowers on the chalkboard, pretend you're a bee, and fly from flower to flower. *3.* Pretend you're a bee and sting Maria.

beer *1.* Pick up the can of beer *(empty container),* pull the tab, and take a drink. *2.* Pretend you're pouring some beer into Pedro's shirt pocket. *3.* Pour some beer *(empty container)* into the glass, put the glass on the tray, and serve it to Maria.

before *1.* Write (hold up) the number that comes before (after) seven. *2.* Pinch the student who has the number that comes before ten *(cc-12)*. *3.* Kick a student who arrived before (at the same time as) Pedro. *4.* Before you cough (clap, cry), point to the door (ceiling).

beg *1.* Stick out your hand and pretend you're begging for money. *2.* Pretend you're a dog begging for food.

beggar Put a coin in the beggar's *(pc)* hand (pocket).

begin *1.* Write the time our class begins (starts, ends). *2.* Draw a house (tree, cat). Begin when I count to three. *3.* Hand your book (notebook, ruler) to a student whose name begins with the letter "m." *4.* Look at the teacher and then begin to laugh (cry).

beginning *1.* Let's sing the song again from the beginning. *2.* Shake a student who was (wasn't) present (absent) at the beginning of the class.

behave Pretend Pedro is your little boy. He isn't behaving, so give him a spanking (have him sit in the corner).

behind *1.* Stand behind (in back of, in front of, next to) the desk (teacher, chair, student wearing a yellow skirt). *2.* Hide behind the desk (door, teacher).

bell *1.* Ring the bell a few (many, several) times. *2.* Dance (cry, laugh, stoop, yawn) when I ring the bell. *3.* Hop (jump) around the class ringing the bell and singing a song.

belly *1.* Touch (point to, pat, rub) your belly. *2.* Put one hand on your belly and the other on your head. Now switch.

belong *1.* If this watch belongs to Maria, give it to her. If not, put it in the bag. *2.* Draw something that belongs in the kitchen (bedroom, living room, bathroom). *3.* Move your desk and then put it back where it belongs.

below *1.* Write a number that's below (under, over, less than, more than) twenty. *2.* Draw a kite (bird, butterfly; an airplane) below (above, over) some clouds.

belt *1.* Pull Pedro to the door by his belt. *2.* Unbuckle (buckle) your belt. *3.* Draw a fat man wearing a wide (narrow) belt. *4.* Belt Pedro with the plastic bottle (bat).

bench *1.* Draw two girls (boys, men) sitting on a bench. *2.* Make a bench using the ruler and two match boxes.

bend *1.* Bend (shape, form) the wire into a **C (S, U, V, J)**. *2.* Pretend you're bending an iron bar. *3.* Draw a road that bends (curves) to the right (left).

bend over *1.* Bend over and touch your toes. *2.* Bend over while Maria scratches your back.

beneath *1.* Put the pen (keys, chalk, cup) beneath the napkin (towel). *2.* Draw a star (butterfly, bird) beneath (over, under) some clouds.

beside *1.* Stand beside (in front of, next to) the desk (fan, door, teacher, chair). *2.* Walk beside (behind) me. *3.* Draw a tree (car) beside a house (church).

best *1.* Applaud the student who got the best (next to the best) grade on the test. *2.* Congratulate the student who made the best imitation of a dog (cat, bird, monkey). *3.* Everybody, draw a picture of your teacher. Now let's vote for the best drawing.

bet Pedro and Carlos are going to race to the door. Use

your play money and bet on the student you think will win.

better *1.* Pretend you have a headache. Take some aspirin. Now smile. You feel better. *2.* I'm going to show you the names of two singers (actors, actresses, movies). Point to the one you like better.

between *1.* Stand between the teacher and the chalkboard (window, desk, door). *2.* Draw a heart (circle, hat, star) between two squares (diamonds, butterflies). *3.* Run to the event that occurred between 1930 and 1950 *(cc-7).*

beyond Draw some hills. Now draw some mountains (trees; a river, lake) beyond the hills.

bib Maria is your baby. Tie the bib around her neck and feed her some baby food *(empty container).*

bicycle *1.* Pretend you're riding a bicycle. *2.* Draw a man riding a bicycle.

bid We're going to have an auction. For each object or picture I hold up, use your play money to make your bid.

big *1.* Draw a big (small, tiny, huge; an enormous) house (circle, car, heart, triangle). *2.* Give a big hello to the next student who walks in the class. *3.* Show the big red circle to the class.

bill *1.* Give Maria the ten-dollar bill (use play money). *2.* Pedro, pretend you're a doctor and check Roberto's pulse. Now give him his bill. *3.* Draw a bird with a long (short) bill (beak).

bind *1.* Bind (tie) my feet (hands, ankles, wrists) together with the rope (string, twine). *2.* Bind the toothpicks (pencils, matches) together with the yarn (a rubber band).

binoculars Pick up the binoculars (telescope) and look at the student who's wearing a beard (tie, mustache, hat, necklace).

bird *1.* Pretend you're a bird, flap your wings, and fly around the room. *2.* Draw a bird flying over a house (cloud, tree, church). *3.* Draw something birds like to eat.

birthday *1.* Today's Maria's birthday. Let's sing "Happy Birthday." *2.* Pull the nose (hair, left ear) of a student whose birthday is in May *(student-made cc)*.

bit *1.* Pour a little bit (a lot) of water into the glass (cup, bowl). *2.* I want you to jump (swim, hop, skip) to the window (door, desk). Wait a bit and then do it. *3.* Tear up the paper into little bits.

bite *1.* Put your finger (pencil) in your mouth and bite it. *2.* Pretend you're eating the apple and bite into it. Chew it slowly. Now swallow. *3.* Pretend you're a dog and bite Pedro.

bitter Pour yourself a cup of coffee. Take a sip and make a face. It's bitter. You forgot to put some sugar. Now add some sugar.

blade *1.* Touch (feel) the blade of the knife (sword). *2.* Draw a sword with a wide (narrow) blade.

blank *1.* Show the class a blank sheet of paper. *2.* Erase one of the words in the sentence on the chalkboard and replace it with a blank. *3.* Fill in the blank with a word that has four letters and begins with "s." *4.* Give me a blank look.

bless *1.* Go (hop, drive) to the church *(pc)* and have the priest bless you. *2.* Pretend you're a priest; put your hands on my head, and bless me.

blind *1.* Pretend you're blind. Close your eyes, extend your hands, and walk to the door (window, desk). *2.* You're blind. Put your hand on my shoulder and let me guide you.

blindfold Put on the blindfold, spin around three times, and try to walk a straight line.

blink Look at me and blink many (a few, several) times.

block *1.* Set the block on the table with the letter "A" facing up. *2.* Build a pyramid with the blocks. *3.* Arrange the blocks into a circle. *4.* Make a pile (stack) of five blocks. *5.* Knock down (over) the tower of blocks. *6.* Block the view of a short student. *7.* Block the door.

blond Give the flower to a student who has blond (red, black, dark brown) hair.

blood *1.* Draw a man with an arrow in his arm and blood dripping from the wound. *2.* Touch something that's the color of blood.

blouse Kneel in front of and propose to the girl who's wearing a yellow blouse (a blouse with big buttons).

blow *1.* Blow the horn (whistle). *2.* Make a tower with the blocks and then blow it down. *3.* Blow the toothpick (match, paper ball) off the desk. *4.* Use the straw to blow some bubbles in the water. *5.* Strike a blow to my head (shoulder) with the bottle (book).

blow out Light the candle (match) and then blow it out.

blow up Blow up (inflate) the balloon.

blunt Touch the blunt (sharp, pointed) pencil.

board *1.* Drive (hammer) the nail into the board. *2.* Hop (run, swim, jump, skip) to the board *(= chalkboard).* *3.* Draw a boy standing on a diving board about to dive into the water.

boat *1.* Sail (row) the boat to Maria. *2.* Draw a boat (ship) in a river (lake).

body *1.* Draw a dog (cat, man) with a big body and a small head. *2.* We're going to draw a man. First draw the body. Now draw the head. Now add the arms and legs. *3.* Shake your body.

boil Put the kettle on the stove and boil some water to make some coffee.

bolt *1.* Tighten (loosen) the nut on the bolt. *2.* Twist the nut off the bolt. *3.* Pretend you're bolting the door.

bomb *1.* Imitate (make) the sound of a bomb exploding. *2.* Draw an airplane dropping three bombs.

bone *1.* Pretend you're a dog and chew on (bury) the bone. *2.* Draw a big bone, cut it out, and give it to the student who's pretending he's a dog.

book *1.* Open (close, read from) the book that's on (under) the table. *2.* Put the pen (pencil) in (on, under, on top of, next to) the book. *3.* Walk around the class with the thick (thin) book on your head. *4.* Set (drop) the book on the floor (desk). *5.* Make a stack (pile) of books.

bookstore Go to the bookstore *(pc)* and buy a book *(use play money)*.

boot *1.* Draw a man (woman) wearing boots and then color the boots red. *2.* Boot (kick) the ball to (out) the door.

border *1.* Write the names of (go to the map and touch) the countries that border your country. *2.* On your map locate some border cities. *3.* Draw a rug. Make it blue with a yellow border.

bored Pretend you're bored. Yawn several times.

boring Write (print, say, shout, whisper) the name of a boring book (movie, subject, activity).

born *1.* Write (print) the month when you were born. *2.* Pinch the cheek (arm, nose) of a student who was born in May (the same month as Pedro) *(student-made cc / cc-2)*. *3.* Give the blue fish to a student who was born in a city located in Europe *(cc-11)*.

borrow *1.* You can borrow a pencil from Pedro *(said to a student who doesn't have a pencil)*. *2.* Touch (point to) the student who had to borrow a pencil because she didn't bring hers to class. *3.* Write some words that English has borrowed from Spanish (French).

both *1.* Raise both hands (feet). *2.* Show both hands (only one hand) to the class. *3.* Put (rest) both elbows on your desk (on Maria's head). *4.* Point to (touch) both eyes (ears, hands, feet, elbows, arms). *5.* Pick up both the triangle and the square.

bottle *1.* Hit me on the head (shoulder) with the plastic bottle. *2.* Pick up the bottle and pour some water onto your left (right) hand. *3.* Lay the bottle on its side and spin it. *4.* Set the bottle on the floor, stand back, roll the ball, and try to knock it over.

bottle caps *1.* Give Maria several (many) bottle caps. *2.* Form a square (an **S**) with the bottle caps. *3.* Make a tower with the bottle caps. *4.* Drop a few bottle caps into the cup. *5.* Put some bottle caps in the glass and then spill them out onto the table.

bottle opener Pick up the bottle opener, open the bottle of soda pop, insert a straw, and take a sip.

bottom *1.* Put the book (eraser, ruler) in the bottom (top, middle) drawer of the teacher's desk. *2.* Turn the paper plate over and draw a star (cloud) on the bottom. *3.* Draw a tall man standing at the bottom (top) of a stairs (mountain, hill).

bounce *1.* Bounce (roll, throw, toss, kick) the ball to Maria. *2.* Toss the ball into the air, let it bounce two times, and then catch it. *3.* Jump to your feet with a bounce.

bow *1.* Sing a song (dance with Maria, juggle the paper balls) and then take a bow. *2.* Pretend you're from Japan, stand in front of Maria, and bow to her. *3.* Bow four times, each time facing a different direction.

bow *1.* Draw a bow and an arrow. *2.* Draw a short girl with a big bow in her hair. *3.* Pick up the ribbon (yarn) and tie a bow in Pedro's hair.

bow tie *1.* Put on (take off) the bow tie. *2.* Draw a tall (fat) man wearing a big (small, huge, wide, narrow) bow tie.

bowl *1.* Pour a little (a lot of) water into the bowl. *2.* Pick up the box of cereal *(empty container)* and pour some cereal into the bowl. *3.* Pretend you're drinking a bowl of soup. *4.* Turn the bowl upside down and cover the sponge (eraser, paper ball).

box *1.* Open (close, tie the string around) the box. *2.* Put the coin (candle, sponge, pencil, ruler) in the box. *3.* Write your name (age, address, telephone number) on the chalkboard and draw a box around it. *4.* Pretend you're boxing.

boy *1.* Shake hands with (pull the hair of) a boy (girl, man, woman). *2.* Draw a boy wearing shorts standing next to a girl with pigtails. *3.* Draw (pick up) an object that boys like to play with.

bracelet *1.* Put on (take off, hold up, show me) the bracelet. *2.* Tie the string (ribbon, yarn) around the finger of a student who's wearing a bracelet. *3.* Draw a girl wearing a bracelet on each arm.

brackets *1.* Put brackets around the second (first, last) word in the sentence I wrote on the chalkboard. *2.* Enclose all of the words that have five letters in brackets.

braid *1.* Braid Maria's hair. *2.* Cut three long pieces of

49

string, tie them together at one end, and then braid them.

brain Touch the part of your body where your brain is located.

branch *1.* Draw a tree with many branches. *2.* Pretend you're a tree and extend your arms to represent the branches.

bread *1.* Draw two slices of bread on a sheet of paper, cut them out, and put them together to form a sandwich. Now eat the sandwich. *2.* Write the name of a brand of bread.

break *1.* Break a toothpick (match, pencil; piece of chalk, string). *2.* The class record for standing on tiptoes is five minutes. Let's see who can break that record. *3.* Draw the sun shining through a break in the clouds. *4.* Break into tears.

breakable Pick up (show the class) an object that is breakable (unbreakable).

breakfast *1.* Toss your comb (book, eraser) to the student who has breakfast at 7:30 *(student-made cc).* *2.* Write the time you had breakfast today. *3.* Count the students who had a big breakfast today.

breath *1.* Take a deep breath and then let it out. *2.* Show the class something that's used to freshen your breath *(e.g., mints).* Now take one out and put it in your mouth.

breathe *1.* Breathe in and then slowly breathe out. *2.* Draw an animal that can breathe under water.

brick Draw a house made of bricks.

bridge *1.* Build a bridge with the match boxes (spools) and the ruler. *2.* Draw a bridge across the river that Maria drew on the chalkboard.

brief Give (make, formulate) a brief (long, complicated; an easy) command.

bright *1.* Draw a bright (dim) light. *2.* Maria, pick up the flashlight and shine it in Pedro's eyes. Pedro, the light is very bright, so put your arm up in front of your eyes.

Brillo pad Pick up the Brillo pad and scrub the pot (pan, frying pan, silverware).

bring *1.* Walk to the desk, pick up the book (ruler, notebook, flower, candle, coin), and bring it to me. *2.* Stand in front of (next to, beside, in back of) a student who forgot to bring (didn't bring) his book today.

broad *1.* Draw a broad (narrow) river (street). *2.* Draw a sword with a broad (narrow) blade.

broken *1.* Draw a circle (square, triangle, heart, rectangle) with broken lines. *2.* Draw a broken vertical (curved, horizontal, diagonal) line.

brooch *1.* Put on (take off) the brooch. *2.* Toss the ball (orange, eraser, coin) to the student who's wearing a brooch.

broom *1.* Pick up the broom and sweep the floor in front of (in back of, next to) the desk. *2.* Sweep the teacher's head with the broom. *3.* Lean the broom against the door (desk, teacher). *4.* Pretend you're a witch and ride the broom around the class.

brother *1.* Write your brother's name and draw a horizontal line over (under, beside) it. *2.* Pull the nose (hair, ears) of a student who has a brother but doesn't have a sister.

brush *1.* Pick up the brush and brush your hair. *2.* Brush the hair of a student who's wearing a blouse that's the same color as Pedro's shirt. *3.* Brush the hair out of your eyes. *4.* Sprinkle some confetti on Pedro's shirt and then brush it off.

bubble *1.* Use the straw to blow some bubbles in the water that's in the glass (cup). *2.* Blow a bubble with the bubble gum.

bubble gum Remove the wrapper from the bubble gum, stick it in your mouth, and blow a big bubble.

bucket *1.* Pour some (a little, a lot of) water into the bucket (pail). *2.* Fill the bucket with books (notebooks, crumpled newspaper). *3.* Put the bucket on your head and walk (skip, hop, run) around the class (desk, teacher).

buckle *1.* Buckle (unbuckle) your belt. *2.* Touch the buckle on your belt (shoe, purse).

build Build (erect, put up, construct, make) a tower (pyramid) with the blocks (match boxes, spools, coins).

building *1.* Show the class a picture of a building cut out from a magazine. *2.* Draw two tall office buildings. *3.* Open the almanac and find the tallest building in the world.

bull Pedro, take the cape (towel) and pretend you're a bull fighter. Carlos, pretend you're the bull.

bullet Draw a bullet coming out of the barrel of a gun.

bump *1.* Bump into the door (teacher, wall, desk). *2.* Bump into Maria and excuse yourself. *3.* Draw a man with a large bump on his head.

bunch *1.* Draw a bunch of grapes (circles, triangles, stars, eyes). *2.* Give (hand, pass) me the bunch of grapes.

burn *1.* Light the match, watch it burn for two seconds, and then blow it out. *2.* Burn a hole in the paper with the cigarette. *3.* Touch the stove and pretend you burned your hand. *4.* Pretend you're walking on the beach and the hot sand is burning your feet.

burp Pedro is your baby. After you feed him the bottle, burp him.

burst *1.* Blow up the balloon until it bursts. *2.* Burst the balloon with the pin (needle, pencil). *3.* Burst through the door. *4.* Burst into (out of) the room.

bury *1.* Pretend you're a dog and bury the bone. *2.* Bury your face in your hands. *3.* Choose a card, look at it, and bury it in the deck. *4.* Pedro and Carlos, carry Roberto to the place where people are buried *(cemetery pc)*.

bus *1.* Drive the bus to the door (desk, teacher). *2.* Draw a bus in front of (in back of) a car.

bus driver Pretend you're a bus driver and drive the bus around the class.

53

bush Draw some bushes next to a house (tree, church).

bushy Draw a man with a long (short) bushy beard.

busy *1.* Write the name of a busy street. *2.* Pretend you're busy (idle).

but *1.* Pick up the circle (triangle), but don't show it to the class. *2.* Shake hands with (pull the hair of) any student in the class but Maria. *3.* Don't show your drawing to anyone but me. *4.* Write a number that's greater than five but less than ten.

butcher *1.* Run to the butcher *(pc)* and sing him a song. *2.* Stand in front of the butcher *(pc)* and pretend you're a cow.

butcher shop Go to the butcher shop *(pc)* and buy some meat *(magazine cutouts)*.

butter *1.* Draw a slice of bread on a sheet of paper and cut it out. Now remove the lid from the butter dish *(empty container)* and butter (spread some butter on) the bread. *2.* Write the name of a brand of butter.

butter dish Remove the lid from the butter dish and pretend you're buttering some bread.

butterfly *1.* Draw an upside-down butterfly (a girl with a butterfly on her nose). *2.* Draw a butterfly between two clouds (stars, birds, flowers). *3.* Pretend you're trying to catch a butterfly with your hands.

button *1.* Sew a button to Pedro's sleeve. *2.* Count the buttons on Maria's blouse. *3.* Draw a woman wearing a dress with big round (square) buttons. *4.* Unbutton and then button your shirt. *5.* Pick up the calculator and press the On (Off) button.

buy *1.* Pick up an object that you can buy for less than ten dollars. *2.* Go to the store *(pc)* and buy (purchase) a radio (television, watch). *(Use play money and magazine cutouts.)*

buzz Buzz like a bee (fly, mosquito).

buzzer Make a sound like a buzzer.

by *1.* Stand by the desk (my side). *2.* Draw (touch) something you buy by the pound (dozen). *3.* Draw a rectangle two inches by six inches. *4.* Count to twenty by fives. *5.* Divide (multiply) fifty by ten. *6.* Write the name of a book written by Agatha Christie.

cactus *1.* Draw a cactus, cut it out, and put it on the empty seat next to Maria. Pedro, sit on the cactus, jump up, and scream "ouch." *2.* Draw a desert scene with a tall cactus and the sun shining brightly.

cage *1.* Draw a bird in a cage. *2.* Pretend you're a lion (tiger) in a circus cage and pace back and forth.

cake *1.* Draw a birthday cake with five candles, cut it out, put it on the tray, and serve it to Maria. *2.* Draw a small cake, cut it out, put it in the toy oven, and bake it.

calculate Draw a rectangle, pick up the ruler, measure its length and width, and then calculate its area.

calculator *1.* Pick up the calculator and press the On (Off) button. *2.* Use the calculator to solve the problem I put on the chalkboard.

calendar *1.* Put (insert) the calendar in Maria's book. *2.* I'm going to put this month's calendar on the chalkboard. Copy it into your notebook. Now cross out (circle, underline) the last day of the month. *3.* Hang the calendar on the wall.

call *1.* Call Maria by her nickname. *2.* When I call your name, stand up (cry, laugh, sigh, groan). *3.* Call the roll for me today. *4.* Pretend you're drowning and call for help. *5.* Flip a coin and call it Heads or Tails. *6.* Pick up the phone and give Maria a call.

call out When I point to you, call out your name (the name of a student wearing something red).

calm *1.* Sit with a calm (nervous, worried, sad) look on your face. *2.* Open the door (walk around the class, pour yourself a cup of coffee) calmly.

camel Draw a camel with two big humps standing next to a cactus (tree, man, house).

camera *1.* Pick up the camera, aim (point) it at me, focus, and take (snap) my picture. *2.* Write the name of a brand (make) of cameras.

can *1.* Shake (open, set the cup on top of, drop a coin into, remove the lid from) the can. *2.* Roll the can to Pedro. *3.* Lay the can on its side. *4.* Cover the can with the towel (napkin). *5.* Count the students in the class who can swim (play the piano).

can opener Pick up the can opener and quickly (slowly) open the can of peas (corn) *(empty containers).*

candle *1.* Strike a match and light the candle. *2.* Measure (cut off a tiny piece of) the candle. *3.* Point to the ceiling with the candle. *4.* Roll (toss, slide) the candle to Pedro. *5.* Light the candle and then blow it out (walk around the room singing).

candy *1.* Unwrap the candy, put it in your mouth, and chew it slowly. *2.* Give (offer) Maria a piece of candy. *3.* Drop a piece of candy into your pocket. *4.* Award the winner of the race a piece of candy.

candy bar *1.* Pick up the knife and cut a piece of the candy bar. *2.* Unwrap the candy bar, bite off a piece, chew it slowly, and then swallow it. *3.* Put the candy bar on the tray and serve it to a student who doesn't have anything on his desk.

cane *1.* Pretend you are very old and are walking with the support (help, aid) of a cane. *2.* Draw an old man who is bent over walking with a cane.

canoe *1.* Pretend you're paddling a canoe. *2.* Draw a canoe in a lake (river). In the canoe there is a man fishing.

cap *1.* Put on (take off) the cap (hat, wig, tie). *2.* Remove the cap from the bottle. *3.* Cap (uncap) the bottle.

cape *1.* Put on (take off) the cape (hat, cap, tie, brooch). *2.* Pick up the cape and pretend you're a bull fighter. *3.* Draw a man wearing a cape.

capital *1.* Print your (my) name in capital letters. *2.* Draw a circle around all the capital letters in the third sentence I wrote on the chalkboard. *3.* Swim (jump, run, hop) to the capital of France *(cc-11)*.

captain *1.* I want each team to choose (elect) a captain.

2. The team captains will now step forward and shake hands.

car *1.* Drive the small red car around the class (desk, teacher, fan). *2.* Drive (race, speed) the car to the door (window, chalkboard) and honk the horn when you get there.

carbon paper Stick a sheet of carbon paper between two sheets of paper and draw a heart (flower, spaceship, canoe, tree). Give the original to Maria and the copy to Pedro.

card *1.* Choose a card from the pile (stack) and perform the command written on it. *2.* Distribute the picture cards *(Appendix B)*. *3.* Pick up the deck of cards and mix (shuffle, deal) them. *4.* Send Maria the birthday (anniversary, get-well, graduation) card.

cardboard Hold up (touch, show the class) an object made of cardboard *(e.g., the box)*.

careful *1.* Pretend you're a careful (reckless) driver. *2.* Draw a street on the floor and cross it carefully (carelessly).

careless Write your name carelessly (sloppily, carefully, neatly).

carpenter *1.* Tug on the sleeve (belt, collar) of the carpenter *(pc)*. *2.* Watch the carpenter *(pc)* drive (hammer) the nail into the board.

carrot *1.* Put the carrot on the tray and serve it to the student sitting to my left (right). *2.* Cut a slice of the carrot and taste it. *3.* Pick up the peeler and peel the carrot. *4.* Tie the string to the carrot and swing it around over your head.

carry *1.* Pedro and Carlos, carry the teacher to the door (chalkboard, window). *2.* Carry the chair (wastebasket) around the class. *3.* Pretend you're carrying a heavy box (suitcase).

carton Pick up the carton of milk (empty container) and pour yourself a glass of milk.

cash *1.* Go to the supermarket *(pc)* and buy some fruit. Pay in cash (with a check). *2.* Go to the bank *(pc)* and cash a check.

cashier Pick up an object from the desk, take it to the cashier *(pc),* and pay for it with the play money.

castle *1.* Give a large sum of money (play money) to the student who lives in a castle *(pc).* *2.* Draw a castle located (sitting) on the top of a mountain. *3.* Wink (blink) at a person who lives in a castle *(king pc).*

cat *1.* Maria, pretend you're a cat. Pedro, pretend you're a dog and chase the cat around the class. *2.* Draw a cat with three ears (eyes) and a long tail.

catalogue Open the catalogue, find something you'd like to buy, and show it to the class.

catch *1.* Throw (toss) the ball (eraser, candle, coin) into the air and catch it. *2.* Sneeze and cough. You've caught a cold. *3.* Pedro, hop and try to avoid being caught by Carlos. Carlos, jump after Pedro and try to catch him.

catch up Walk far behind Maria. Now run and catch up

with her.

cause *1.* Pick up (touch, point to) something that causes you to sneeze (cry) *(e.g., the pepper, onion).* *2.* Tickle Pedro and cause him to laugh.

cautious *1.* Drive the car around the class. Pretend you're a cautious (reckless) driver. *2.* Draw a street on the floor and cross it cautiously (carelessly).

cease I want everyone to cry (sing, talk, laugh, hum, make a lot of noise). When I clap (whistle, sneeze, stand up), you will cease (stop).

ceiling *1.* Throw (kick, toss, boot) the ball to the ceiling. *2.* Draw a light hanging (suspended) from the ceiling. *3.* Point to the ceiling with your thumb (pencil, little finger, elbow, foot).

celebrate *1.* Sit next to (in back of) the student who celebrates her birthday in May *(student-made cc).* *2.* Hop (run, skip) to the event we celebrate in January *(cc-3).*

cemetery *1.* Light the candle and walk to the cemetery *(pc).* *2.* Pedro, pretend you're dead. Now I want four strong male students to carry him to the cemetery *(pc).*

center *1.* Stand in the center (middle) of the class (of the circle you drew on the floor). *2.* Draw a cat (happy face, heart, butterfly) in the center of your paper. *3.* Draw a small heart, cut it out, and tape it to the center of Maria's forehead.

chain *1.* Measure (count the links on) the chain. *2.* Walk to (brush the hair of) the student who's wearing a gold chain. *3.* Write the name of a chain of supermarkets (drugstores).

chair *1.* Stand in front of (in back of, behind, next to, on) the chair. *2.* Set (place) the chair on top of the desk. *3.* Put the chair on your head and walk (run) around the class. *4.* Pick up the chair with one hand. *5.* Jump (leap) over the chair. *6.* Turn the chair around.

chalk *1.* Show a piece of chalk to the class. *2.* Break the chalk in half. *3.* Hide (crumble) a piece of chalk. *4.* Put (place) a piece of chalk in your pocket.

chalkboard *1.* Write (print) my name on the chalkboard. *2.* Run (jump, hop, skip) to the chalkboard. *3.* Erase the chalkboard slowly (quickly, from left to right, from top to bottom).

champion *1.* Shake hands with (congratulate, award the trophy to) the class champion tic-tac-toe player. *2.* Write the name of a champion boxer (tennis player, golfer).

chance Roll the ball and knock over the bottle. You have three chances (trys).

change *1.* Line up five students in front of the class. Now change their order. *2.* Draw something and then change it. *3.* You're happy. Now change and become sad (angry, worried). *4.* Change papers with a friend and then correct your friend's paper.

change places Change places with a student who's wearing a beard (mustache, long-sleeved shirt, red skirt, checked blouse; glasses).

channel Change the channel on the television.

chapter *1.* Write the page number that chapter 10 begins (ends) on. *2.* Open your books (turn to) chapter 5.

chase *1.* Hop after and chase the student who's jumping and trying to get away from you. *2.* Pedro, pretend you're a dog. Maria, pretend you're a cat. Now the dog is going to chase the cat.

cheat *1.* Pretend you're taking a test and are cheating by looking over Maria's shoulder. *2.* Play a game of cards and try to cheat.

check *1.* Copy these sentences into your notebook and put a check next to the ones that you agree with. *2.* You're a policeman. Stop the student who's driving the yellow car and check her documents. *3.* Pick up the checkbook and write your teacher a check.

check off Make a list of five students from the class and then say hello to each one of them. As you say hello, check off their names.

checkbook Pick up the checkbook, write a check to a student who's wearing a necklace (bracelet, green blouse), tear it out, and give it to her.

checked Draw a woman with a checked (striped) dress (skirt, blouse, hat, purse, umbrella).

cheek *1.* Touch (point to, pinch) your (Pedro's) cheeks. *2.* Draw a happy (sad) face with a flower (heart, star) on each cheek.

cheer Pedro and Carlos are going to have a jumping race

to the door. This half of the class will cheer for Pedro shouting, "Come on Pedro" and that half will cheer for Carlos shouting, "Go Carlos."

cheese *1.* Serve the piece (slice) of cheese to the student who's sitting (standing) in the corner. *2.* Hop (run, jump) to the student who's eating a piece of cheese.

chest *1.* Pretend you're a doctor, put the stethoscope to Pedro's chest, and listen to his heart beat. *2.* Hold a book (notebook, magazine) against your chest. *3.* Tie the rope (string, yarn) around Pedro's chest (arm, leg). *4.* Draw a chest of drawers.

chew Pick up the apple (cookie, cracker, banana), take a bite, chew it slowly (quickly), and then swallow it.

chicken Imitate (pretend you're) a chicken (dog, cat, cow).

chief Make a list of the chief (principal) products that your country exports (imports).

child Draw a family with only one child (with three children).

children *1.* Draw a family with two children. *2.* Form a circle, join hands, and sing a children's song. *3.* Write the names and ages of your children. *4.* Draw (pick up, show the class) an object that children like to play with.

chimney Draw a chimney on the roof of the house you just drew. There's smoke coming out of the chimney.

chin *1.* Touch your right knee with your chin. *2.* Stand

63

behind a student who's seated and put (rest) your chin on her head (shoulder). *3.* Draw a man with a pointed (round, square) chin.

choice You have a choice of either hopping or jumping to the door. Indicate your choice by performing the action.

choke Pretend you're going to choke (strangle, hit) the teacher.

choose *1.* Choose (select, take) a card and perform the command that's written on it. *2.* Choose a friend to perform the dialogue with you.

chop *1.* Give the teacher a karate chop. *2.* Break the pencil that I'm holding with a karate chop. *3.* Pedro, pretend you're a tree. Maria, pretend the pencil is an ax (hatchet) and chop (cut) down the tree *(Pedro would then fall down).*

Christmas *1.* Sing (hum, whistle) a Christmas song. *2.* Go (hop, jump, swim) to the month in which we celebrate Christmas *(cc-2).*

church *1.* Go to the church *(pc)* and pray. *2.* Sing hello to the student who's at church *(pc).* *3.* Perform an action you typically do in church. *4.* Draw a church with a big cross on top of it. *5.* Write the name of the church you attend.

cigar *1.* Light (measure) the cigar. *2.* Pretend you're smoking the cigar (pipe, cigarette).

cigarette *1.* Offer Pedro a cigarette. *2.* Cut one of your cigarettes in half. *3.* Measure (bend) a cigarette. *4.* Stick the cigarette behind your ear. *5.* Light Maria's cigarette for her. *6.* Draw a fish (cat) smoking a cigarette. *7.* Balance the pack of cigarettes on your thumb.

cigarette lighter *1.* Turn up the flame on the lighter. *2.* Pick up the lighter and light my cigarette. *3.* Wrap the lighter as a present and give it to Pedro.

circle *1.* Put the big blue circle on the small green triangle. *2.* Stand up, join hands, and make a circle. *3.* Form two concentric circles. Everybody in the outer (inner) circle will now circle to the left (right). *4.* Draw a row (column) of tiny (large) circles. *5.* Circle (draw a circle around) your name.

circular Make a circular motion with your hand (foot, finger, thumb, head).

city *1.* Write (shout) the name of an important city in Brazil. *2.* Jump (run, swim) to a city in Europe (Asia) *(cc-11).* *3.* On the map locate a city that's near a river (an ocean, the coast, some mountains).

clap *1.* Throw the ball into the air and see how many times you can clap before it lands (you catch it). *2.* Clap seven (a few, many) times. *3.* Walk (run, jump) around the class clapping. *4.* Clap softly (as loud as you can).

clasp *1.* Everybody, clasp (join) hands and form a circle (square, triangle). *2.* Clasp hands with the person standing in front of you and spin around together. *3.* Unfasten (fasten) the clasp on the necklace (bracelet, brooch, badge).

class *1.* Walk (jump, run, swim, hop, skip) around the class. *2.* Write the time our class begins (ends). *3.* Count the students in our class.

65

claw *1.* Draw a cat with long claws. *2.* Pretend your fingers are claws and claw Maria.

clay *1.* Roll the clay into a ball (cylinder). *2.* Flatten the clay. *3.* Form (make) a ring (snake, face) with the clay.

clean *1.* Clean the chalkboard with the eraser (sponge, napkin). *2.* Clean your glasses on your shirt. *3.* Pick up the rag (a sheet of paper) and clean the seat where you're going to sit. *4.* Draw a boy with a clean (dirty) face.

clear *1.* Clear everybody out of the room (everything off of your desk). *2.* Clear the table after Maria sets it. *3.* Clear your throat (the calculator). *4.* Draw a picture with a clear (cloudy) sky. *5.* Give Pedro a command mumbling (speaking clearly).

clerk Go to the supermarket (bank, drugstore) *(pc's)* and talk to (smile at, pull the ears of) the clerk.

climate Write the name of (go to the map and touch) a country (place) noted for its hot (cold) climate.

climb *1.* Climb onto the chair (desk). *2.* Draw a man climbing a mountain (ladder, tree).

clip *1.* Count (distribute) the clips. *2.* Drop some clips into the can (bowl, cup). *3.* Unbend a clip and bend it into a square (circle; an *S).* *4.* Fasten these papers together with a clip. *5.* Clip the papers together.

clippers Pick up the clippers and clip (cut, trim) your fingernails.

clock *1.* Set the clock to 7:30. *2.* Put the small (hour) hand on the three and the big (minute) hand on the six. *3.* Draw a clock showing ten after eight.

clockwise Walk (swim, fly, run) around the class (desk) clockwise (counterclockwise).

close *1.* Stand close to (far from, near) the window (door, desk, teacher). *2.* Write the name of a city that's close to (far from) here. *3.* Write a word putting all of the letters close together (far apart).

close *1.* Close (open, shut) the door (window, book; your hand, mouth). *2.* Write (shout, whisper) the time that the bank (supermarket) closes (opens).

cloth *1.* Touch something made of cloth (wood, leather, plastic). *2.* Pick up the cloth (cardboard, paper) triangle and show it to the class.

clothes *1.* Touch your clothes. *2.* Touch some objects in the class that are the same colors as the clothes Pedro's wearing.

clothespin *1.* Draw a happy face and attach it to the back of Pedro's shirt with a clothespin. *2.* Attach the clothespin to my right ear.

clothing store Write the name of a clothing (hardware) store.

cloud *1.* Draw a cloud over a house (tree, bird, kite; an airplane). *2.* Draw a star (butterfly, flower, happy face) between (under) two big (small) clouds. *3.* Draw a cloud shaped like a mushroom (heart).

cloudy Draw a picture showing a cloudy (sunny) day.

67

clown *1.* Blow up the balloon and give it to the clown *(pc).* *2.* Pretend you're a clown and try to make Maria laugh.

club *1.* Club me on the head with the bat (bottle, book, notebook). *2.* Draw a man holding a club. *3.* Write the name of a club you're a member of.

clumsy *1.* You're clumsy. Knock over the bottle (bump into the chair, trip and fall down). *2.* Walk across the room in a clumsy (graceful) manner.

coast Go to the map and touch a city located on the East (West) Coast.

coat Put on (take off) your coat (glasses, ring, necklace, hat).

coffee *1.* Serve (pour) me a cup of coffee. *2.* Drink your coffee slowly (quickly). *3.* Blow on the coffee to cool it. *4.* Open the jar of instant coffee *(empty container),* put a teaspoonful in your cup, and add some boiling water from the kettle.

coffee pot Pick up the coffee pot and pour a cup of coffee for the girl who's sitting across from (behind, next to) Pedro.

coil *1.* Coil the rope (twine, yarn,). *2.* Draw a snake coiled around a tree (man, flagpole).

coin *1.* Hide the coin and I will try to find it. *2.* Flip a coin to see who will give the commands. *3.* Roll (slide) a coin to the wall (out the door). *4.* Arrange the coins into a square (circle, heart). *5.* Drop a coin into the can (cup, glass; your pocket).

cold *1.* Pretend you're cold and shake (shiver). *2.* Write (whisper) the name of a place where it's cold (hot) all year long. *3.* Pretend you have a cold and sneeze and cough.

collapse *1.* Collapse into the chair. *2.* Stack (pile) the coins (blocks, spools) on top of each other until they collapse. *3.* Open and then collapse the umbrella.

collar *1.* Turn up (down) your collar. *2.* Tug on (pin the cloth circle to) Pedro's collar.

collect *1.* Collect the homework (cards, slips of paper, tests). *2.* Show the class something that people collect.

color *1.* Draw a man and color his shoes (hat, pants, tie, shirt) blue. *2.* Pinch the nose (cheek, ear, shoulder) of a student whose blouse is the same color as your shirt.

column *1.* Form (get into) a column in front of the teacher's desk. *2.* Draw a column of six triangles (circles, hearts, eyes). *3.* Draw five stars (rectangles, doors) in a column (row). *4.* Divide your paper into four columns.

comb *1.* Comb (brush) your hair quickly (slowly; with your right hand). *2.* Stick (leave) the comb in your hair. *3.* Draw a girl combing her hair.

come *1.* Come to me. *2.* Write the number that comes before (after) ten. *3.* Swim (hop) to the student who comes from Japan *(cc-4)*. *4.* Walk around the class and when you come to Maria, sing a song. *5.* Go out and come in running (crying, smiling).

comfortable Sit in a comfortable (an uncomfortable) position.

comic book *1.* Open the comic book and circle the last word on page seven. *2.* Read to the class from the comic book. *3.* Trade the comic book for something Maria has in her purse.

command *1.* Command Pedro to touch his toes (stretch, make a paper airplane). *2.* Write a command that ends with the word *table* (with a word that has five letters). *3.* Congratulate the student who successfully carried out my command.

common *1.* Write a common girl's (boy's) name from your country. *2.* Draw a picture of (pick up) an object that's commonly found in a classroom (kitchen, woman's purse).

communicate Communicate these feelings without speaking: hunger, happiness, sadness, surprise.

company Write the name of a company that produces (makes) televisions (cars, refrigerators, computers).

compare *1.* Compare Pedro and Carlos, and push the taller of the two to the window (out the door). *2.* Compare these two sticks (pieces of string) and give me the shorter (longer) one. *3.* Compare these two lists to see if they are the same.

compass *1.* Pick up the compass and draw a circle. *2.* Pick up the compass and face north.

complete *1.* Complete this command: "Stand in ..." *2.* Write your complete name. *3.* Count the cards to see if the deck is complete. *4.* When you complete (finish) the exercise, raise your hands. *5.* Touch the circle that's completely (partially) shaded in.

concentrate I'm going to put a pebble under one of these three paper cups and then mix them up. Concentrate and touch the one it's under.

concert Pretend you're giving a piano concert.

confess *1.* Stand next to the priest *(pc)* and confess. *2.* When I go out of the room, I want someone to hide my pen. When I come back in, I want the person who hid it to stand up and confess.

congratulate *1.* After Pedro jumps over the chair (touches his toes), congratulate him by patting him on the back (shaking his hand). *2.* Congratulate the student who came in first in the race.

connect *1.* Connect the dots that Maria drew on her paper. *2.* Draw a picture of something you connect (associate) with a table (church, door, tree, dog).

construct Construct (build, erect, make) a tower with the blocks (spools, coins, bottle caps).

consult I'm going to write some words on the chalkboard. Consult your dictionary to see what they mean.

contain *1.* Pick up the glass (cup) that contains a little (a lot of) water. *2.* Draw a square containing many (a few) hearts (stars, flowers, triangles). *3.* If the sentence Pedro wrote contains a mistake (an error), go and correct it.

contents *1.* Empty the contents of the purse (box, can, jar, bag) onto the table. *2.* Turn to the table of contents in your book.

contest We're going to have a contest to see who can stand on one foot the longest.

continue *1.* Clap your hands. Don't stop. Continue. *2.* When I count to three, you're going to dance (jump, cry, shake your body). Continue until I tell you to stop.

convert Convert ten pounds into kilos (five inches into centimeters, two miles into kilometers).

cook Pick up the pot (frying pan) and pretend you're cooking (preparing) dinner.

cookie *1.* Take a cookie out of the bag and offer (serve) it to Pedro. *2.* Unwrap the package of cookies and give one to a girl who has dark (light) hair. *3.* Cut the cookie in half (quarters). *4.* Reward the student who won the race with a cookie.

cool Pour yourself a cup of coffee (tea; bowl of soup). Now blow on it to cool it.

copy *1.* Copy the words (sentences) I wrote on the chalkboard into your notebook. *2.* Draw a picture of a house (fat man, cat; your teacher), make a carbon copy, and show the copy (original) to Maria.

cord *1.* Tie the cord (rope, yarn, string) around Pedro's arm (leg, ankle, waist). *2.* Wrap the cord around the fan. *3.* Draw a lamp (fan, television) with a long cord.

cork *1.* Put the cork in the bottle. *2.* Drop the cork on my head (shoulder). *3.* Toss (drop) the cork into the wastebasket (top drawer of the teacher's desk). *4.* Float the cork in a glass of water. *5.* Stick the pin into the cork. *6.* Cork the bottle.

corn *1.* Pretend you're eating the corn on the cob. *2.* Open the can of corn *(empty container),* pour some corn into the pan, heat it over the stove, and serve it to Maria.

corner *1.* Stand (stoop, sit) in the corner. *2.* Put (place) the teacher (chair, wastebasket, fan) in the corner. *3.* Push Maria (the desk, your chair) into the corner. *4.* Extend the towel (napkin, rag) on the desk and raise (lift up) a corner.

correct *1.* Some of the words I wrote (put) on the board are spelled wrong. Correct them. *2.* Raise your hand (foot) if you think Pedro performed the correct action. *3.* If Maria answered correctly, congratulate her (give her the flower).

cost *1.* Pick up an object on the desk and tell the class how much you think it costs. *2.* Touch (draw) something that costs very little (a lot).

cotton *1.* Touch (show me) something made of cotton. *2.* Wipe your face (chin, nose, cheek, forehead) with the cotton balls.

cough *1.* Put your hand to your mouth and cough three times. *2.* Pretend you're a doctor, put your ear to Pedro's back, and listen to him cough. *3.* Pretend you have a slight (bad) cough.

cough medicine You have a bad cough. Remove the cap from the bottle of cough medicine *(empty container),* pour some into the spoon, and taste it. Make a face because it tastes awful (terrible, horrible).

count *1.* Count to ten slowly (quickly). *2.* Count the windows (chairs, students, females, males) in the class. *3.* Count the triangles (circles, stars, hearts, vertical lines) that Pedro drew. *4.* Count to fifty by tens.

country *1.* Write the name of a country in Europe (Asia, Africa, South America). *2.* Swim (hop) to the student who lives in a country in Central America *(cc-4).*

couple *1.* Give me a couple of clips (bottle caps, coins, matches, toothpicks). *2.* Draw a couple of (many, a few) flowers (hats, chairs, doors, trees). *3.* Draw a couple holding hands.

cover Cover the pencil (book, bottle, teacher's face) with the towel (newspaper, napkin).

cow Imitate (draw, pretend you're) a cow (cat, dog, bird).

crack *1.* Draw a cup (vase, plate) with a crack in it. *2.* Open the door wide (a crack). *3.* Crack (hit) Pedro on the head (shoulder) with the bottle (book, notebook, magazine). *4.* Break a toothpick (pencil) and listen to it crack.

cracked Draw a cracked mirror (plate, cup).

cracker *1.* Unwrap (cut open) the package of crackers. *2.* Eat a cracker. Now you're thirsty, so take a drink of water. *3.* Crumble a cracker and throw the crumbs in the wastebasket.

crash *1.* Crash the red car into the wall (door, desk). *2.* Draw an airplane on fire about to crash. *3.* Drop the can onto the floor and listen to the crash.

crawl *1.* Pick up the baby *(child's toy)* and have it crawl on top of the table. *2.* Pretend the rope is a snake crawling on the floor.

crayon *1.* Pass (hand) a red crayon to Maria so that she can color the heart (house, boat) she just drew. *2.* Take out (put away) your crayons.

crazy *1.* Pretend you're crazy. *2.* Give a crazy (silly) command to Pedro.

creak Open the door slowly making a creaking sound.

cream *1.* Apply some cold cream *(empty container)* to your face. *2.* Pick up the creamer (packet of cream) and add some cream to your coffee.

credit card Take a credit card out of your wallet and show it to the class.

creep *1.* Creep to the door (window, desk, back of the class). *2.* Creep up behind the teacher and scare her.

criminal Pedro, you're a policeman. The student wearing the mask is a criminal. Take him to jail *(pc)*.

crooked *1.* Draw a long (short) crooked (straight, wavy, curved) line. *2.* Walk to the desk (chalkboard, teacher, door) in a crooked line.

cross *1.* Draw a cross on top of a church. *2.* Cross your legs. *3.* Sit with your legs crossed. *4.* Draw a street on the floor in chalk, look both ways to see if any cars are coming, and then cross the street.

cross out *1.* Cross out the third word in the last sen-

75

tence. 2. Cross out all the words that begin with the letter "s" (have more than five letters).

crowd *1.* I want everybody to crowd (gather) around Maria (the desk). *2.* The students in this row will now form a crowd in front of the door (window, chalkboard).

crown *1.* Put on (take off) the crown. *2.* Draw a man wearing a crown. *3.* Hop (run) to the man who's wearing a crown *(king pc)*.

crumple Crumple a sheet of paper into a ball and toss (throw) it into the wastebasket.

crush *1.* Step on the paper cup and crush it. *2.* Pretend you're crushing an ant with your thumb. *3.* Shake hands with Pedro and crush (squeeze) his hand.

cry *1.* Cry like a baby. *2.* Touch (point to) the teacher and cry. *3.* Pretend you're drowning and cry for help. *4.* Walk (jump, run, hop) around the class crying (laughing, humming).

cry out *1.* Hit your finger (thumb) with the hammer and cry out in pain. *2.* Stub your toe and cry out.

cube *1.* Draw a cube. *2.* Draw a glass with some ice cubes in it.

cucumber *1.* Pick up the peeler and peel the cucumber. *2.* Pretend you're slicing the cucumber and the tomato to make a salad. *3.* Hop to the student who's wearing a striped (checked) shirt and put the cucumber in his pocket.

cup *1.* Drink a cup of coffee (tea). *2.* Set (place) the cup next to the glass (plate, fork, spoon). *3.* Put the cup of coffee on the tray and serve it to me. *4.* Tie the string (yarn) to the handle of the cup.

cure *1.* You have a bad cough. Go to the drugstore *(pc)* and buy some cough medicine *(empty container)* to cure your cough. *2.* Maria has the hiccups. See if you can cure them by scaring her.

curly Draw a man with curly (straight, wavy) hair.

current Pretend you're in a river swimming against a strong current.

curtain Draw a window with checked (striped) curtains.

curve *1.* Draw a road that has many curves (that curves to the left). *2.* Draw a curved (straight, diagonal, vertical) line. *3.* Draw a circle with four curved arrows.

cut *1.* Cut the string (yarn, thread, paper in half). *2.* Pretend you cut your finger. Now put a Band-Aid on the cut. *3.* Pick up the scissors and cut my (your, our) hair. *4.* Pick up the clippers and cut (trim) your nails. *5.* Cut the deck of cards.

cut down Draw a tree on the chalkboard. Pretend the pencil is an ax and cut it down *(erase the tree and draw it in a horizontal position).*

cut off Cut off a piece of the candle (string, yarn, thread).

cut out *1.* Draw a fish (circle, happy face, heart) and cut it out. *2.* Cut out the fat man (tall woman, car, boat) that Maria drew.

cylinder *1.* Show the cylinder to the class. *2.* Lay the cylinder on its side. *3.* Look at me (the door) through the cylinder. *4.* Drop a coin (bottle cap, pencil) through the cylinder.

damp Touch (wipe) your forehead (cheek, chin, nose) with the damp (moist) cloth.

dampen Dampen the towel (handkerchief) and wipe your forehead (chin, cheek, nose).

dance *1.* Dance with the doll. *2.* Draw a fat man dancing with a thin woman.

danger Draw a symbol that indicates danger.

dangerous *1.* Draw (touch, pick up) a dangerous object. *2.* Hop (swim) to a man who has a dangerous profession *(policeman pc).*

dark *1.* Draw (Pretend you are) an animal that can see in the dark. *2.* Turn out (off) the lights to make the room dark. *3.* Draw a circle (triangle, heart, house) with dark (light) lines.

darken Draw a heart (circle, triangle) with light lines. Now darken the lines.

dash *1.* Dash to the door (window, chalkboard, desk). *2.* Dash around the class (desk). *3.* Write the word *soup* putting a dash between the letters.

date *1.* Write today's date (the date you were born). *2.* Write a note to Maria and date it.

daughter *1.* Draw a family. The daughter has a purse

(cup) in one hand and an umbrella (toothbrush) in the other. 2. Write (tell us) your daughter's name.

day *1.* Circle (underline) a month that has 28 (30, 31) days. *2.* Jump (walk, run) to a month that has 30 days *(cc-2)*.

dead *1.* Write the name of an actor (actress, author; a singer, painter) who is dead (still alive). *2.* Pretend you're dead. *3.* Shake hands with (pull the nose of) a person who has been dead for more than twenty years *(cc-8)*.

deaf Cup your hand to your ear and pretend your slightly deaf.

deal *1.* Pick up the deck and deal five cards to Maria. *2.* Jump (skip, limp) to a subject that deals with numbers (important dates, words) *(cc-6)*.

death Swim (hop, jump) to the person whose death occurred (took place) in 1922 *(cc-8)*.

decide I want either Pedro or Maria to come to the desk. Decide who will come by flipping a coin.

deck *1.* Show the deck of cards to the class. *2.* Cut (shuffle) the deck of cards and then deal me five cards.

declare *1.* Write the date that your country declared its independence. *2.* Kneel in front of Maria and declare that you love her.

decline *1.* When Pedro asks you to dance, decline by shaking your head (kicking him, slapping him). *2.* Draw a car going down a gentle decline.

decorate Draw a woman wearing a long dress decorated with flowers (hearts, stars, diamonds).

decrease Draw some hearts (flowers, stars, butterflies) on the chalkboard. Now decrease (increase) the number you drew by two.

dedicate Open this book and tell the class who it was dedicated to.

deep *1.* Draw a boy swimming in deep (shallow) water. *2.* Speak in a deep (high) voice. *3.* Pretend you're in a deep sleep. Maria will try to wake you by shaking you, but don't wake up.

defend Everybody, make a paper ball and when I count to three, throw it at Pedro. Pedro, defend (protect) yourself with your notebook.

degree *1.* Cut the hair of (throw the ball to) the student who has a degree in mathematics *(cc-6)*. *2.* Touch (kick) a student who has a degree from a university that was founded in 1636 *(cc-13)*. *3.* Pick up the protractor and draw a forty-degree angle.

delay *1.* I'm going to give you a command. Delay your action for ten seconds. *2.* Jump (walk, swim) to the door. Do it without any (after a short) delay.

deliver *1.* Deliver the book (notebook, magazine, envelope, package) to Maria. *2.* Pick up the bottle (plastic bat) and deliver a blow to Pedro's shoulder (arm, back).

demonstrate Pick up two pencils and demonstrate how to eat with chopsticks.

dense *1.* On the map locate an area that has a dense (sparse) population. *2.* Draw a chimney with dense smoke coming out of it. *3.* Draw a dense forest.

dentist *1.* Push (pull, shove) Pedro to the dentist *(pc)*. *2.* Maria, draw a face with a big open mouth. Pedro, you're a dentist. Examine the teeth in the mouth that Maria drew.

department store Accompany Maria to the department store *(pc)* and help her select a present for the teacher *(use magazine cutouts)*.

deposit *1.* Go to the bank *(pc)*, fill out a deposit slip, and deposit some money (make a deposit). *2.* Deposit the book (tray, box, toy) on the table.

desert *1.* Draw a plant found in the desert. *2.* Locate a desert on your map. *3.* Write the name of a famous desert.

deserve Maria wrote a perfect (nearly perfect) test. She deserves a big round of applause (a pat on the back).

design Design the car (house) of the future.

desire Hop (fly the plane, drive the car) to a country you desire (would like) to visit *(cc-4)*.

desk *1.* Jump to (sit on, walk around) the desk. *2.* Clear off the desk. *3.* Help Pedro move the desk. *4.* Push the desk against the wall. *5.* Stand in front of (in back of, next to, near, on) the desk.

destroy Pedro, write a note (letter) to Maria. Maria read it and then destroy it by tearing it up.

detach Detach (tear out) a sheet of paper from your notebook.

detective *1.* Write the name of a famous detective *(e.g., Sherlock Holmes).* *2.* Pretend you're a detective and follow Maria around the class.

devote *1.* I want you to devote the next ten minutes to working in pairs. *2.* Write how much time you devoted to your English lesson last night.

dial Pick up the phone and dial Maria's number. As you dial each number, call it out.

dialogue *1.* Practice (review, study, look at) the dialogue with your partner. *2.* Act out the dialogue in front of the class. *3.* Choose a part in the dialogue. *4.* Write a short dialogue.

diameter *1.* Draw a circle with a diameter of ten inches. *2.* Draw two circles. Make the diameter of the first circle the same length as (twice as long as) that of the second. *3.* Measure the diameter of a coin (bottle cap, button).

diamond *1.* Draw a diamond (heart, star, house). *2.* Add the numbers seven and ten, and put (enclose) the sum inside a diamond (square).

dice *1.* Roll the dice and put the number on the chalkboard. *2.* Put the dice in the glass, cover the opening with your hand, shake the glass, and roll (throw, spill) the dice out on the desk.

dictate *1.* Dictate one of the commands to your partner. *2.* I'm going to dictate some commands to you. After each command, I will pause for you to write it down.

dictionary *1.* Show your dictionary to the class. *2.* Look up the word *car* in your dictionary. *3.* Tie the ribbon (string, yarn) around the dictionary. *4.* Open your dictionary to page 25 and write the first (last) word on the chalkboard.

die *1.* Pull the nose (hair, left ear) of a person who died less than thirty years ago *(cc-8)*. *2.* Touch the chin (cheek, forehead, neck) of the person who died in 1968 *(cc-8)*.

differ Touch (pick up, point to) two geometric figures that differ in size (shape, color).

different *1.* Hold up two geometric figures that have different colors (sizes, shapes). *2.* Touch (point to) two different students. *3.* Put a number on the chalkboard. Now put a different (the same) number in Maria's notebook.

difficult *1.* Put a difficult (an easy) math problem on the chalkboard. *2.* Point to (hold up, give me) a subject you find difficult *(cc-6)*. *3.* Formulate (write) a difficult (simple) command.

dig *1.* Pick up the shovel (spade) and pretend you're digging a hole. Throw the dirt over your shoulder. *2.* Draw a picture of a tool you use to dig with.

dinner Cut the hair of (shake hands with) a student who usually has dinner at 7:30 *(student-made cc / cc-10)*.

dip Dip your finger (thumb, elbow) into the water that's in the bowl (pail, glass, cup).

83

direct *1.* Direct the class for the next five minutes. *2.* Stand up and close your eyes. I'm going to direct you to the desk. *3.* Put the candle in direct contact with the ruler (book, eraser, pen). *4.* Walk directly to the door (window, chalkboard).

dirt Draw a boy with some dirt on his face (forehead, chin).

dirty *1.* Draw a boy with a dirty (clean) face (tie, shirt, hat). *2.* Show us a dirty (clean) sheet of paper.

disappear Pretend you're a magician and make the coin (paper ball, Maria) disappear.

discover *1.* Write the name of the man who discovered America. *2.* Go out of the room. I'm going to hide a piece of chalk. Come back and see if you can discover (find) where I hid it.

disease Look at the chalkboard and you will see the word *cancer*. Cancer is a disease. Next to it write the name of another disease.

dissolve Dissolve an aspirin (some salt) in a glass (cup) of water.

distance *1.* Draw two circles (flowers, hearts, stars) on your paper and measure the distance between them. *2.* Measure the distance between Maria's eyes (from her elbow to her wrist).

distant *1.* Point to (smile at) a student who's distant from you. *2.* Place the can (chalk, book, ruler) distant from (close to) the glass. *3.* Speak with a distant (strong) voice.

distribute Distribute the papers (command cards, clips, test booklets, answer sheets).

dive *1.* Pretend you're on a diving board and are about to dive into the water. *2.* Draw a man diving into a swimming pool (lake). *3.* Fly the plane and make it dive.

divide *1.* Divide the students in the class into four groups. *2.* Draw a square (rectangle, circle) and divide it in half with a horizontal (vertical, diagonal) line. *3.* Divide twenty by five (five into twenty).

dizzy *1.* Pretend you're dizzy. *2.* Spin around until you become dizzy.

do *1.* Do whatever I do. *2.* Do the exercises on page ten. *3.* Do me a favor. Please open the window (erase the chalkboard, take the attendance). *4.* I have two books (pencils, coins) on my desk. If you do too, raise your left (right) hand.

doctor *1.* You're a doctor. Take Pedro's temperature with the thermometer (feel Maria's pulse, examine my eyes). *2.* Pedro is sick. Roberto and Carlos, carry him to the doctor *(pc)*.

dodge Maria, throw the ball (sponge, cork, paper ball) at Pedro. Pedro, dodge it.

dog *1.* Imitate (bark like) a dog. *2.* Pretend you're a dog. Growl and chase the cat *(another student pretends she's a cat)*.

doll *1.* Kiss (hug, shake hands with, dance with) the doll. *2.* Tie the ribbon (yarn) in the doll's hair. *3.* Rock the doll to sleep.

dollar *1.* Draw a big (huge, tiny) dollar sign. *2.* Swim (jump, run) to the student who has twenty dollars *(cc-9)*.

donkey Bray like (pretend you are) a donkey.

don't *1.* Pick up the small red triangle, but don't show it to the class. *2.* Walk (run, hop, jump) around the class (desk, teacher). Don't stop until I tell you to.

door *1.* Open (close, kick, hop to) the door. *2.* Open the door wide (a crack, a little bit). *3.* Stick your head (foot, hand) out the door. *4.* Draw a house with two doors. *5.* Erase the door on the house you drew.

doorknob *1.* Slowly (quickly) turn the doorknob and open the door. *2.* Hang the towel (hanger, picture of your teacher) on the doorknob.

doorway *1.* Stand (sit, stoop, squat) in the doorway. *2.* Draw a girl (fat man) standing in the doorway holding a flower.

dot *1.* Make some dots (dashes) on your paper. *2.* Draw a circle (square, triangle, heart) and fill it with dots.

dotted *1.* Draw a long (short) dotted line. *2.* Sign (print) your name on the dotted line that Pedro drew on the chalkboard.

double *1.* Write a number that's double (half) the number I say. *2.* Draw double the number of circles (hearts) that Pedro drew. *3.* Hit double the number of students that Maria pinched (slapped). *4.* Write the number that's double the sum of seven plus three.

down *1.* Sit down. *2.* Pick up the book (key, triangle, ruler, purse), show it to the class, and then put it down. *3.* Stand on the chair (desk). Now get down. *4.* Look down (up, to your left, over your shoulder).

dozen *1.* Give me a dozen paper balls (coins, toothpicks, bottle caps, matches). *2.* Draw a dozen circles (chairs, eyes, hearts, triangles).

drag Drag the chair (teacher) to the door (window, desk, chalkboard).

draw *1.* Draw the moon surrounded by stars (clouds, hearts). *2.* Draw a cat (happy face, fat man). *3.* I'm going to draw a number from the hat. Whoever has that number will perform the next command. *4.* Draw Maria aside and whisper something in her ear.

drawer *1.* Open (close, pull out, push in) the drawer. *2.* Put your wallet (pen, pencil, notebook) in the top (bottom) drawer. *3.* Draw a dresser with four drawers.

drawing *1.* Draw a picture of your teacher and then show your drawing to the class. *2.* Let's vote for the best drawing. *3.* Congratulate (shake hands with) the student whose drawing was voted the best.

dream Lay down your head and pretend you're sleeping. Smile (frown) because you're having a good (pleasant, bad) dream.

dress *1.* Point to (stand beside, smile at) a woman who's wearing a dress (skirt). *2.* Draw a woman wearing a striped (plain, checked) dress.

dressmaker Go to the dressmaker *(pc)* and have her

design a dress (blouse) for you.

drink *1.* Drink the glass of water very slowly. *2.* Pick up the can of beer *(empty container)* and take a drink. *3.* Put the tea bag in the cup and pretend you're drinking a cup of tea. *4.* Draw a woman (man) drinking a cup of coffee (glass of water).

drip Wet the towel (handkerchief, rag) and drip some water on the teacher's head (hand, nose).

drive *1.* Drive the jeep (truck, motorcycle, ambulance) to the window (door). *2.* Drive the blue car around the class (desk, teacher). *3.* Drive the nail into the board and then pull it out.

drop *1.* Drop the bottle caps (coins) into the can (glass) one by one. *2.* Drop the book (notebook, candle, eraser) onto the floor. *3.* Pick up the eyedropper and squeeze a few drops of water on Maria's nose. *4.* Sing loudly and then have your voice drop off.

drown *1.* Pretend you're drowning and call out for help. *2.* Throw the rope to the student who's drowning.

drugstore *1.* Go (skip, swim) to the drugstore *(pc)* and buy some medicine *(use play money)*. *2.* Write the name of a drugstore.

drum *1.* Pretend the can is a drum and the pencils are drumsticks. *2.* Drum your fingers on the table.

drunk *1.* Pick up the can of beer *(empty container)*, take a drink, and then pretend you're drunk. *2.* Walk (act) as if you were drunk.

dry *1.* Dry your hands (face) on the towel. *2.* Cry, stop crying, pick up the napkin (paper towel), and dry your eyes. *3.* Draw two big circles on the chalkboard. Throw some water at one of the circles. Now touch (stand in front of) the dry (wet) circle.

duck *1.* Quack like a duck. *2.* Draw a duck swimming in a lake. *3.* When I throw the sponge (paper ball, cork), duck so that I don't hit you.

dull *1.* Touch (feel) the point of the dull (sharp) pencil. *2.* Sharpen the dull pencil.

dump *1.* Dump the books (notebooks, papers, bottle caps) on the desk. *2.* Everybody, make a paper ball and put it in the bowl. Pedro, dump the contents of the bowl on the teacher's head (into the wastebasket).

dust Pick up the rag (duster) and dust the furniture in the classroom.

duster Pick up the duster and dust the teacher's head (shoes, desk).

each *1.* Give each student in the first (second, last) row a coin (slip of paper, bottle cap, toothpick). *2.* Tell some students to stand up. Point to each one as he or she stands up. *3.* Stand in front of a friend and pull each other's hair (nose, ear, ears).

ear *1.* Pull (touch, point to) an ear (both ears, a friend's ears). *2.* Hang the hanger on my left ear. *3.* Put the pencil in back of your ear. *4.* When Maria sings (shouts), stick your finger in your ears. *5.* Draw a man with big (small, pointed) ears.

early *1.* Touch (point to, shake) a student who came to class early (late) today. *2.* Sing (whisper, shout, write) the name of a student who gets up early *(student-made cc)*.

earn *1.* Congratulate (shake hands with) the student who earned an "A" on the test. *2.* Hop to the person who earns his living by cutting hair (working in a hospital, flying airplanes) *(pc's)*.

earring *1.* Put on (take off) the earring (bracelet, necklace). *2.* Draw a woman wearing big (tiny, enormous, oval, triangular, round) earrings.

earth Draw a picture of the solar system and have an arrow pointing to the earth (sun, second planet from the sun).

east *1.* Face east (west, north, south). *2.* Write the name of a city located on the East (West) Coast.

easy *1.* Put an easy (a hard) math problem on the chalkboard and then solve it. *2.* Give Maria an easy (a difficult) command. *3.* Walk (swim) around the class at an easy (a fast) pace.

eat *1.* Pretend you're eating. *2.* Jump (hop, swim, run) to the student who's eating a carrot *(distribute plastic food items)*. *3.* Wink at the student who eats dinner at 6:30 *(student-made cc)*. *4.* Pick up two pencils and demonstrate how to eat with chopsticks.

echo *1.* Maria is going to speak and you will be her echo. *2.* Echo everything I say.

edge *1.* Sit on the edge of your chair. *2.* Put (set, place) the book (pen, bowl, eraser) on the edge of the desk. *3.* Touch the edge (blade) of the knife. *4.* I want this row (group of students) to form a crowd. Pedro, edge your way through the crowd.

egg *1.* Put the fried egg on the plate and serve it to Maria. *2.* Fry the egg in the frying pan. *3.* Draw an egg and color the yolk yellow. *4.* Pretend you're cracking an egg.

either *1.* Give (hand) me either a pen or a pencil. *2.* Place a chair (student) on either side of the desk (teacher).

elastic Touch something that is elastic (that stretches) *(e.g., a rubber band).*

elbow *1.* Rest your elbows on the desk (on Pedro's head, shoulders). *2.* Stand next to Maria and elbow her. *3.* Touch your right knee with your left elbow.

elect *1.* Congratulate (give the flower to) the student who was just elected class president. *2.* I want each group to elect (choose, select) a leader.

electricity Touch (draw) an object that uses electricity.

elephant Imitate (pretend you are) an elephant (airplane; a dog, cow).

eliminate Eliminate all the words that begin with the letter "s" (end with the letter "k," have five letters).

else *1.* Point to (touch, look at, smile at) Pedro. Now point to someone else. *2.* Pick up the ball (book, ribbon, pencil, cup). Now put it down and pick up something else.

empty *1.* Empty the bottle (glass, cup) into the pail. *2.* Pick up the empty (full, half-full) glass and show it to the class. *3.* Fill the cup with paper (chalk, bottle caps) and then empty it. *4.* Empty the wastebasket (ashtray).

enclose *1.* Write your name and then enclose it in parentheses (brackets). *2.* Draw a heart (happy face, house, car) enclosed in a square (triangle, rectangle).

encourage Encourage your teammate in the contest by shouting, "Come on, you can do it!"

end *1.* Hold the string (ruler) by both ends. *2.* Tie a knot in the end of the rope (yarn). *3.* Tie one end of the rope to the doorknob. *4.* Write a word that ends (begins) with the letter "r." *5.* Write a command that ends with the word *table*.

enemy Write the names of two countries that are (were) enemies today (in World War II).

engaged *1.* Give the flower (heart) to a student who's engaged to be married. *2.* Pull the hair (ears, nose) of the student who's engaged in drawing circles (stars) on the chalkboard.

engine Touch the part of the car where you find the engine.

engineer Draw a bridge (church, house, tall building) and take it to the engineer *(pc)*.

enjoy *1.* Write the name of a movie (book, play) that you enjoyed (liked, found interesting). *2.* Pretend you're playing a sport (game) that you enjoy.

enormous Draw an enormous (a big, small, tiny) house (heart, triangle, happy face).

enough *1.* I'm going to pour some water into your glass. Whistle (cry, raise your hand) when it's enough. *2.* Walk (run) to the student who has (doesn't have) enough money to buy a car (house, radio, notebook) *(cc-9).*

enter *1.* Enter (come in) the class smiling (crying, laughing, dancing, singing). *2.* Write the year you entered the university.

entire *1.* Write the entire alphabet on the back of the envelope. *2.* Say hello to the entire (whole) class. Now, only to this half. *3.* Pick up an object that's made entirely (partly) of plastic (rubber, wood, paper, metal).

entrance *1.* Stand (stoop, squat, sit) in the entrance of the door. *2.* Come in the class making a dramatic entrance.

envelope *1.* Address (tear open, cut open, glue shut) the envelope. *2.* Write a letter to Maria, insert it in the envelope, and deliver it to her. *3.* Write a check, put it in the envelope, and hand it to Pedro.

equal *1.* Make two equal stacks of coins (match boxes, blocks). *2.* Give Maria seven coins and then give an equal (lesser, greater) number to Pedro. *3.* Write two numbers whose sum equals twenty. *4.* Draw the equal sign under (inside) a square.

erase *1.* Erase the chalkboard slowly (quickly, from left to right). *2.* Draw a heart (circle, fat man, tree, church) and then erase it with your right (left) hand. *3.* Write a word that has four letters and then erase the two end (middle) letters.

eraser *1.* Put (place) the eraser on your head and walk around the class slowly (quickly). *2.* Drop the pencil eraser into Maria's purse (my pocket, the cup).

erect *1.* Erect (set up, build, construct) a tower with the spools (match boxes, blocks). *2.* Stand erect (stooped over).

error *1.* Correct the errors (mistakes) in the sentence on the chalkboard. *2.* Congratulate the student who had the fewest (least) errors.

escape *1.* Go to the jail *(pc),* pick up the saw, saw the bars, and escape. *2.* Pedro and Carlos, hold Roberto tight. Roberto try to escape (get away).

establish Give (hand) Maria the university that was established (founded) in 1636 *(cc-13)*.

estimate Maria, draw many small circles (hearts, chairs) on the chalkboard. Pedro, estimate (guess) the number of circles she drew. Carlos, count them and tell us the exact number.

even *1.* Draw a big triangle. Now draw another one that's even bigger. *2.* Divide the coins evenly between Pedro and Maria. *3.* Write all the numbers from one to twenty. Now circle (cross out, underline) the even (odd) numbers.

evening Write the name of a program that's on tv Monday evening (morning, afternoon).

event Walk around (change places with) the student

who has the event that happened (took place) in 1492 *(cc-7)*.

ever If you've ever been to London (eaten lobster, been late to class, climbed a mountain, driven a car), raise your right (left) hand (foot).

every *1.* Touch (slap, shake hands with) every student in the last (back, front) row. *2.* Wave to (smile at) every student in the class. *3.* Every time I point to the ceiling, stand up and clap (cry, sneeze).

every other *1.* Draw a row of triangles (stars, eyes, hearts). Now cross out (underline, draw a circle around) every other triangle. *2.* Touch the nose (forehead, chin, head) of every other student in the first row.

everybody I want everybody to stand up (be seated, take a seat, laugh, cough).

everything *1.* Take everything off of your desk and put it under your seat. *2.* Touch (pick up, point to) everything that's on (some of the things that are on) the teacher's desk.

exact *1.* Maria, draw many stars. Pedro, tell the class the exact number of stars that Maria drew. *2.* Draw a horizontal line that's exactly (approximately) five inches long. *3.* Draw a line that's exactly (almost, nearly) as long as the one that Pedro drew.

exaggerate *1.* Draw many small flowers (hats, chairs). Exaggerate the number. *2.* Draw a man. Exaggerate the size of his eyes (nose, mouth, ears).

examine *1.* You're a doctor. Examine Pedro's eyes (back, neck, heart, hands). *2.* Run to the supermarket *(pc)* and examine the apple (orange, banana).

exceed Pedro, draw some cars (stars, hearts, boats, happy faces, clouds). Maria, draw some cars, too. I want the number of cars that you draw to exceed the number that Pedro drew by three.

except Touch (point to, shake hands with, smile at) every student in the class except (but) Pedro.

exchange *1.* Exchange places with a friend. *2.* Exchange tests with the person sitting next to you. Now correct each other's test.

excuse *1.* Bump (walk, run) into a student and excuse yourself. *2.* Sneeze loudly and then say "Excuse me."

exercise *1.* Do some physical exercises and then sit down panting. *2.* Do (work) the exercises on page 55.

exhale *1.* Inhale, hold your breath for ten seconds (until I count to ten), and then exhale. *2.* Hold your breath as long as you can and then exhale.

expand Fill the balloon with air and watch it expand. Now release it and watch it contract (shrink, fly away).

expect *1.* Pedro and Carlos are going to race to the door. Touch (wink at, write the name of) the one you expect to win (lose) the race. *2.* Shake hands with the student who's expecting a baby *(in relation to a student who is pregnant).*

expensive Pick up (draw, touch) an expensive (a cheap) object.

experiment Pick up the test tube and pretend you're a scientist doing (performing) an experiment.

explode Make (imitate) the sound of a bomb exploding.

extend *1.* Extend your left hand (right hand, left foot; both feet). *2.* Extend your hands palms up (down). *3.* Extend (stretch out) the ribbon (string, rope) on the table (floor).

extra *1.* Draw a hand with an extra finger (a foot with an extra toe). *2.* Maria, if you have an extra pen, lend it to Pedro. *3.* Draw a circle (square, kite, happy face). Make it extra small (big).

extract *1.* You're a dentist. Pick up the pliers and extract (pull out) one of Pedro's teeth. *2.* Extract the square root of the number I put on the chalkboard.

eye *1.* Point to an eye (both eyes, one of your two eyes). *2.* Stand in front of (behind) a student who has blue (brown) eyes. *3.* Draw a sad face with triangles (hearts, diamonds, stars) for eyes. *4.* Stick the thread through the eye of the needle.

eyebrow *1.* Draw a sad (happy) face with bushy (thick, thin) eyebrows. *2.* Walk (run, swim, skip) to Maria and touch (point to) one (both) of her eyebrows.

eyelash Draw a girl (woman) with long eyelashes.

face *1.* Draw (make) a happy (sad, surprised) face. *2.* Make a face at Pedro. *3.* Deal me five cards face up (down). *4.* Face the door (teacher, chalkboard, window, other way). *5.* Draw an airplane facing the upper (lower) left-hand corner of your paper.

fade *1.* Draw a horizontal (vertical, diagonal) line that begins dark and slowly fades away. *2.* Count to ten. After each number your voice will fade a little until it finally disappears.

fail Point to (smile at, make a face at) the student who failed (was unable) to catch the ball (knock over the bottle, perform the command).

faint *1.* When you see the mouse (spider), scream and then faint. *2.* Pedro, pretend you're Dracula (a monster). Maria, look at him and faint. *3.* Say hello to Pedro in a faint (loud) voice. *4.* Draw a heart (kite, cloud) with faint (light, dark, heavy) lines.

fall *1.* Stand up, walk five steps, and then fall down. *2.* Toss the ball (coin, book) into the air and watch it fall. *3.* Count to ten. Begin speaking loudly, but after each number have your voice fall (drop) a little until it's only a whisper.

false *1.* Shake your head if you think the sentence on the chalkboard is false; nod if you think it's true. *2.* Take a bill out of your wallet and examine it to see if it's false.

familiar Sing (hum, whistle) a song that everybody (nobody) is familiar with.

family *1.* Write your full name on the chalkboard. Circle (cross out) your first name and draw a rectangle (triangle) around your family name. *2.* Draw a family with a tall father, a short mother, a fat son, and a thin daughter.

famous Write the name of (show the class the picture of) a famous singer (actor, actress, scientist, statesman).

fan *1.* Plug in (turn on, turn off) the fan. *2.* Fold the paper into a fan and fan the teacher (student sitting to your right; yourself).

fancy Draw a woman wearing a fancy (plain) dress (blouse).

far *1.* Stand far from (near) the window (door, desk, fan). *2.* Write the name of a city that's far from (near) here. *3.* Throw the ball (paper ball, bottle cap, sponge) as far as you can.

farm Imitate (pretend you are) an animal you see (find) on a farm (in the city).

farmer 1. Take the corn (cucumber, tomato) to the farmer *(pc)*. *2.* Drive the tractor (jeep, truck) to the farmer *(pc)*.

farther *1.* Pinch the cheeks (arm, nose) of the student who threw (kicked) the ball farther than Pedro did. *2.* Move (go, step) back a little farther. *3.* Throw (toss, hand, roll) the ball to someone who's sitting farther from the window than Maria is.

fast *1.* Walk (swim, hop) around the class (desk, teacher, chair) fast (very slowly). *2.* Count to twenty (draw a cat) as fast as you can. *3.* We're going to have a race to see who the fastest student is. *4.* Hold Pedro fast so that he can't move.

fasten *1.* Fasten the papers together with a clip (staple). *2.* Draw a picture of your teacher and fasten it to the wall. *3.* Fasten (attach) the handkerchief to Pedro's shirt with the clothespin (safety pin).

fat Draw a fat (thin) man wearing a hat (beard, mustache, wide belt, narrow tie).

father Draw a family. The father has a short beard (long nose, big mustache; curly hair, pointed ears).

fault *1.* Pedro, crash your car into Maria's. Lucia, touch (point to, pull the hair of) the student who was at fault. *2.* If the accident was Pedro's fault, twist (take hold of) his arm and take him to jail.

favor Do me a favor. Please close the door (open the window, erase the chalkboard, bring me a piece of chalk, sharpen my pencil).

favorite *1.* Write the name of your favorite singer (actor, actress, song, movie, book). *2.* Drive the car (bus, jeep) to the student whose favorite singer's (actor's) name begins with the letter "s" *(student-made cc).*

fear *1.* Stand in front of the class with a look of fear on your face. *2.* Write the name of (show the class the picture of) an animal you fear.

feather *1.* Draw (imitate) an animal that has feathers. *2.* Measure (touch your nose with, tickle me with) the feather.

feed *1.* Pretend Pedro's your baby. He's hungry. Open the jar of baby food *(empty container)* and feed him. *2.* Pedro, pretend you're a dog. Maria, feed him the bone.

feel *1.* Close your eyes, feel the object I put in your hand, and guess what it is. *2.* Feel the point of the pencil to see if it's sharp. *3.* Feel Pedro's pulse. *4.* Feel my forehead to see if I have a fever. *5.* Draw a man who's feeling happy (sad, angry).

feet *1.* Touch (point to, raise, lift) your feet. *2.* Stand on (put the book on) Maria's feet. *3.* Draw a boy (girl, man, woman) with big (pointed, small) feet.

female *1.* Count (smile at) the females in this room. *2.* Give the flower (candy bar, cookie) to a female student.

fence Draw a house with a fence around the front (back) yard.

fever *1.* Feel my forehead to see if I have a fever. *2.* Pretend the pencil is a thermometer, stick it under your arm, and check your temperature to see if you have a fever.

few Touch a place on the map where few (many) people live.

fight *1.* Pretend you're fighting with Pedro. *2.* I want this row of students to form a crowd in front of the door. Maria, fight your way through the crowd.

file *1.* Pick up the nail file and file (shape) your nails. *2.* Stand in (form) a single (double) file line.

fill *1.* Fill the glass (pitcher, cup) up to the top (halfway up) with water (crumpled newspaper, paper balls). *2.* Fill my pocket with paper (bottle caps). *3.* When Maria drives her car to the gas station *(pc)*, the attendant will fill her tank for her.

fill in Fill in the blanks in the sentences I wrote (put) on the chalkboard.

101

film *1.* Pretend you're loading a roll of film into the camera. *2.* Write the name of a film that's playing now (that was on tv last night). *3.* Whistle (laugh, smile, wink) at a student who saw (went to) the same film you did last week *(student-made cc)*.

find *1.* Go out of the room, come back in, and try to find the piece of chalk that Maria hid. *2.* Draw a picture of something you find in the kitchen (living room, bedroom, bathroom). *3.* Find a student who was born in the same month as you *(student-made cc)*.

fine *1.* Maria, drive the car very fast. Pedro, you're a policeman. Give her a fine (ticket) for speeding. *2.* Squeeze the hand (foot, nose) of the student who said he's feeling fine.

finger *1.* Measure (tie the string around) one of Pedro's fingers. *2.* Put your finger in your mouth and bit it. *3.* Draw a hand with long (short) fingers.

finish *1.* Write five commands. When you finish, look up. *2.* Begin to draw a happy face, stop, kick Pedro, and then finish it. *3.* Finish the drawing that Maria started (began). *4.* Run to the student who finished first (last) in the race.

fire *1.* Draw a house on fire. *2.* You're going to execute Pedro. Pick up the rifle. Ready, aim, fire. Don't forget to make the sound of the rifle.

fireman *1.* Draw a house on fire, cut it out, and take it to the fireman *(pc)*. *2.* Pretend you're a fireman and the rope is a fire hose.

firetruck When Maria lights the candle (match), you will drive the firetruck to her and blow it out.

firm *1.* Take a firm hold of Maria's wrist (arm, elbow). *2.* Give me a firm (weak) handshake. *3.* Firmly push Pedro down into his seat.

first *1.* Write the first (last) letter of the alphabet and circle it. *2.* Draw a rectangle around your first name and erase your last name. *3.* Wink at the student who came in first in the race. *4.* You're going to draw a cat (house), but first you will point to the door (window).

fish *1.* Put (place) the red fish under (next to, in front of, in back of, on top of) the blue fish. *2.* Draw a fish with pointed teeth (three eyes, two feet). *3.* Pretend you're fishing.

fist *1.* Make a fist. *2.* Threaten Pedro with your fist. *3.* Pretend you're angry and shake your fist in front of my face.

fit *1.* Pick up (touch) an object that will (won't) fit in your pocket (purse). *2.* Draw a man wearing a hat that doesn't fit because it's too big (small). *3.* Pedro, remove (take off) your ring. Maria, try on Pedro's ring to see if it fits.

fix *1.* Pretend the tv is broken and try to fix it. *2.* Draw a picture of your teacher and fix (attach) it to the wall (door, window, chalkboard). *3.* Fix your eyes on Maria.

flag *1.* Hold up (wave) the flag. *2.* Stick the flag in your (my) pocket. *3.* Draw your country's flag.

flame *1.* Turn up (down) the flame on the cigarette lighter. *2.* Light the candle and hold the flame under

103

the can (pass the scissors through the flame). *3.* Draw a candle with a big (small) flame.

flap *1.* Pretend you're a bird and flap your wings. *2.* Tuck the flap into the envelope.

flash Use the mirror to flash (reflect) some light into my eyes (face).

flashlight *1.* Shine the flashlight on the floor (door, ceiling, chalkboard). *2.* Take the flashlight apart and then put it back together. *3.* Unscrew the cap and remove the batteries from the flashlight.

flat *1.* Pick up a flat object. *2.* Draw a house with flat land in front of it and hilly land in back of it. *3.* Draw a car with a flat tire.

flatten Roll the clay into a ball (cylinder) and then flatten it.

flexible Pick up a flexible (rigid) object *(e.g., a straw, ruler).*

flip *1.* Flip a coin and call it Heads or Tails in the air. *2.* Flip (turn) the record (tape) over and play the other side. *3.* Flip (thumb) through the pages of your English book.

float *1.* Pour some water into the pail (bowl, cup, glass) and float the cork (sponge) in it. *2.* Hold a sheet (piece) of paper horizontally in front of your nose, let go, and watch it float down.

floor *1.* Point to (touch, sit on, throw your notebook on) the floor. *2.* Draw a house and erase the floor (door, roof, walls). *3.* In slow motion, punch Pedro in the jaw and floor him.

flow *1.* Write the name of a river that flows into the Atlantic Ocean (Pacific Ocean, Gulf of Mexico). *2.* Draw a girl with long flowing hair.

flower *1.* Give (present, offer) the flower to Maria. *2.* Put the flower in Pedro's pocket. *3.* Draw many (a few) small flowers enclosed in a square (rectangle, triangle). *4.* Pick up the watering pot and water the flower. *5.* Smell the flower.

flute Pick up the pencil (pen, rod) and pretend you're playing the flute.

fly *1.* Extend your arms, pretend you're an airplane, and fly around the class (teacher, desk). *2.* Make a paper airplane and fly it to the window (out the door). *3.* Roll up the newspaper and pretend you're swatting a fly (mosquito).

focus Focus the camera and take (snap) my picture.

fold 1. Fold the towel (handkerchief, napkin, paper) into a triangle. 2. Fold the paper and insert (put) it in the envelope. 3. Fold your arms. 4. Fold your hands and pray.

follow 1. Write the number that follows ten (the letter that follows "c"). *2.* The student who has the number that follows (precedes) two will now sneeze (cry, sing) *(cc-12). 3.* Pretend you're a detective and follow Maria.

food *1.* Write the name of a restaurant that serves Chinese (Mexican, Japanese, Italian) food. *2.* Pretend

Maria is a baby, pick up the jar of baby food *(empty container)*, and feed her.

fool Close your eyes. Some students will stand in back of you. They will say hello to you and try to fool you by disguising their voices. See if you can guess who's speaking.

foot *1.* Point to (touch, show me, raise, lower) a foot. *2.* Put your left foot in the wastebasket (on the chair). *3.* Stand (put the notebook) on Pedro's right foot. *4.* Draw a boy standing at the foot (top) of a stairs (hill, mountain).

for *1.* Jump (hop, dance, sing, clap) for ten seconds. *2.* Draw a happy face with hearts (stars, diamonds, triangles) for its eyes. *3.* Hold open the door for Maria. *4.* Please take the attendance for me today.

force *1.* Squeeze my hand gently. Now squeeze it hard applying some force. *2.* Force your way through the crowd of students blocking the exit (door).

forearm *1.* Measure (draw a heart on) Pedro's forearm. *2.* Cut a piece of string the same length as my (your) forearm. *3.* Wrap the rope (yarn, string) around Maria's forearm (wrist, ankle).

forehead *1.* Touch (point to, tap) your forehead. *2.* Draw a boy with a star (flower, heart, diamond, triangle) on his forehead (chin). *3.* Draw a small heart (happy face), cut it out, wet it, and stick it to Maria's forehead.

forest *1.* Draw (imitate) an animal that's found in the forest. *2.* Draw a forest with many tall trees.

forget Kick (shake hands with) the student who usually forgets to bring his book to class.

fork *1.* Pick up the fork and pretend you're eating. *2.* Stick the fork into the potato (carrot, sponge). *3.* Walk around the class hitting (banging on) the can with the fork. *4.* Draw a road that has a fork in it.

form *1.* Form a circle with your hands. *2.* Form a triangle (square) with the bottle caps (coins, matches, toothpicks). *3.* Form the letter **C (L, V, M)** with the wire. *4.* Form (roll, shape) the clay into a ball.

forward *1.* Take three steps forward and two backwards. *2.* Form a single (double) file line and slowly (quickly) move (advance) forward. *3.* Come forward and sit up front.

found Hop (swim, jump) to the student who studies at a university that was founded (established) in 1636 *(cc-13)*.

frame *1.* Draw a picture of your teacher. Now draw a black frame around the picture and hang it on (fasten it to) the wall. *2.* Touch the frame of your (my) glasses.

free *1.* Hold the purse (book, notebook) in one of your hands and wave to me with your free hand. *2.* Pedro, tie Carlos up with the string. Maria, free him by cutting him loose. *3.* Touch (draw) an object that's free *(e.g., a leaf)*.

freeze *1.* Everyone, walk about the room. When I shout "freeze," you must remain perfectly still without moving. *2.* Touch a place on the map where it's always (usually) freezing cold.

frequently Walk around the class frequently stopping

107

(waving, coughing, sneezing).

fresh Open the window (door) to let in some fresh air.

friend *1.* Say (whisper, sing, shout) hello to a friend. *2.* Change places (shake hands) with a friend.

frighten Pedro, growl (pretend you're a monster, make a face) and frighten (scare) Maria.

from *1.* Walk (jump, hop) from Pedro to Maria. *2.* Smile at the student who's from Japan *(cc-4)*. *3.* Take the pen (pencil, book) from Pedro's desk and put it on Maria's. *4.* Stand far from (near) me. *5.* Read to the class from your history (math, biology) book.

front *1.* Stand in the front (back) of the class. *2.* Go to the front (back, middle) of the line. *3.* Draw a house with a tree in the front (back) yard. *4.* Show the class the front page of the newspaper.

frown *1.* Frown (smile, laugh, wink) at Maria. *2.* Walk (swim, jump) around the class with a frown (smile, grin) on your face.

fruit *1.* Put a piece of fruit on the tray and serve it to Pedro. *2.* Touch (pick up) a fruit that's usually red (that monkeys like to eat). *3.* If you ate some fruit today, raise your hand (foot).

fry Fry the egg in the frying pan.

frying pan *1.* Put the egg (fish) in the frying pan and place the frying pan on the stove. *2.* Draw a woman holding a frying pan with some fish in it. *3.* Hit me on the head with the frying pan.

full *1.* Pick up the full (empty) glass (cup). *2.* Hold your breath for a full minute. *3.* Write your full (first, middle, last) name. *4.* Swim (hop, jump, run) to the student whose pocket is full of paper (bottle caps, pencils).

funnel *1.* Use the funnel to pour some water from the glass (cup, bowl) back into the bottle. *2.* Walk around the class (teacher, desk, fan) with the funnel on your head.

funny Make (draw) a funny (sad, happy, serious) face.

furniture *1.* Draw (show me a picture of) a piece of furniture you find in the living room (bedroom, kitchen, classroom). *2.* Touch some of the furniture in our classroom. *3.* Write the name of a furniture store.

furniture polish Pick up the bottle of furniture polish *(empty container),* put some polish on the rag, and apply it to the teacher's desk.

further *1.* Twist the arm (ear, foot) of the student who threw (hit, kicked, batted) the ball further than Pedro did. *2.* Write the name of a city that's further from Los Angeles than San Francisco is.

gain *1.* Walk (swim, run) around the desk three times. Each time gain a little speed. *2.* Draw a picture of a man. Now draw another picture of the same man after he has gained (lost) ten kilos.

game *1.* If you're going to a football (basketball, baseball) game this weekend, raise your left (right) hand. *2.* Play a game of cards (tic-tac-toe) with me.

gap Draw a happy (sad) face with two teeth. There's a gap between the teeth.

garden *1.* Take the cucumber (tomato, carrot) to the man who works in a garden *(gardener pc)*. *2.* Draw a flower garden. *3.* Pick up the watering pot and water the plants in the garden you drew on the chalkboard.

gardener Give the flowers (pear, cucumber, carrot) to the gardener *(pc)*.

gas Drive the car (jeep, motorcycle) to the gas station *(pc)* and get some gas.

gas station *1.* Write the name of the intersection where the nearest gas station is located. *2.* Drive the red car to the gas station *(pc)*.

gather I want everyone in the first (last) row to gather around the teacher (my desk, Maria).

gather up Gather up the homework (tests, exercises, answer sheets, booklets).

generous You're a generous person. Give some money *(play money)* to all of the students in the second row.

gentle *1.* Give Pedro a gentle (rough) shove. *2.* Say hello to Maria in a gentle (harsh) voice. *3.* Hit Pedro on the head with the book (bottle, magazine, notebook, bat) gently (hard).

get *1.* Go to another classroom and get me an eraser. *2.* Stand on the chair. Now get down. *3.* Run to the door and cry when you get there. *4.* Get into three groups. *5.*

Pretend you're getting dressed. 6. Touch the student who's got a lot of money *(cc-9)*.

get up Swim (run, hop, jump) to the student who gets up at 7:30 *(student-made cc)*.

giant *1.* Take one small (tiny) step and then take two giant (big) ones. *2.* Pretend (make believe) you're a giant. *3.* Write the name of a children's story in which there is a giant (prince, princess, king, queen).

gift *1.* Give the gift (present) to the student who's celebrating his birthday today. *2.* Go to the department store *(pc)* and buy (purchase) a gift for Pedro *(use magazine cutouts and play money)*.

giraffe Draw a giraffe next to a house (church, tree, tall building).

girl *1.* Put the orange (pear, banana, cup of coffee) on the tray and serve it to a girl. *2.* Draw (pick up, touch) an object that you associate with girls (boys). *3.* Draw a girl with pigtails (a ponytail).

give *1.* Give the pen (eraser, book) to the student sitting in the corner. *2.* Give Pedro a kick (smile, pinch). *3.* Give the doll a kiss. *4.* Take the pen (purse) from Maria's desk, show it to the class, and then give it back (return it) to her.

glance *1.* Glance (stare) at the student sitting to your right (left). *2.* Glance at your (my, Pedro's) watch.

glare *1.* Glare (smile, frown) at a student who's wearing a tie (bracelet, beard, watch, ring). *2.* When Maria shines the flashlight in your eyes, put up your hand to block the glare.

glass *1.* Touch (pick up) something made of glass. *2.* Pour me (Maria, the teacher) a glass of water. *3.* Pour some (a little, a lot of) water into the glass (cup). *4.* Fill the glass with paper (leaves, bottle caps).

glasses *1.* Put on (take off) your glasses. *2.* Clean (wipe) your glasses on your shirt (the napkin). *3.* Pull the hair (nose, left ear) of a student who wears (doesn't wear) glasses. *4.* Draw a fat (thin, tall, short) man wearing glasses.

glove *1.* Put on (take off) the glove. *2.* Slap Pedro with the glove. *3.* Turn the glove inside out.

glue *1.* Cut out and glue a small circle to a big triangle. *2.* Spread some glue on a coin and glue it to a scrap of paper. *3.* Pick up the tube of glue, remove the cap, squeeze some glue onto the envelope, and glue it shut.

go *1.* Go to the desk (chalkboard, window, fan, door). *2.* Go to the supermarket (church, department store, clothing store) *(pc's)*. *3.* Go out the door (out of the class) crying (laughing, smiling, frowning, clapping).

going to *1.* When I count to five, you're going to stand up (cry, pull your nose, walk to the door, sneeze several times). *2.* Touch the student who's going to open the door (erase the chalkboard, turn off the lights).

gold Touch (point to) something made of gold (silver, plastic, metal, wood, paper, glass, leather).

good *1.* Congratulate (applaud) a student who got a good (an excellent) grade on the test. *2.* Write (spell) the

112

name of a good (bad) actor (actress, singer).

gorilla Pretend (make believe) you're a gorilla and beat your chest.

grab *1.* Grab Maria's purse (notebook, wallet, pencil, pen, eraser) and run. *2.* When Pedro runs (walks, hops) past you, grab him. *3.* Walk beside Pedro, slip (trip), and grab his arm.

graceful *1.* Pretend you're graceful dancer. *2.* Walk around the room gracefully (clumsily).

grade Shake hands with (applaud, smile at) the student who got the best (next to the best) grade on the test.

gradual *1.* Draw a graph showing a gradual (sudden) increase (decrease). *2.* Draw a hill with a gradual (steep) slope.

graduate *1.* Sing a song to the student who graduated with a degree in biology *(cc-6)*. *2.* Walk (jump, swim) around a student who graduated from a university that was founded in 1636 *(cc-13)*.

grapes *1.* Pretend you're eating the grapes (banana, orange). *2.* Serve the grapes to a student who's wearing tennis shoes. *3.* Draw a man (woman) eating a bunch of grapes.

grasp *1.* Grasp Pedro's wrist (arm, elbow, ankle). *2.* Grasp the glass (candle, stick, ruler).

grass *1.* Draw some grass under a tree. *2.* Go out of the class and come back with some grass. *3.* Pretend you're an animal that eats grass.

grave *1.* Draw a grave with some flowers on it. *2.* Sit in front of Pedro with a grave (serious, sad, happy, surprised) look on your face.

great *1.* Write the name of a person you think was a great world leader. *2.* Write a number that is greater than ten but less than twenty.

greet When the next student comes in (arrives), greet him or her with a smile (song, round of applause; silence).

grin *1.* Grin (smile, laugh, frown) at the student who's sitting behind (in front of, to the left of) Pedro. *2.* Walk (hop, run, swim) around the class with a grin (smile, frown).

grip *1.* Grip Pedro's shoulder (elbow, wrist, arm). *2.* Take a firm grip on the rope (stick, broom, back of the chair).

groan *1.* When Pedro drives the car (truck, jeep) into you, you will groan. *2.* Walk (jump, hop) around the class groaning.

ground *1.* Draw a bird (butterfly; an airplane) on the ground (in the air). *2.* Walk out of the classroom and touch the ground.

group *1.* Divide the class into four groups. *2.* Touch (change places with) a student who is in another group. *3.* Walk (hop) to the group sitting in the back (front) of the class.

growl Pretend you're a dog and growl (bark, howl, bite Pedro).

guard Pick up the gun (rifle) and stand in front of the

bank *(pc)*. You're a bank guard.

guess *1.* Close your eyes and stick out (extend) your hand. I'm going to put something in your hand. Guess what it is. *2.* Guess the number I wrote on my slip of paper.

guide Pedro, pretend (make believe) you're blind. Maria, guide him to the door (desk, window, chalkboard).

guitar *1.* Pretend you're playing the guitar (flute, piano, drums, trombone). *2.* Draw a man (woman, heart) playing the guitar.

gum *1.* Unwrap (remove the wrapper from) the gum, put (stick) it in your mouth, and chew it. *2.* Offer (serve, award) a stick (piece) of gum to the student who won the race. *3.* Blow a bubble with the bubble gum.

gun Aim the gun at Maria, pull the trigger, and shoot her saying, "bang."

had better You forgot (didn't bring) your book today. You'd better (you'll have to) share with Maria.

hair *1.* Pull (touch, pick up the scissors and cut) your (my) hair. *2.* Pull a friend's hair, jumping (hopping). *3.* Draw a man with long (short, curly, wavy) hair.

hairbrush Pick up the hairbrush and brush my (your, our) hair.

hairdresser Go to the hairdresser *(pc)* and have your hair done (combed, brushed, cut).

hairpin *1.* Form a square (triangle) with the hairpins. *2.* Bind the hairpins together with the string (yarn, rubber band). *3.* Put the hairpin in your hair.

half *1.* Draw a square (circle) and divide it in half with a vertical (diagonal) line. *2.* Tear (cut) the paper in half. *3.* Give half of the bottle caps (coins) to Maria. *4.* Draw ten hearts (stars, flowers) and then erase (cross out) half of them.

halfway *1.* Fill the glass halfway up with water (small paper balls, crumpled paper). *2.* Walk (jump, swim) across the class. When you reach the halfway point, turn around and go back to your seat.

halt Pretend you're a soldier and march around the class. When I raise my left (right) hand, you will halt (come to a halt).

hammer *1.* Pick up the hammer and hammer (drive) the nail into the board. *2.* Hold the hammer by the head (handle). *3.* Hit Pedro on the head (shoulder, thumb, back) with the plastic hammer.

hand *1.* Show me both hands (your right hand). *2.* Shake hands with me. *3.* Tie Pedro's hands together. *4.* Draw a clock with the big hand on the twelve and the little hand on the three. *5.* Put your hands on (over) your head. *6.* Give me a hand moving the desk. *7.* Hand (toss) Pedro the ball (book, pen).

hand in Hand in your papers (answer sheets, test booklets, homework).

handbag *1.* Put the pencil (eraser, pen) in Maria's handbag. *2.* Throw (toss, set) the handbag on the floor (desk).

handkerchief *1.* Fold the handkerchief once (twice, in half). *2.* Cover the glass (pen; your head) with the handkerchief (napkin). *3.* Stuff the handkerchief in your shirt pocket. *4.* Tie (make) a knot in the handkerchief.

handle *1.* Tie the string (yarn) to the handle of the cup. *2.* Touch (hold) the handle (head) of the hammer. *3.* Draw a cup with two handles.

handsome Write the name of a handsome actor (singer).

hang *1.* Hang the towel (handkerchief) on the back of Maria's chair (on the doorknob). *2.* Hang the hanger on the teacher's left (right) ear. *3.* Draw a picture of your teacher and hang it on the wall. *4.* Make a noose with the string and hang the doll.

hanger *1.* Hang the towel (handkerchief) on the hanger. *2.* Slide the hanger along the floor to Pedro. *3.* Draw a series of five small hangers (hearts, hats) in a row (column).

happen Walk (run, jump, swim) to the event that happened in 1492 *(cc-7)*.

happy *1.* Make (draw) a happy (sad, crazy, surprised) face. *2.* Draw a happy face with diamonds (triangles, hearts, stars) for its eyes. *3.* Draw a big (small) happy face with big (small) eyes (ears, teeth; with only one eye).

hard *1.* Pick up a hard (soft) object. *2.* Put a hard (an easy) math problem on the chalkboard.

hardly any Pull the nose (hair, ears, left foot) of the

student who has hardly any money *(cc-9)*.

harmful Show the class a harmful (useful) object *(e.g., the cigarettes, can opener)*.

harp *1.* Pretend you're playing the harp (piano, flute, drums). *2.* Draw a picture of a man (woman) playing the harp.

harsh Give Pedro a command in a harsh (soft, sweet, loud) voice.

hat *1.* Put on (take off) the hat (cap, tie, watch). *2.* Draw a fat man (happy face, sad face) wearing a big (small, triangular) hat.

have *1.* Slap the student who has the red car. *2.* Jump to the student who has dinner at 6:30 *(student-made cc)*. *3.* Hit all the students who have blue eyes. *4.* You have five minutes to write ten commands. *5.* Have (take) a look at Pedro's drawing.

head *1.* Touch (put the book on, place both elbows on) Maria's head. *2.* Stand at the head (rear) of the line. *3.* Draw a boy with a big (tiny) head. *4.* Make a list of famous actors and then erase the name that heads the list.

headache *1.* Pretend you have a headache. Hold your head and groan. *2.* Take an aspirin for your headache.

headline Unfold (spread out) the newspaper and cut out the headlines from the front page.

heal Maria, limp to Pedro. Pedro, put your hands on her

head. Maria, walk away without limping. You're healed.

heap *1.* Put a heap (pile) of papers (books, notebooks) on the teacher's desk. *2.* Maria, pretend you're serving Pedro and heap the food on his plate.

hear *1.* If you can hear me, raise your hand (shake your feet). *2.* Whenever you hear the word *circle (table, ceiling)*, I want you to stand up (cry, smile, cough, sing).

heart *1.* Draw a heart, cut it out, and give it to Maria. *2.* Draw a row (column) of seven big (small) hearts. *3.* Draw an arrow through (pointing to) the heart that Pedro just drew. *4.* Draw a girl with a heart (flower) on her forehead (chin, cheeks).

heat *1.* Pour some water into the can and heat it with the candle. *2.* Touch (draw) something that's used to heat food.

heavy *1.* Pretend you're carrying (picking up) a heavy object. *2.* Touch (draw, write the name of) a heavy (light) object.

heel *1.* Walk on your heels (toes). *2.* Jump into the air and touch (click) your heels together. *3.* Stand with your heels touching the wall.

height *1.* Draw a horizontal line in chalk on the wall at a height of exactly three feet from the floor. *2.* Pick up the tape measure and measure Pedro's height (waist).

help *1.* Help Maria carry the desk (erase the chalkboard, collect the answer sheets, pass out the tests). *2.* Pedro didn't understand the command. Give him some help. *3.* Pedro, sit on the floor. Carlos, help him up.

here *1.* Come here. *2.* Stand here, next to me. *3.* Put the book (notebook, towel) here on the desk.

hesitate *1.* Run (jump) around the class. Hesitate for ten seconds before you begin. *2.* Hesitate when you hear my command and then carry it out. *3.* Draw a street on the floor in chalk. Look both ways, hesitate, and then cross the street.

hide *1.* Hide behind the desk (teacher, door). *2.* I'm going out of the class. Hide the bottle cap, call me back, and I will try to find it.

high *1.* Jump as high as you can and make a chalk mark on the wall. *2.* Write a high (low) number. *3.* Speak in a high (deep) voice. *4.* Draw a man standing on a ladder with a cat on the same ladder, but higher up. *5.* Drive the car at a high (low) speed.

hill *1.* Draw a boy (girl) walking up (down) a hill. *2.* Draw a mountain surrounded by low hills.

hinge *1.* Open the door and touch the hinge. *2.* Pretend the hinge is rusty and make a creaking sound as you slowly open (close) the door.

hip Put your hands on your hips (on one of your hips).

hit *1.* Hit me on the head with the bottle (book). *2.* Make a paper ball and hit it with the bat (your notebook). *3.* Hit every (every other) student in the second row on the shoulder. *4.* Write the name of a song that's a recent (an old) hit.

hold *1.* Hold the paper (string) while I cut it. *2.* Hold the glass while Pedro pours some water into it. *3.* Hold the book in front of my face. *4.* Hold Pedro tight so that he can't escape. *5.* Draw a girl holding a purse (an umbrella). *6.* Take hold of the stick (rope) by both ends (by the middle).

hole *1.* Make (punch) a hole in the paper with your finger (pen, pencil). *2.* Look at Maria through the hole in the paper (record). *3.* Stick the straw (pencil, pen) though the hole in the paper. *4.* Pick up the shovel and dig a hole.

holiday Hop (run, jump, swim) to the holiday that's celebrated in July *(cc-3)*.

hollow Pick up (show the class) an object that's hollow (solid) *(e.g., a straw, pencil)*.

holy Write the name of a holy city (book).

homework *1.* Turn in (hand in) your homework. *2.* Collect (pick up) the homework for me.

honk Drive the car (bus, truck, jeep) around the class honking the horn.

hook *1.* Bend the wire into a hook. *2.* Form a hook with your thumb and hang the towel (handkerchief) on it. *3.* Draw a man with a hook for a hand. *4.* Draw a fish about to eat a worm that's on a fishhook.

hop Hop (run, swim, jump, limp) to the window (door, chalkboard, desk, fan).

horizon Draw the ocean with some clouds (birds) in the sky and a ship (boat, canoe) on the horizon.

horizontal *1.* Draw a horizontal (vertical, curved, diagonal) line under (in, over) a circle (square). *2.* Draw a short (long) horizontal line between two curved lines. *3.* Hold the pencil (pen) in a horizontal (vertical) position under your nose (chin).

horn *1.* Blow the horn. *2.* Drive the car (jeep, truck, bus) honking the horn.

horse Imitate (pretend you're) a horse (cow, pig, dog, cat).

hose *1.* Pretend the rope is a hose and water the flower (the grass in the front yard of the house you drew on the chalkboard). *2.* Draw a house on fire, pick up the rope, pretend it's a hose, and put out the fire.

hospital Limp (run, hop, drive the ambulance) to the hospital *(pc)*.

hot *1.* Blow on your coffee (tea) to cool it. It's too hot to drink. *2.* Draw the sun on the chalkboard. It's a very hot day. You're sweating. Wipe your forehead. *3.* Draw a plant that grows in a hot place. *4.* Locate a hot (cold) place on the map.

hotel *1.* Swim (drive the car, fly the airplane) to the hotel *(pc)*. *2.* Pick up the suitcase, go to the hotel *(pc)*, and check in (sign in). *3.* Write the name of a famous chain of hotels.

hour *1.* Calculate the number of hours in a week (month, year, decade, century). *2.* Draw a clock with the hour hand on the two and the minute hand on the six.

house *1.* Draw a house that has two chimneys (three windows, two doors; a tree in front yard). *2.* Draw a house between two trees (cars). *3.* Draw a house missing (lacking, without) a door (window, wall, roof, floor).

how *1.* Show the class how to eat with chopsticks. *2.* Raise your hand (clap, jump up and down) if you know how to swim (dance, cook, ski, play the piano).

howl Howl like a wolf (dog).

hug Hug the doll (the student sitting next to you).

huge Draw a big triangle (circle, square, heart) next to (under) a huge one.

hum *1.* Hum (whistle, sing) "Happy Birthday." *2.* Walk (run, jump) around the class humming (crying, laughing).

hungry You're hungry. Hold your belly. Lick your lips. Now eat a banana (cracker, pear; some grapes).

hurry *1.* Hurry (rush, speed) to the door (window, desk, fan, chalkboard). *2.* Erase the chalkboard (draw some flowers, make a tower with the blocks). Hurry (take your time). *3.* Draw some circles (triangles, flowers, stars). Do it in a hurry.

hurt Pretend you hurt your finger (wrist, elbow, head). Hold it and cry (groan).

husband *1.* Draw a family. The husband is fat, and has short hair and a long beard. *2.* Write your husband's (wife's) name on the chalkboard.

hypnotize Hypnotize Pedro and give him some commands.

ice cube Draw a glass with some (many) ice cubes in it.

ice-cream cone 1. Draw an ice-cream cone, cut it out, and offer it to Maria. 2. Lick the ice-cream cone.

identify Close your eyes. A student will stand in back of you and address you disguising his or her voice. See if you can identify (guess) who's speaking.

if *1.* If today's Monday, draw a circle (square, triangle). If not, draw a heart (sad face, flower, door). 2. If I point to the ceiling (window, fan), clap (sing, whistle, sneeze). But if I point to the door (floor, chalkboard), stretch (stoop, hum).

ignore *1.* Maria, when Pedro speaks to you, you will ignore him. 2. When the next student walks in the class, everybody will ignore him. Nobody will talk to him.

ill *1.* You're feeling ill. Take an aspirin. 2. Maria is feeling ill (sick). Take her to the doctor *(pc)*.

imagination Use your imagination and draw a picture of a man from Mars (of life in the year 2500).

imagine Imagine life in the year 2500 and draw a picture of it.

imitate Imitate a dog (cat, car, bird, chicken, clown, drunk, train).

imitation Let's take a vote to see who did the best

124

imitation of a horse (cat, bird, dog).

immediately Walk to the door (window, television, chair). Do (don't do) it immediately.

important *1.* Write an important date on the chalkboard and then tell the class in your native language why it's important. *2.* Make a list of ten important people in the world today.

impossible *1.* Draw a picture of an object which is impossible for you to carry. *2.* Give Pedro an impossible command.

improve Pedro, draw a bad picture of a dog (house, tree, man, cat). Maria, see if you can improve Pedro's drawing.

in *1.* Put the pen (eraser, coin) in the purse (glass, drawer, book). *2.* Stand in the center of the class (in a corner). *3.* Draw a fish (canoe, boat) in a lake. *4.* Cut (tear) the paper in half. *5.* Write your name on a slip of a paper in ink (pencil, chalk).

in back of Stand in back of (behind, in front of, next to) the desk (chair, teacher, student who has the blue fish).

in front of Stoop (stretch, yawn, cry, squat, take a seat) in front of (behind, next to) the teacher (desk, fan).

inch *1.* Draw a seven-inch horizontal (vertical, diagonal) line. *2.* If the ribbon (string) is more than ten inches long, tie it in your hair. If not, wrap it around your finger (thumb, wrist).

include Make a list of five important cities (countries, rivers). Include at least two from Europe and one from Asia.

increase Draw a few circles (triangles, stars, hearts, flowers). Now increase (decrease) the number of circles you drew.

independence Write the year your country gained (won, obtained) its independence.

index *1.* Turn to the index in my (your) book. *2.* Show the class your index (ring, little) finger.

indicate *1.* Show the class an object that indicates the time (temperature, date). *2.* I'm going to make some statements. If you agree, indicate it by extending your left hand, thumb up. If you disagree, indicate it by showing your right hand, thumb down.

inflate Inflate (blow up) the balloon.

inhale *1.* Stand at the window and inhale (breathe in) deeply. *2.* Inhale, mentally count to ten, and then exhale (breath out).

initial *1.* Write your initials on a slip of paper, fold it, and hand it to the person sitting to your left (right). *2.* Draw a picture of your teacher and then initial it.

injure You injured your wrist (elbow, arm, shoulder). Hold it and groan (cry).

ink Write your name (address, telephone number) in ink (pencil, chalk).

inner *1.* Draw two concentric circles. Color the inner circle red and the outer one blue. *2.* Fill the inner circle with dots (hearts, triangles) and the outer circle with crosses (flowers, stars).

insert *1.* Write a note to Maria, insert it in the envelope, and deliver it to her. *2.* Copy this command: "Draw a house." Now insert the word *big*. *3.* Copy this command and insert the missing words: "Stand front the desk."

inside *1.* Draw a heart inside (beside, under, over) a rectangle (square, triangle, circle). *2.* Stand inside (outside) the square (circle, triangle) that you drew on the floor.

inside out Turn the glove inside out.

inspect Inspect Pedro's documents (driver's license, ID card).

instant Pick up the jar of instant coffee (empty container), prepare a cup of coffee, and serve it to Maria.

instead *1.* Walk (run, jump) to Pedro. Walk to Maria instead *(said as student begins to walk)*. *2.* Pull Pedro's hair (nose, ears). No, on second thought, pull yours (mine) instead.

instrument *1.* Pick up a musical instrument and play it. *2.* Draw a musical instrument. *3.* Pretend (make believe) you're playing a musical instrument.

interesting *1.* Write the name of an interesting book (movie, tv program). *2.* Jump (swim, limp) to a subject you find interesting *(cc-6)*.

interrupt *1.* Every time I begin to speak, interrupt me. *2.* Interrupt the class three times in the next five minutes.

interval *1.* Stand up, clap, and sit down at intervals of twenty seconds. *2.* Draw a long horizontal line. Draw circles (triangles, vertical lines) on this line at intervals of two inches.

into *1.* Draw a circle (square) on the floor in chalk. Jump (step) into (out of) the circle. *2.* Drop the eraser (coin, pen)into the bag (purse). *3.* Walk into the room with a smile (frown, grin) on your face. *4.* Drive the car (jeep, truck) into the wall.

introduce Introduce the student who's wearing the tie (hat, cap, necklace) to the student sitting in back of (next to) the student with the yellow blouse.

invert *1.* Invert the glass (bowl, cup, funnel) *2.* Draw an inverted triangle.

invite Walk up to Maria (call Maria on the phone) and invite her to go for a walk (go to the movies, have dinner with you).

involve Pedro, crash you car into Maria's car. Roberto, take the two people who were involved in the accident to the hospital *(pc)*.

iron 1. Pick up the iron and iron the towel (handkerchief; my head, back, shirt). 2. Touch something made of iron. 3. Draw a house with iron bars protecting (in front of) the windows.

irregular Draw a row of hearts (triangles, circles) in an irregular (a regular) pattern.

island *1.* Locate a famous group of islands in the Pacific Ocean. *2.* Draw a river (lake) with an island in it.

jacket Button up (unbutton, zip up, unzip) your jacket.

jacks *1.* Play a game of jacks with Pedro. *2.* See how many jacks you can pick up before the ball bounces a second time.

jail *1.* Pull the nose (ear) of the student who's in jail *(pc)*. *2.* Put on the badge, pretend you're a policeman, arrest the student who's wearing the mask, and take him to jail *(pc)*.

jar *1.* Shake (open, twist the lid off) the jar. *2.* Put the clips (coins, bottle caps, paper balls, pebbles) in the jar. *3.* Lay the jar on its side. *4.* Turn the jar upside down.

jaw *1.* Land a punch in slow motion to Pedro's jaw and knock him out. *2.* Touch your lower (upper) jaw.

jeans Say (sing, shout) hello to a student who's wearing jeans.

jeep Drive the jeep (truck, car) around (to) the desk (teacher, fan, student standing in the center of the class).

jingle Hop (walk, run) around the class jingling the coins (bottle caps) in your pocket.

job *1.* Salute (wave to) the person whose job involves protecting people (fighting fires, fixing cars, praying) *(pc's)*. *2.* Wink (smile) at the person who has a dangerous (fun, difficult, boring) job *(pc's)*.

join *1.* I want the students in the last row to stand up, join hands, and form a circle (triangle, rectangle, heart). *2.* You can join this group. *3.* Join (fasten) the papers together with a clip.

join in When I give the signal, this group will join in the song.

judge Pedro, Carlos, and Maria will draw a picture of a cat (dog; the teacher). You will judge the pictures and award the best artist a trophy that you cut out, out of a sheet of paper.

jug *1.* Pick up the jug and pretend you're drinking some wine. *2.* Pour some water from the jug into the glass (cup).

juggle Make three paper balls and see if you can (make an attempt to, try to) juggle them.

juice Pick up the orange and pretend you're squeezing it to make some orange juice. Now serve Maria the glass of orange juice.

jump *1.* Jump to (around) the desk (chair). *2.* Jump as high as you can and make a chalk mark on the wall. *3.* Jump into the air and clap twice before you land. *4.* Jump over the rope that Carlos and Maria are holding. *5.* Let's see who can make the longest jump.

just Wink at (smile at, sing a song to) the student who just came in (finished the exercises, drew a picture on the chalkboard, wrote her name in your notebook).

kangaroo *1.* Jump around the class like a kangaroo. *2.* Touch a place on the map where kangaroos are found.

keep *1.* Run to the place where people keep their money (bank pc). *2.* I'm going to make funny faces to try to make you laugh. Keep a serious face. *3.* Keep jumping until I tell you to stop. *4.* Pedro, stand outside the class and try to come in. Roberto, keep him out. *5.* Keep score for this contest.

kettle Put the kettle on the stove, heat some water, and make yourself a cup of coffee (tea).

key *1.* Insert the key into the lock, turn the key, and unlock it. *2.* Drop the key into the cup (bowl, glass; your pocket). *3.* Tie the ribbon (string, yarn) to the key.

key chain *1.* Shake (rattle) the keys on your key chain. *2.* Remove a key from your key chain and show it to the class.

kick *1.* Kick the door (wall, desk, fan, teacher). *2.* Kick (toss, throw, roll) me the ball. *3.* Try to kick the rolling (bouncing) ball. *4.* Walk up to Pedro and give him a kick.

kill *1.* Pick up an object that's used to kill. *2.* You're going to pick up the gun (knife) and kill Pedro by shooting (stabbing) him. *3.* Draw an ant (spider) on the floor in chalk and kill it by stepping on it.

kind *1.* Pretend you're a kind (nice) person and gently pat Pedro on the head. Now pretend you're unkind and give him a kick. *2.* Draw two different kinds of flowers (cars, hats, weapons, tools).

131

king *1.* Kneel in front of (bow to) the king *(pc)* *2.* Write the name of a country that has a king.

kiss *1.* Kiss the doll (your hand). *2.* Throw a big kiss to the happy (sad) face Maria drew on the chalkboard.

kitchen *1.* Draw (pick up, touch) an object you find in the kitchen. *2.* Go to the kitchen *(pc)* and fry an egg.

kite *1.* Draw a boy (girl) flying a kite. *2.* Draw a kite over (under, beside) a cloud (house, tree, butterfly, bird).

knee *1.* Bend your knees. *2.* Touch the desk (wall) with your left (right) knee. *3.* Cover one of your knees with the towel (napkin, newspaper).

kneel 1. Kneel in front of Maria and give her the flower. *2.* Kneel next to (in front of, behind) the teacher's desk and pray. *3.* Go to the church *(pc),* kneel, and pray.

knife *1.* Pick up the knife and the fork, and pretend you're eating. *2.* Use the knife to cut off a small piece of the candle. *3.* Feel the edge (blade) of the knife to see if its sharp or dull. *4.* Draw a blunt (pointed) knife.

knit Pick up the knitting needles and pretend you're knitting a sweater.

knitting needle *1.* Pick up the knitting needles and the yarn, and pretend you're knitting. *2.* Measure the knitting needle. *3.* Use the knitting needle to make a hole in the paper.

knock *1.* Knock on the door (desk, wall; Maria's head). *2.* Knock me on the head with the bottle (sponge, newspaper). *3.* Set the bottle on the floor, step back, roll the ball, and knock it over (down). *4.* Knock (bump) into Pedro.

knock out Pretend you're a boxer, land a punch in slow motion to Pedro's jaw (chin), and knock him out.

knot Tie a knot in the rope (string, handkerchief, yarn).

know *1.* Toss your pen (pencil, book) to the student who knows how to speak French *(cc-5)*. *2.* Raise your hand if you know the answer. *3.* If you don't know the words to the song, you can hum.

lack *1.* Draw a house lacking (without) a door (roof, wall; windows). *2.* Draw a man (woman) lacking (missing) an eye (ear; a hand, foot, nose).

ladder Draw a ladder leaning against a house (tree, church, skyscraper).

lake Draw a lake surrounded by mountains (hills, trees, houses). There's a canoe (boat, ship, shark) in the lake.

lamp Draw a lamp on a table (chair, desk, bookcase).

land *1.* Fly the airplane and land it on Maria's desk (head, shoulder). *2.* Go to the map and touch some land (water).

language *1.* Hold up the card that shows the language people speak in France *(cc-5)*. *2.* Jump (run, hop, skip) to a student who speaks a language that begins with the letter "g" *(cc-5)*.

lap *1.* Cover your lap with the towel (newspaper, napkin). *2.* Pretend you're a baby and sit on Maria's lap.

large *1.* Pick up (point to) the large (small) blue triangle. *2.* Draw a large (small) number of circles (hearts, stars). *3.* Go to the map and touch a large (small) city.

lash Draw a girl with long eyelashes.

last *1.* Wave to the last student to come in. *2.* Pedro, Carlos, and Roberto are going to race to the wall. Touch the student who came in last (first). *3.* Sit in the last row. *4.* Draw a row of fifteen hearts. Now erase the last few. *5.* Write your last name.

late Point to (touch) the student who arrived to class late (early, on time) today (yesterday).

laugh *1.* Look at (point to, sit on, wave to) the teacher and laugh. *2.* Laugh at the funny (sad, crazy) face Maria drew. *3.* When Maria makes a funny (silly) face, you will laugh (cry).

lay *1.* Lay (set, place) the book (paper, notebook, flower) on the table (floor). *2.* Lay the can (cylinder, cup, glass) on its side. *3.* Lay your head on your desk (shoulder).

layer Draw a birthday cake with three layers.

lead *1.* Lead (guide, take) Maria to the door (window, teacher, desk). *2.* Draw a path leading up a hill.

leader *1.* I want each group to elect (select, choose) a leader. *2.* Will the group leaders please raise their hands.

leaf *1.* Go outside and pick a leaf from the tree (plant). *2.* Draw a leaf, cut it out, and give it to Maria.

leak Make a hole in the bottom of the paper cup with the pin (pen, pencil). Fill the cup with water and watch it leak.

lean *1.* Lean against the wall (door, desk; Pedro). *2.* Lean the ruler (pencil) against the box. *3.* Lean out the door (window).

leap *1.* Leap into the air. *2.* Leap (jump, hop) around the class (desk, teacher).

least *1.* Touch the nose (left ear, chin; both cheeks) of the student who drew the least (most) circles (hearts, chairs, hats). *2.* Hop (run, limp) to the student who has the least money *(cc-9)*.

leather *1.* Touch (point to, pick up) something made of leather. *2.* Stand next to (beside, behind) a student who's wearing a leather belt. *3.* If your purse (wallet) is made of leather (cloth, plastic, straw), hold it up.

leave *1.* Leave the room silently (noisily, slowly, quickly). *2.* Leave your book on the desk and walk away. *3.* Pretend you're leaving. *4.* Leave the door open. *5.* If four from seven leaves three, stand up and cry. *6.* Erase the chalkboard, but leave my name on it.

left *1.* Raise (hold up, touch, shake) your left foot (hand). *2.* Turn left (right, around). *3.* Put (place) your left hand on your right knee (shoulder, ear).

leg *1.* Touch (point to, raise) a leg. *2.* Draw a man (woman, boy, girl) with long (short) legs (arms). *3.* Tie the rope (string, yarn) to a leg of the (desk, chair).

lemon *1.* Pretend you're squeezing the lemon to make

135

some lemonade. *2.* Put the lemon in the glass, pretend it's a glass of lemonade, and serve it to the teacher.

lemonade Serve me the glass of lemonade you just made.

lend Lend (loan) me your pencil (pen, book, ruler, scissors, notebook).

length *1.* Measure the rope (string, stick, yarn) and write its length on the chalkboard. *2.* Draw a rectangle whose length is three times its width. *3.* Walk the length of the classroom.

lengthen Draw a horizontal (diagonal, vertical, curved) line. Now lengthen (shorten) it.

less *1.* Write a number that's less (more) than twenty. *2.* Walk to a student who has less money than Maria *(cc-9).* *3.* Pour some water into two glasses and give me the one that has less water. *4.* If seven less three leaves four, clap. If not, cry (whistle).

lesson *1.* Open your books to lesson seven. *2.* Write the number of the page on which lesson three begins (ends).

let *1.* Raise your left (right) hand. Now let (put) it down. *2.* I want the students in the first row to stand in front of the door blocking it. When Pedro goes to the door, let (don't let) him out(through). *3.* Let's begin class. Please be seated.

let go Hold the candle (book, box, ball) in front of your nose, count to three, let go, and watch it fall.

letter *1.* Count the letters in the word you wrote. *2.* Write a word that begins (ends) with the letter "k." *3.* Form a word with the letters on the chalkboard. *4.* Cross out the third letter of the fourth word. *5.* Write a word that has five letters. *6.* Write a letter to Pedro and take it to the post office *(pc)*.

level *1.* Fill two glasses with water to the same level (to different levels). *2.* Hold the book (notebook, pencil) in a level (an unlevel) position.

library *1.* Take (return) a book to the library *(pc)*. *2.* Go to the library *(pc)* and check out a book.

license *1.* Take out your driver's license and show it to the class. *2.* Pretend you're a policeman and check the driver's license of the student driving the red car.

lick *1.* Lick the postage stamp and stick it on the envelope. *2.* You're very hungry. Lick your lips.

lid *1.* Remove the lid from the can. *2.* Spin the lid. *3.* Roll (hand, give) the lid to Pedro. *4.* Hold the can and press down on the lid. *5.* Pretend the lid is a tray (mirror).

lie *1.* Lie down. *2.* Pick up the book (notebook, can, ruler) that's lying on the floor (desk). *3.* Go to the map and touch a state that lies to the north of California. *4.* Stand up and tell the class a lie.

life Give your book (notebook, watch, bracelet) to the man (woman) who had a long (short) life *(cc-8)*.

lift *1.* Lift (raise) your hands (a foot, both feet). *2.* Lift (pick up) the desk (teacher) with Pedro.

light *1.* Touch a light (heavy) object. *2.* Walk to a student who has light (dark) hair. *3.* Draw a circle and color it light (dark) blue. *4.* Touch Pedro lightly on the nose (head). *5.* Turn on (off) the lights. *6.* Light the candle (match, cigarette, pipe).

light fixture Point to (look at, throw the paper ball to) the light fixture.

lightning Draw some lightning shooting out of a cloud.

like *1.* Hit the student who likes fried chicken *(student-made cc)*. *2.* Pinch the student who likes to play tennis *(student-made cc)*. *3.* Write the name of a food (sport, tv program, author, actor) you like. *4.* Bark like a dog. *5.* Act like a drunk (clown).

limp *1.* When Maria kicks Pedro in the knee (leg, foot, ankle), he will limp to the hospital *(pc)*. *2.* Limp (run, hop, skip, swim) to (around) the desk (teacher).

line *1.* Draw a horizontal (vertical, curved, diagonal, wavy, broken, dotted, crooked) line. *2.* Get in line behind the teacher. *3.* Form a single (double) file line. *4.* Draw a river and line it with trees (houses).

line up Line up in front of (behind) the desk (teacher, student wearing the blue blouse).

link *1.* Draw a chain with ten links. *2.* Count the links on the chain.

lion *1.* Roar like a lion. *2.* Pedro, pick up the chair and pretend you're a lion tamer. Carlos, be the lion.

lip *1.* Touch (put your finger to) your lips. *2.* Draw a face with thick (thin) lips.

lipstick *1.* Open your purse, take out your lipstick, and pretend you're putting it on. *2.* Draw a heart (happy face) on a piece of paper in lipstick. *3.* Write your name in lipstick.

list *1.* Make a list of actors (actresses, restaurants, streets, animals). *2.* Make a list of the students who have a dog (cat, car, younger sister). *3.* List the students who come from Asia.

listen *1.* Let's listen to the song on the tape before we try to sing it. *2.* Listen to my (your) watch tick. *3.* Pretend you're a doctor and use the stethoscope to listen to Pedro's heart.

little *1.* Put the little square (circle) on the big triangle (rectangle). *2.* Draw a little house (car, church, triangle) next to a big cat (square, heart, door). *3.* Pour a little bit (a lot) of water into the glass (cup, bowl).

live *1.* Smile at the student who lives on Elm street *(student-made cc)*. *2.* Jump (hop) to the student who lives in London *(cc-11)*. *3.* Pull the nose (hair) of a famous person who lived for 70 years *(cc-8)*. *4.* Draw an animal that lives in a tree.

living room Draw something that you find in the living room (kitchen, bathroom, garage).

load *1.* Pedro, extend your hands. Maria, load a pile of books (notebooks) on Pedro's hands. *2.* Pretend you're loading the rifle (gun).

loan Loan (lend) Maria your pen (pencil, ruler, book).

local Write the name of a local soccer team (baseball team, newspaper, university).

locate *1.* Go to the map and locate a desert (mountain range, river, large city). *2.* Swim (jump, hop, run) to a student who lives in a city located in Europe (South America, Asia) *(cc-11).*

lock *1.* Put (insert) the key in the lock and open it. *2.* Pick up the key and pretend you're locking the door (car). *3.* Draw a big (small) lock. *4.* Cut a lock of your hair and give it to Pedro.

long *1.* Draw a long (short) horizontal (vertical, diagonal, curved) line. *2.* Draw a man (woman) with long (short) hair (arms, legs). *3.* Measure the long (short) string (rod). *4.* Kick the student who has the longest (shortest) first (last) name.

look *1.* Look down (up, to your left). *2.* Look over the shoulder of the person sitting (standing) in front of you. *3.* Look out the window (door). *4.* Look at me and smile. *5.* Give Maria a serious look. *6.* Look angry (sad, happy, surprised).

look for When you come back into the room, you will look for the coin (piece of chalk) that Pedro hid.

look up Copy the list of words I wrote on the chalkboard and then look them up in your dictionary.

loose *1.* Pick up the jar and twist the lid so that it's loose (tight). *2.* Tie the rope (string) to the chair loosely (tightly). *3.* Tie a loose (tight) knot. *4.* Pedro, loosen your shoelaces. Maria, shake the student whose shoelaces are loose.

loosen Loosen your belt (shoelaces; the knot in the rope).

lose *1.* Write the name of the team you think will win (lose) the soccer match (football game) tonight. *2.* If Pedro loses the race, cry. If he wins, jump up and down. *3.* Pretend you're walking a tightrope and you lose your balance and fall off.

lot *1.* Draw lots of circles (triangles, hearts, hats). *2.* Write the name of a student who has lots of (very little) money *(cc-9)*. *3.* Pull the nose (ear, ears) of a student who's a lot taller (shorter) than Maria.

lotion *1.* Put some lotion *(empty container)* on your hands and rub them together. *2.* Apply some lotion to your face.

loud *1.* Say hello to Pedro in a loud (soft) voice. *2.* Sing (cry, hum, laugh, snore, clap) loudly (softly). *3.* Speak a little louder (softer).

love *1.* Draw something that symbolizes (is a symbol for) love. *2.* Sing a song that has the word *love* in it.

low *1.* Draw a low (tall) building. *2.* Speak in a low (high, loud, deep) voice. *3.* Draw an airplane flying low (high). *4.* Draw (pick up) an object that has a low (high) price. *5.* Write a low (high) number.

lower *1.* Raise and then lower your arm (foot, hand, feet). *2.* Fasten a picture to the wall. Now lower (raise) it a little. *3.* Tie the string to the candle (cup, scissors), stand on the chair, and slowly lower it to the floor. Now raise it.

luck Draw a symbol that stands for good (bad) luck.

lunch *1.* Write what you had for lunch today (yesterday). *2.* Stand beside (behind, in front of) the student who has lunch at 12:30 *(student-made cc).*

mad *1.* Pretend you're mad (= crazy). *2.* Pretend you're mad (= angry) and pound your fist on the desk (make an angry face).

made of Touch (show the class) something made of plastic (wood, leather, cloth, glass, metal).

magazine *1.* Open the magazine to page 30 and read. *2.* Hit me on the head (knee, arm, left shoulder) with the magazine. *3.* Roll the magazine into a cylinder. *4.* Tie the string (yarn, ribbon) around the magazine. *5.* Make a list of five magazines.

magnifying glass *1.* Write your mother's (father's, brother's)name in very small letters and look at it through the magnifying glass. *2.* Look at Maria's left (right) eye through the magnifying glass.

maid *1.* Pretend you're a maid, pick up the broom, and sweep the floor in front of (in back of, next to) the desk (teacher). *2.* Pull the nose (ear, hair) of the maid *(pc).*

mail *1.* After Maria addresses the envelopes, deliver the mail to the students in the class. *2.* Write a letter to a classmate, take it to the post office *(pc),* and mail it.

mailman *1.* Pretend you're a mailman and deliver the letter to the student (person) it's addressed to. *2.* Take the letter to the mailman *(pc).*

major *1.* Draw a square (triangle, rectangle, heart) and color the major part of it blue. *2.* Count the buttons on the shirt of the student who's majoring in history *(cc-6)*.

majority *1.* Take the majority of the bottle caps (coins) out of the can and put them on (under) the chair (desk). *2.* Shake hands with the majority of the students in the first row. *3.* Draw ten small hearts (stars, doors, hats) and then erase the majority of them.

make *1.* Make a paper ball (paper airplane, sad face, fist). *2.* Make a tower with the blocks (spools, match boxes). *3.* Make a list of the students whose names have five letters. *4.* If two and two makes four, jump to the desk. If not, point to the ceiling.

male *1.* I want a male (female) student to stand up and sing (cry, dance, yawn). *2.* Walk (run, swim) to a male and then throw the paper ball (sponge, book) to a female.

man *1.* Stand in front of (behind, in back of, next to) a man (woman). *2.* Draw a man wearing a beard (tie, bow tie, hat). *3.* If the third student in the first row is a man, give me the pen (notebook, pencil). If not, squeeze my hand (nose, elbow).

many *1.* Draw many (a few) stars (hearts, hats, circles, eyes). *2.* Give many bottle caps (pieces of chalk, clips, pebbles, coins) to a friend. *3.* Jump up and down (walk around the chair, sneeze, blink) many (several) times.

map *1.* Hang the map on the wall. *2.* Locate a mountain (river, city, ocean, island) on the map. *3.* Draw a map of your city.

march *1.* Pretend you're in the army, salute me, and then march around the class. 2. March to the door (desk, chalkboard).

margin *1.* Open your book to page 35 and write your (my) name in the left (right) margin. *2.* Draw a heart (happy face, triangle) in the margin of your book.

mark *1.* Make a mark at the top (bottom) of your paper. *2.* Mark the bottom of your paper with a star (cross, heart). *3.* For this contest Pedro will mark the points. *4.* Maria, mark a point for your (the other) team.

married *1.* Touch something that shows (symbolizes) that you're married (engaged). *2.* Say (whisper, sing) hello to a student who is married (single, engaged). *3.* Write the year you got married.

marry Pedro, stand at the church *(pc),* pretend you're a priest, and marry Maria and Carlos.

mask *1.* Put on the mask, pick up the gun, and rob the bank *(pc).* *2.* Give (show) the flower (book, ring, purse) to the student who's wearing the mask.

match *1.* Light a match and blow (shake) it out. *2.* Break a match in half. *3.* Form a triangle with the matches. *4.* Match the words to the drawings. *5.* Pinch the student who matched Pedro's record for bouncing the ball. *6.* Draw and color a man wearing a shirt that matches (doesn't match) his pants.

match box *1.* Pick up the box of matches, take out a match, light it, and then blow it out. *2.* Make (build, set up) a tower with the match boxes. *3.* Walk (jump, hop) around the class shaking the match box. *4.* Put the match box in Pedro's shirt pocket.

maximum Congratulate the student who got (obtained, earned) the maximum number of points on the test.

meanwhile Maria is going to slowly walk (swim) around the class. Meanwhile (in the meantime) everyone else will sing (hum, cry, clap, groan).

measure *1.* Pick up the ruler and measure your nose (thumb). *2.* Draw a long (short) diagonal (horizontal, vertical) line and measure it. *3.* Measure the candle (string, pencil, pen, rod). *4.* Draw a rectangle measuring ten inches by six inches.

meat Give the knife to the man who sells meat *(butcher pc)*.

mechanic *1.* Draw a wrench, cut it out, and give it to the mechanic *(pc)*. *2.* Drive your car to the mechanic *(pc)*.

medicine *1.* Pull the nose (ears) of the student who studies medicine *(cc-6)*. *2.* Go to the drugstore *(pc)* and buy some cough medicine *(empty container)*. *3.* Cough and take a spoonful of cough medicine *(empty container)*.

meet *1.* Meet me at the drugstore (bank, post office, church) *(pc's)* in fifteen seconds. *2.* Pedro, fly the plane to the airport *(pc)*. Maria, go (drive) to the airport and meet him.

melt Light the candle, melt some wax, and drip it on the saucer (plate, desk, floor).

member *1.* Count the members of your group. *2.* Join (jump to) the group that has seven members. *3.* List the members of the group that's next to the window. *4.*

Write the name of a club you're a member of.

men *1.* Touch (point to) the nose (ears, shoulder, chin) of three men. *2.* Draw two tall (short) men standing next to a house (tree, church, happy face).

menu Go to the restaurant *(pc),* pick up the menu, and show the waiter what you want to order (eat).

message Maria is staying at the hotel *(pc).* Go there and leave a message for her.

messy *1.* Scatter some papers and other objects on the desk so that it's messy. *2.* Write your name with a messy (neat) handwriting.

metal Touch something made of metal (glass, wood, steel, tin, plastic, wax, cotton, paper, cardboard).

microphone Pretend (make believe) the pencil (pen, candle) is a microphone and you are a singer. Sing a song for us.

middle *1.* Stand in the middle of the class and pretend you're a bird. *2.* Hold the rope (ruler) by the middle (an end). *3.* Draw a row (column) of seven hearts (hats) and erase the middle one. *4.* Draw a big circle and in the middle (center) put a square (cat).

midnight Draw a clock (watch) showing midnight.

milk *1.* Pretend Pedro is your baby, pick up the baby bottle, and give him some milk. *2.* Pick up the carton (bottle) of milk *(empty containers)* and pour me a glass. *3.* Drink the glass of milk slowly (quickly). *4.* Imitate an animal that gives us milk.

minus If six minus two is (leaves) four, point to the floor (ceiling, door, desk, teacher). If not, cry (stoop, laugh).

minute *1.* Everybody, clap for one minute and ten seconds. Pedro, look at your watch, time us, and tell us when the time is up. *2.* Draw a clock with the hour hand on the three and the minute hand on the eight. *3.* The minute I come back in, everyone will cry.

mirror *1.* Look at yourself in the mirror. *2.* Hop to the student who's looking at herself in the mirror. *3.* Hold the mirror so that you can see the student sitting in back of you. *4.* Use the mirror to reflect some light into my face.

miss *1.* Throw the ball (candle, sponge, eraser) into the air, try to catch it, but miss. *2.* Write the name of a student who is (isn't) missing (absent) from class today. *3.* Draw a girl missing her nose (mouth, left ear, right eye).

mistake *1.* Circle (underline, cross out) the mistake in the sentence on the chalkboard. *2.* If you had less than five mistakes on the test, raise your hand. *3.* Congratulate (applaud) the student who didn't have any mistakes on her test.

mix Everybody, write a command on a slip of paper, fold the paper, and put it in the bag. Maria, shake the bag to mix the slips, stick your hand in the bag, take out a command, and read it for Pedro to perform.

model Maria, put on the earring and the necklace. Now walk around the room like (as if you were) a model.

moist Dip a corner of the rag (towel, handkerchief) into

147

the water, wring it out, and wipe your cheek (nose, chin, forehead) with the moist cloth.

moisten Moisten the rag (towel, handkerchief) and wipe your forehead (chin, cheeks).

money *(Use play money.)* *1.* Take the money out of the wallet and count it. *2.* Give some (a little, a lot of) money to Pedro. *3.* Put the money in your wallet (purse, back pocket, shirt pocket). *4.* Smile at the student who has little (lot's of) money *(cc-9).*

monkey *1.* Imitate (pretend you're) a monkey. *2.* Pick up (draw) a fruit that monkeys like to eat.

monster Draw (pretend you're) a monster.

month *1.* Jump (hop) to the month that comes before (after) June *(cc-2).* *2.* Hold up (show the class) the month that begins with the letter "d" *(cc-2).* *3.* Say (whisper) hello to the student who was born in the same month as Maria *(student-made cc).*

mood Pretend you're in a good (bad) mood.

moon Draw the moon between (under, over) two clouds (trees, stars, doors, houses).

more *1.* Write a number that's more than ten but less than twenty. *2.* Pour some (a little) water into the glass (cup, bowl, pail). Now pour some more. *3.* Draw some circles (triangles, hats, hearts). That's not enough. Draw some more.

morning Draw a picture of the sun coming up in the morning (setting in the evening).

mosquito There's a mosquito on your arm. Swat it and scratch your arm.

most *1.* Kick the student who drew the most (least) circles. *2.* Put most (none) of the coins under (on) the desk. *3.* Touch most (all, several) of the students in the first row. *4.* Draw a square and color it red and blue. Make it mostly blue.

mother *1.* Write your mother's (father's, sister's, brother's) name on the chalkboard. *2.* Draw a family. The mother is tall (short, thin) and is wearing a hat (skirt, necklace, bracelet).

motion *1.* Shave (comb your hair, brush your teeth) in slow motion (quickly). *2.* Motion for Maria to sit down (stand up, come to you, be quiet).

motorcycle Drive the motorcycle to the window (door, chalkboard, desk, teacher).

mountain *1.* Draw a mountain surrounded by clouds (stars). *2.* Write the name of a famous mountain. *3.* Open the almanac and find the tallest mountain in North (South) America.

mouse When you see the mouse at your feet, scream (run away, faint, stand on the chair).

mouth *1.* Raise the glass to your mouth. *2.* Open your mouth wide. *3.* Close your mouth tight. *4.* Put your finger in your mouth and bite it. *5.* Cover your mouth with both hands. *6.* Draw a man with a square (rectangular, round, big, small) mouth.

move *1.* Move your head (left hand, right foot; both feet).

2. Move the chair to the back (front, other side) of the class. 3. Move the paper ball across the table by blowing on it. 4. Move forward (backwards) two (several) steps.

movement 1. Walk across the room with graceful (awkward) movements. 2. Make a circular movement with your hand (head, foot, finger).

movie 1. Write the name of (show an advertisement for) a movie playing near here. 2. Write the name of a movie you liked (enjoyed, disliked).

much 1. Draw two tall men. Make the one on the left much taller (shorter, fatter, thinner). 2. Draw two horizontal lines one above the other. Make the lower (upper) line much longer (shorter). 3. Kick a student who has much (little) money *(cc-9)*.

multiply 1. Multiply four by ten. 2. If five multiplied by (times) six equals thirty, sit down (stand up). If not, write your name on the chalkboard (pretend you're a dog).

mumble Mumble a command (your name, hello, good morning) to Maria.

murder Pick up the knife (sword, gun) and pretend you're going to murder (kill) the teacher.

muscle When Pedro makes a muscle, Maria will jump (walk, swim) to him and feel it.

museum Draw a picture of your teacher and take (sell) it to the museum *(pc)*.

music If you like to listen to classical (pop, rock, country) music, pull your nose (hair, ear). If not, touch your mouth.

mustache *1.* Push Maria to the student who wears (has, uses) a mustache. *2.* Draw a fat man (thin man, fish, happy face) with a mustache (beard).

nail *1.* Hammer the nail into the board. *2.* Form a square with the nails. *3.* Put the rubber band (tie the string) around the nails. *4.* Pick up the clippers and cut one of your nails. *5.* Pick up the nail polish *(empty container)* and paint (do) your nails.

nail file Pick up the nail file and shape your nails.

nail polish Open the nail polish *(empty container)* and paint your nails.

name *1.* Write your first (last, middle, family) name. *2.* Draw a funny face and put a friend's name under it. *3.* Draw a circle (rectangle) around your first (last) name. *4.* Erase your nickname. *5.* Name the months of the year (days of the week).

napkin *1.* Put the napkin on your lap. *2.* Wipe your mouth with the napkin. *3.* Wrap the cookie (banana) in the napkin. *4.* Fold the napkin into a triangle. *5.* Draw a picture of your teacher on the napkin. *6.* Punch a hole in the napkin.

narrow *1.* Put on the narrow (wide) tie. *2.* Draw a fat (thin) man wearing a narrow (wide) tie (belt). *3.* Draw a narrow road that gradually becomes wider.

native Say hello to the class in your native language.

near Stand near (far from, close to) the door (window, chalkboard, fan, teacher).

nearly *1.* Touch the student who is nearly twenty *(cc-1).* *2.* Draw a house (car). When you're nearly (almost) finished, stand aside and take a bow. Then finish your drawing. *3.* Draw a fat man and a thin man. Make the fat man nearly as tall as the thin man.

neat *1.* Write your first (last) name with a neat (messy) handwriting. *2.* Arrange the teacher's desk so that it's neat (messy).

neck *1.* Touch (point to, tie the ribbon around) your (my) neck. *2.* Draw a short (fat, tall, thin) man with a long (short, thick) neck. *3.* Touch the neck of the bottle.

necklace *1.* Put on (take off) the necklace (ring, bracelet, watch). *2.* Count the beads on the necklace. *3.* Draw a woman wearing a necklace (bracelet).

need Draw (touch) an object that needs electricity (batteries) to work.

needle *1.* Thread the needle. *2.* Stick the needle into the cork (sponge, potato). *3.* Pick up the needle and use it to sew the button to the corner of the handkerchief.

neighbor *1.* Shake hands with (pull the hair of) your neighbor (classmate) on your right (left). *2.* Write the names of the countries that are neighbors of your country.

neither Look at Maria and Pedro. If either or both of them has a triangle, hop to the door (window, teacher). But if neither of them has one, point to the ceiling (floor, desk, chalkboard).

neither . . . nor If neither Pedro nor Maria is standing next to (behind, in front of) the desk, touch your nose (neck, throat, chin). But if one of them is, shake your hand (foot, head).

nervous Pretend you're nervous and bite your nails (pace the floor).

net *1.* Draw a girl trying to net a butterfly. *2.* Pedro and Carlos, stretch the rope tight and pretend it's a net. Maria, toss the ball over the net. *3.* Pretend you're playing a sport that uses a net.

neutral Walk (swim, run) to a student who's wearing an article of clothing that's a neutral (loud) color and touch it.

never Smile (wink, laugh) at a student who has never (has already) been to Spain *(student-made cc)*.

new Everybody, welcome (say hello to) the new student.

newspaper *1.* Read the newspaper to the class. *2.* Hit Maria on the head with the newspaper. *3.* Tear the newspaper in half. *4.* Spread the newspaper on the floor and jump over it. *5.* Hold the newspaper upside down. *6.* Crumple the newspaper into a ball.

next *1.* I'm going to say a number. Write the number that comes next. *2.* If next month is March, touch your nose (chin). If not, sneeze (cry). *3.* When the next student comes in, I want everybody to stand up (breathe in, snore, clap).

next to *1.* Stand next to (in front of, behind, beside) the desk (fan, door, teacher). *2.* Draw a fat (tall, thin, short) man next to a house (tree, church, rocket).

nickname *1.* Write (print) your nickname on the chalkboard (in Maria's notebook). *2.* Call Maria by her nickname.

night *1.* Draw an object you usually see at night. *2.* Write the name of a program that's on television Monday night.

nightmare Lay your head down. Pretend you're sleeping and are having a nightmare (pleasant dream).

nobody *1.* Put the book (notebook, can, eraser) where nobody can see it. *2.* Stand (sit) where nobody (everybody) can see you. *3.* Speak in a voice so low that nobody can hear you.

nod Nod to (wink at) the student sitting behind you (to your right, to your left).

noise *1.* Make some noise by humming (stamping your feet, clapping, hissing, pounding on your desk). *2.* Draw something that makes a lot of noise.

noisily Walk around the class (teacher, fan, desk) noisily (silently).

nominate We're going to have an election for class president. Pedro, nominate someone. Now Maria, you nominate someone else. Carlos, write the nominations on the chalkboard.

noon Draw a picture showing the sun at noon.

normal *1.* Draw a girl (boy) whose head is a normal (an abnormal) size. *2.* Draw a hand (foot) that has (doesn't have) the normal number of fingers (toes).

north *1.* Face north (south). *2.* Go to the map and touch the state that's to the north of California.

nose *1.* Touch (point to, pull) Maria's nose (ears). *2.* Draw a sad face with a long (short, pointed, crooked) nose. *3.* Draw a happy face with a circle (triangle, heart, star) for its nose. *4.* Draw a circle (rectangle) in the air with your nose.

note *1.* Write a short note to Maria inviting her to go to a movie (out to dinner). *2.* Draw a musical note.

notebook *1.* Write your name (age, address, telephone number) in my notebook. *2.* Hit Pedro on the knee with your notebook. *3.* Place (set, put) the notebook on (under) the chair. *4.* Walk around the class with the notebook on your head.

nothing *1.* Walk to a student who has nothing on her desk and put the book (purse) on it. *2.* Put everything under your desk. Leave nothing on it. *3.* If seven minus seven leaves nothing, touch the floor. But if it leaves something, point to the ceiling.

notice Notice (look at) the student sitting behind Pedro. If she has blue eyes (light hair, dark hair, a yellow blouse), throw her the ball (eraser, purse). If not, pull your hair (nose, ears).

now *1.* Raise your right (left) hand (foot). Now put it down. *2.* Say (whisper, sing) hello to the student who is now (who was) sitting next to Pedro. *3.* Look at your watch,

155

and if it's now 2:15, hit Maria on her left shoulder with your book (pencil).

number *1.* Write the numbers I call out. *2.* Write a number that's more than ten but less than twenty. *3.* Write two numbers whose sum equals seven. *4.* Draw a large number of hearts. *5.* Write your telephone number. *6.* Draw a row of squares and number them.

nurse *1.* Swim (hop, run, limp) to the nurse *(pc)*. *2.* Pretend you're a nurse, pick up the syringe, and give Pedro a shot in the arm.

nut *1.* Tighten (loosen) the nut. *2.* Twist the nut off the bolt. *3.* Pick up the nutcracker, crack a nut, put a piece in your mouth, and eat it.

nutcracker Use the nutcracker to crack a nut.

nylon Touch an object made of nylon (cotton, wool, plastic, rubber).

object *1.* Draw (hand me) a small (big, round, heavy, light, dull, colorful, sharp, pointed, dangerous, thin, flat) object. *2.* Pick up an object that's used to cut (measure, sew, write, erase).

obtain Write the year your country obtained its independence.

occupy I want the five students sitting (standing) in the back of the class to occupy the empty seats in the front row.

occur *1.* Run to the student with the card showing the event that occurred in 1910 *(cc-7)*. *2.* Show the class the

156

holiday that occurs (is celebrated) in December *(cc-3)*. 3. Write a word in which the letter "t" occurs twice (doesn't occur).

ocean *1.* Go to the map and touch the Atlantic (Pacific) Ocean. *2.* Write the name of an island located in the Pacific Ocean. *3.* Write the name of the ocean on which New York (Tokyo) is located.

o'clock *1.* Set the clock to ten o'clock. *2.* Draw a clock (watch) showing seven o'clock. *3.* Write the name of a program that's on television Sunday night at eight o'clock.

odd *1.* Circle (underline, cross out) the odd (even) numbers. *2.* If there's an odd (even) number of students in the first row, turn off the lights (stamp your feet, pretend you're a dog). *3.* Do something in an odd (strange) way.

of *1.* Touch something made of wood (rubber, plastic, metal, paper). *2.* Write the name of the student who's wearing something red. *3.* Touch one of your hands (feet, knees, shoulders). *4.* Tie the yarn to the leg of the chair (table).

off *1.* Blow the paper ball off the desk. *2.* Draw a beach with a ship (canoe, whale) off shore. *3.* Take the cup (glass, plate) off the table. *4.* Clear off your desk. *5.* Take off your hat (watch, necklace). *6.* Turn off (on) the fan (lights).

offer *1.* Offer Maria a cigarette (cup of coffee, piece of candy, glass of water). Without speaking, offer Maria a seat.

office building Drive the blue car to the office building *(pc)*.

oil *1.* Pretend the pencil is an oil can and oil the hinge on the door. *2.* Pedro, pretend you're a rusty robot. Move stiffly making a creaking sound. Maria, pick up the oil can *(empty container)* and oil him. Pedro, now walk smoothly.

old *1.* Pull the nose (hair, ears) of the oldest (youngest) student *(cc-1)*. *2.* If Pedro is older (younger) than Maria, pretend you're a dog (cat, car, cow). If not, stand up and cry (laugh, hum, wink).

omit *1.* Make a list of the students in your group (row), but omit two names. *2.* Copy the command I wrote on the chalkboard omitting one of the words.

on *1.* Put the book on the desk. *2.* Draw a heart on the wall with the chalk. *3.* Stand on one foot. *4.* Smile at the student on your right. *5.* Write the name of a program that's on tv tonight. *6.* Put on the hat (glasses, tie). *7.* Turn on (off) the lights.

on top of *1.* Place (set, put) the book (can, eraser, notebook) on top of the desk. *2.* Put the small red triangle on top of (under) the big black square.

once Write your name (sneeze, cough, bounce the ball, walk around the teacher) once (twice, several times).

one *1.* Touch one (both) of my ears. *2.* Pick up the red fish and the blue fish. Put the red one on the floor (desk) and the blue one on (in) Maria's book. *3.* Draw two circles. Erase one and draw a vertical (horizontal) line under (over, next to) the other.

one at a time Drop the coins (bottle caps, pebbles) into the can (bowl) one at a time (one by one).

onion *1.* Smell the onion and cry. *2.* Pick up the knife and slice the onion. *3.* Toss the onion into the air and catch it with your right (left) hand.

only *1.* Pick up (touch) several (only one) of the objects on the desk. *2.* If only one student is wearing something green, touch your nose (head, shoulder, knee). If not, stand next to the desk (door). *3.* Listen to this command. I'm going to say it only once.

onto *1.* Drop (throw) the book (pencil, eraser, notebook) onto the floor. *2.* Jump onto the chair.

open *1.* Open the door (window; your eyes, hand, mouth). *2.* Open your book (notebook, dictionary) to page 10 and read. *3.* Hop (swim, jump) to the student whose eyes are open (closed). *4.* Sit on the desk (floor) with your eyes open and your mouth closed.

opera Pretend you're an opera singer.

opposite *1.* Stand on the opposite side of the class from Pedro. *2.* Sit (stand) opposite Maria. *3.* Walk towards Pedro, turn around, and hop (run) in the opposite direction. *4.* For each word I say, write a word that means the opposite.

or *1.* Class, do you want Pedro to run or jump? *2.* Give the pen (flower, eraser) to Maria or Pedro. It doesn't matter which one you give it to.

orange *1.* Peel the orange (banana) and offer it to Maria. *2.* Throw (toss) the orange into the air and catch it. *3.*

Roll the orange to the student sitting on Pedro's left. *4.* Put the orange in your purse.

order *1.* Put the words you see on the chalkboard in alphabetical order. *2.* Order the five students who are standing in front of the class from tallest to shortest. *3.* The teacher's desk is messy. Order the papers to make it neat.

organize Class, I want you to organize yourselves into four groups, each with the same number of students.

original Draw a flower (heart, sad face, fat man, picture of yourself) on a piece of paper making a carbon copy. Hang the original on the wall and give the copy to Maria.

other *1.* Pick up two circles. Put one on your head and the other under the chair. *2.* Touch an eye. Now touch your other eye. *3.* Draw a hat. Now turn your paper over and write your name on the other side. *4.* Show me a hand. Now show me your other hand.

out *1.* Go out and come back in. *2.* Throw the paper ball out the window. *3.* Step into the circle you drew on the floor. Now jump out of it. *4.* Look (lean) out the door. *5.* Copy this sentence, but leave out the third word. *6.* Light the match and blow it out.

outer Draw two concentric circles. Color the outer circle red and the inner one blue.

outside *1.* Touch the outside (inside) of the box (can, glass, cup). *2.* Stand (sit) outside the door. *3.* Go (step) outside and see if the sun is shining. *4.* Draw a circle on the floor with the chalk. Stand with one foot inside and one foot outside the circle.

oval Draw a man (woman, girl, boy) with an oval (a round, square, triangular) head (mouth).

oven Pretend you're putting something in the toy oven.

over *1.* Hold your hands over your head. *2.* Draw a cloud over a house. *3.* Jump over the book. *4.* Put the towel over the bottle. *5.* Trip over Pedro's feet. *6.* Touch something that costs over (under) twenty dollars. *7.* Hit me over the head with the bottle. *8.* Roll the ball and knock over the candle.

owl Draw (hoot like) an owl.

own *1.* Pick up the scissors and cut my hair. Now cut your own hair. *2.* If you own (have) a dog (cat, car, bicycle), raise your hand (foot).

owner *(Take articles from the students and put them on the desk.)* I want the owner of the book (watch, pen, notebook, shoe, bracelet) to clap (sing, pray, jump to the door).

pace *1.* Walk forward three paces. *2.* Draw many circles (squares, hearts, chairs). Work at a slow (fast) pace. *3.* You're nervous. Pace the floor.

pack *1.* Draw a suitcase and cut it out. Pretend you're packing the suitcase. *2.* Draw a big circle (square) on the floor and see how many students you can pack into it. *3.* Put the pack of cigarettes in your purse (pocket).

package *1.* Give the package to Maria. *2.* Cut open the

161

package of soup *(empty container)* and pour the contents into the pan.

paddle Pick up the stick (pencil), pretend you're in a canoe, and paddle around the class.

page *1.* Open your book to page twenty. *2.* Draw a circle (star) at the top (bottom) of page five. *3.* Turn the page. *4.* Print your first (last, full) name in the margin (at the bottom) of page ten. *5.* Write the page that lesson five begins (ends) on.

pail *1.* Pour some water into the pail (glass, cup). *2.* Swing the pail back and forth. *3.* Put the pail (box) on your head and walk (jump, swim, hop) around the class.

pain You have a pain in your neck (side, back, upper arm, belly). Hold it and groan.

paint *1.* Pick up the paint brush, pretend you're a house painter, and paint the back wall. *2.* Pick up the brush, pretend you're a famous artist, and paint a picture of Maria.

painter Write the name of a famous French (Italian, Dutch, Spanish) painter.

pair *1.* Arrange yourselves in pairs. *2.* Pretend you're putting on a pair of pants. *3.* Pair up and practice the commands.

palm *1.* Extend your left (right) hand palm up (down). *2.* Draw a heart (flower, sad face) on the palm (back) of Maria's hand. *3.* Draw a palm tree.

pamphlet *1.* Show the pamphlet to the class. *2.* Open the pamphlet (book, magazine, comic book) to page 25 and read. *3.* Write the title of the pamphlet on the chalkboard and underline (cross out, circle) the last (first) two words.

pan *1.* Pour some water into the pan. *2.* Pick up the can of soup *(empty container),* pour the contents into the pan, put the pan on the stove, and stir the soup. *3.* Walk around the class banging on the pan with the spoon. *4.* Hit me on the head with the pan. *5.* Fill the pan with crumpled paper.

pants *1.* Pretend you're putting on a pair of pants. *2.* Walk (jump, swim) to the student who's wearing brown pants (trousers). *3.* Draw a man wearing striped (checked) pants.

paper *1.* Take (tear) out a sheet of paper. *2.* Fold (cut, tear) the paper in half. *3.* Crumple the paper and toss it into the wastebasket. *4.* Burn a hole in the paper with a cigarette. *5.* Make a hole in the paper with the pen. *6.* Make a paper airplane (ball). *7.* Turn your paper over.

paragraph *1.* Count the lines (words, sentences, commas) in the paragraph. *2.* Circle the first word in the paragraph and draw a rectangle around the last (next to the last).

parallel *1.* Draw two long (short) parallel vertical (horizontal, diagonal) lines. *2.* Draw two lines (streets) running parallel (perpendicular) to each other.

parents *1.* Draw a family with fat (thin, tall, short) parents. *2.* Jump to a student whose parents were born in Paris *(student-made cc).*

park *1.* Draw a boy (girl) flying a kite in a park. *2.* Walk (hop, jump) to the student who's at the park *(pc)*. *3.* Park the blue car next to the red car.

parrot Pretend you're a parrot and repeat everything I say.

part *1.* Draw a square (circle, rectangle) and divide it in three equal (unequal) parts. *2.* Say (whisper) hello to part (all) of the class. *3.* Draw a circle (heart, triangle) and color it part red and part blue. *4.* Pick up the comb and part your hair.

participate Stand in front of (point to, wave to) a student who hasn't participated (taken part) today.

partly Draw a square (rectangle, circle) and fill it partly (and completely fill it) with dots (stars, hearts, flowers).

partner *1.* When the music stops, change partners. *2.* Do the exercises with your partner.

pass *1.* Pass me the salt (pepper, butter dish, plate, fork). *2.* Pedro and Maria, you're both driving. Maria, your car is behind Pedro's. Now pull out from behind him and pass him. *3.* Take a card (paper, test booklet) and pass the rest along.

pass out Pass out the geometric figures (picture cards, test booklets, answer sheets).

past *1.* Shout the name of a student who hasn't been in class the past few days. *2.* Write the name of a past president (minister) of your country. *3.* When Maria walks past you, stand up (cry, laugh, frown). *4.* Throw the ball (pencil, bottle cap) past Pedro.

pat *1.* Pat me on the back (arm, head, shoulder). *2.* Pretend Pedro is your dog and pat him on the head.

patch *1.* Draw a man wearing a patch over one of his eyes. *2.* Pick up the square piece of cloth, pretend it's a patch, and tape it to Pedro's back pocket.

path *1.* Draw a narrow path going up a hill. *2.* Maria, drive your car towards Pedro as if you were going to run him over. Pedro, jump out of the path (way) of the car.

patient *1.* Pedro, you're a doctor and Carlos is your patient. Feel his pulse and listen to his heart with the stethoscope. *2.* Imitate (pretend you're) a patient (an impatient) person.

patriotic Sing a patriotic (romantic, funny, children's) song.

pause *1.* Count to ten. When you reach the number seven, pause for three seconds, then continue. *2.* Walk around the class pausing in front of every other student. *3.* Press the Pause button on your tape recorder.

pay *1.* Maria, go to Pedro and buy a cigarette (an eraser, his signature). Pay him ten cents. *2.* Go to the department store *(pc)* and buy something. Pay for it in cash (with a check). *(Use play money and magazine cutouts.)*

peach *1.* Pretend you're eating the peach (banana, apple). *2.* Put the peach on the tray and serve it to Maria.

peak *1.* Draw a mountain with a flag (tree, girl standing) on its peak. *2.* Draw a graph showing three peaks.

pear *1.* Eat the pear. *2.* Pick up the knife and pretend you're slicing the pear. *3.* Draw a pear between two stars (flowers, hats, hearts).

peas Pick up the can opener, open the can of peas *(empty container),* pour the contents into the pan, and heat it over the stove.

pebble *1.* Put (drop) a few pebbles in the teacher's shirt pocket. *2.* Place a stone between two pebbles. *3.* Put some pebbles in the can and walk around the class shaking the can.

peel *1.* Throw the orange peel on the floor. *2.* Pick up (touch, smell, show me) the orange peel. *3.* Pretend you're peeling a banana. *4.* Make a label, glue it to the jar, and then peel it off.

peeler *1.* Use the peeler to peel the potato (apple, cucumber). *2.* Pretend you're peeling Pedro's finger (nose, elbow) with the peeler.

pen *1.* Measure (tie the string around, cover) the pen. *2.* Put the pen in (on, under, next to) the box (glass). *3.* Take (remove) the pen from Pedro's pocket and put it in your own. *4.* Pick up the pen (pencil, chalk) and draw a cat (sad face, fat man).

pencil *1.* Stick the pencil in the sharpener and sharpen it. *2.* Measure (feel the point of) the sharp (dull) pencil. *3.* Point to the door with the pencil. *4.* Break the pencil in half. *5.* Balance the pencil on your thumb. *6.* Write my name in pencil (ink, chalk).

pencil sharpener Use the pencil sharpener to sharpen the pencil.

people *1.* Count (touch) all the people in the class. *2.* Draw a picture with five people, two animals, and three plants in it. *3.* Touch a place on the map where many (few) people live.

pepper *1.* Smell the pepper and sneeze. *2.* Throw some pepper (salt) over your shoulder. *3.* Pretend you have some food on your plate, and season it with the salt and the pepper.

perfect Congratulate (shake hands with) the student who got a perfect (nearly perfect) score on the test.

perform *1.* Perform (do) a dance for the class. *2.* Perform an action that you do at church (in a restaurant).

performance *1.* Award the cookie to the student who had the best performance in the race. *2.* Several students are each going to sing a song. Then we're going to vote for the best performance.

perfume *1.* Smell the perfume *(empty container)*. *2.* Put some perfume on your neck (arm). *3.* Write the name of the perfume you use.

period *1.* Write a sentence (command) on the chalkboard and put a triangle around the period. *2.* Write a sentence, but omit the period. *3.* Erase the period in the sentence that you wrote.

permit *1.* Touch an object that permits (allows) light and air to enter the classroom. *2.* I want the students in the first row to block the entrance to the door. When Maria stands up and walks (swims, hops) to the door, you will (won't) permit her to leave.

perpendicular *1.* Draw two long (short) perpendicular (parallel) lines. *2.* Write the names of two streets that run perpendicular to each other.

person *1.* Hop (swim, jump, skip) to a person who's wearing something red. *2.* Touch (point to, pull the nose of) the person who's sitting behind (next to, in front of, to the left of) you.

photograph Look at the photograph and see if you can guess who it is. *(The students have brought photographs of themselves as children.)*

photographer You're a photographer. Pick up the camera and take (snap) a picture of the student who's wearing a blue shirt.

piano *1.* Pretend you're playing the piano (pushing a piano up a flight of stairs). *2.* Draw a piano.

pick *1.* Pick someone to help you carry the teacher around the class. *2.* Pick a number between one and thirty, and perform the command on the card with that number. *3.* Pick a command card from the pile. *4.* Go outside, pick a flower, and give it to Maria.

pick up *1.* Pick up the circle (square, rectangle, triangle) and show it to the class. *2.* Pick up the book (notebook, pen, pencil, eraser) that you threw (set, placed) on the floor. *3.* Walk around the class gradually picking up speed.

picture *1.* Draw a picture of your teacher (your family; life in the year 3000). *2.* Cut out a picture from the magazine and tape it to the wall. *3.* Pick up the camera and take my picture.

piece *1.* Take out (give me) a piece (sheet) of paper. *2.* Tear (cut) the paper into pieces (strips). *3.* Break a piece of chalk in half. *4.* Pick up the scissors and cut a piece of the string (yarn, thread). *5.* Serve me a piece (slice) of cheese.

pierce Pierce (make a hole in) the paper (paper cup, paper plate) with the pin (pencil, pen; your finger).

pig Imitate (pretend you're, oink like) a pig.

pigtails Draw a short (tall, fat, thin) girl wearing pigtails (a ponytail).

pile *1.* Pile (stack) your books (notebooks) on the teacher's desk. *2.* Make a pile of books (notebooks).

pill *1.* Shake the bottle of pills. *2.* Arrange the pills into a circle (square, triangle). *3.* Draw a happy (sad) face and glue two pills for the eyes. *4.* Crush the pill with your thumb.

pillow *1.* Put (lay, rest) your head on the pillow and pretend you're sleeping. *2.* Throw (toss, give, hand) the pillow to the teacher. *3.* Hit me on the head (shoulder, back) with the pillow.

pilot *1.* Jump (run, walk) to the pilot *(pc)*. *2.* Draw an airplane with a pilot who is wearing a hat (beard). *3.* Pilot (fly) the airplane to the door (window, desk, teacher).

pin *1.* Feel (touch) the point of the pin and say "ouch." *2.* Stick the pin into the cork (potato, sponge). *3.* Blow up the balloon and pop (burst) it with the pin. *4.* Pin the cloth square to your shirt. *5.* Carlos and Pedro, pin me to the wall.

pinch *1.* Pinch yourself (Pedro's cheeks). *2.* Blow up the balloon, pinch the neck so that the air doesn't escape, and tie a knot. *3.* Sneak up behind Pedro and give him a pinch.

pineapple *1.* Pick up the knife and pretend your're cutting (slicing) the pineapple (cucumber, apple). *2.* Walk (run, hop) to the student who's eating the pineapple. *3.* Draw a girl (fat woman) with a pineapple on her head.

pipe *1.* Pretend you're smoking the pipe (cigarette). *2.* Draw a cat (happy face, sad face, fat man) smoking a pipe. *3.* Look at me through the pipe *(= tube)*. *4.* Drop some paper balls (coins) through the pipe (cylinder) into the glass (cup; my pocket).

pistol *1.* Pick up the pistol (gun) and shoot the teacher. *2.* When Maria aims the pistol at Pedro, he will stick up his hands (run away, duck, hide behind the teacher).

pitcher *1.* Pick up the pitcher and pour some water into the glass (cup, bowl, pail). *2.* Cut open the package of fruit drink *(empty container),* pour the contents into the pitcher, add some water and sugar, stir it, and serve a glass to the teacher.

place *1.* Walk to a place where you pray (study) (pc's). *2.* Jump to the door and then go back to your place. *3.* Change places with a friend. *4.* Draw a circle, erase it, and draw a cloud in its place. *5.* Place the book on the floor. *6.* Run in place. *7.* Hop to the event that took place in 1910 *(cc-7)*.

plain *1.* Draw a woman wearing a plain (fancy) dress. *2.* Place the book (notebook, wastebasket, eraser) somewhere where it is (isn't)in plain sight.

plan *1.* Shake hands with the student who plans to become a nurse (doctor, pilot) *(pc's)*. *2.* If you plan (intend) to go to the movies (beach) this weekend, raise your hand (foot).

plant *1.* Pick up the spade, dig a hole, and plant the flower. *2.* Pick up the watering can and water the plant you drew on the chalkboard.

plastic Touch (pick up, show the class) an object made of plastic (wood, glass, metal, leather, cardboard).

plate *1.* Put the apple (orange, cookie, banana) on the plate. *2.* Spin the plate. *3.* Draw a sad (happy) face on the paper plate. *4.* Write the number of your license plate.

play *1.* Pretend you're playing soccer (baseball, volleyball, basketball, tennis; the drums, piano, flute, guitar). *2.* Play a game of tic-tac-toe. *3.* Write the name of a play written by Shakespeare. *4.* Write the name of a movie playing near here. *5.* Pick up (draw) an object that boys (girls) like to play with.

pleasant Lay your head on your desk and pretend you're sleeping. Smile (frown), you're having a pleasant (bad) dream.

please Please open the door (close the window, erase the chalkboard, pass out the tests).

plenty *1.* Pour plenty (a little bit) of water into the pail (glass, cup). *2.* Draw plenty of circles (hearts, houses, doors). *3.* Drive the car (jeep, bus) to the student who has plenty of (very little) money *(cc-9).*

pliers *1.* Take the pliers to the electrician (mechanic) *(pc's).* *2.* Pretend you're tightening Pedro's nose (Maria's ear, the nut) with the pliers (wrench).

plug *1.* Go to the tape recorder and touch the plug. *2.* Punch a hole in the paper cup with the pencil. Plug the hole with your finger (some clay). Now fill the cup with water.

plug in Plug in (unplug) the tape recorder (lamp, fan).

plus *1.* Draw a plus sign and then draw a circle (rectangle,square) around it. *2.* Write the sum of two plus two. *3.* If six plus four equals nine, cry (laugh, sigh). If not, frown (yawn, stoop).

pocket *1.* Put the candle (flower, pen, eraser, tea bag, bottle caps) in Pedro's pocket. *2.* Draw a man wearing a shirt with two pockets. *3.* Fill my pocket with crumpled paper (paper balls, pencils).

point *1.* Point to the ceiling (your nose, an eye). *2.* Touch an object that has a point. *3.* Touch the point of the pencil. *4.* Draw a road that curves to the left. At the point where it curves, draw a house. *5.* Count the points to see who won. *6.* Pinch the student who just scored a point.

pointed *1.* Touch a pointed object *(e.g., the pencil).* *2.* Draw a man with a pointed nose (head, chin; ears).

poisonous Write the name of something that is (isn't)

poisonous.

pole *1.* Go to the map and touch the North (South) Pole. *2.* Draw a boy with a fishing pole over his shoulder. There's a big fish hanging from the pole.

policeman *1.* Pretend you're a policeman, put on the badge, arrest Pedro, and take him to jail *(pc)*. *2.* Pull the nose (ear, hair) of the policeman *(pc)*.

polish *1.* Put some furniture polish (empty container) on the cloth (rag) and polish the teacher's desk. *2.* Pick up the nail polish (empty container) and polish your nails. *3.* Apply some polish (empty container) to your shoes. Now polish them.

politician Write the name of an important (a prominent) politician.

ponytail Draw a girl wearing a ponytail (pigtails).

pool *1.* Draw some boys swimming in a swimming pool. *2.* Pretend you're playing (shooting) a game of pool.

poor *1.* Give some money (a few coins) to the poor man *(beggar pc)*. *2.* Take some money from a rich person and give it to a poor person *(cc-9)*.

pop 1. Blow up (inflate) the balloon until it pops (bursts). *2.* Blow up the paper bag and pop it. *3.* Offer a can (bottle) of pop *(empty containers)* to Maria.

popular Write (say) the name of a popular tv program (singer, song, actor, actress).

population Make a list of five cities with a population of over one million (under five hundred thousand).

pose *1.* Maria, draw a beautiful scene on the chalkboard and pose in front of it. Pedro, pick up the camera and take her picture. *2.* I'm going to take your picture. Hold your pose. *3.* Pose for a picture with Maria.

position *1.* Hold the pen (ruler) under your nose (chin) in a horizontal (vertical, diagonal) position. *2.* Sit in a comfortable (an uncomfortable) position. *3.* Sit in a position so that you can (are able to) see the papers on the desk in front of you.

possible Classify each sentence you hear (read) as possible or impossible.

post *1.* Draw a fence. Using your ruler, place (put) the posts exactly five centimeters apart. *2.* Make a "No Smoking" sign and post it on the wall. *3.* Go to the post office *(pc)* and post (mail) a letter.

post office *1.* Write a letter to Maria, put it in the envelope, and take it to the post office *(pc)*. *2.* Walk (run, jump, swim, limp, skip) to the post office *(pc)* and mail a letter.

postcard *1.* Send the postcard to the student who's sitting behind (next to) Maria. *2.* Stick the postcard in my book (notebook).

pot *1.* Pick up the can opener, open the can of corn (peas) *(empty containers),* pour the contents into the pot, put the pot on the stove, and stir it. *2.* Fill the pot with water (crumpled newspaper). *3.* Scrub the pot with the Brillo pad (sponge).

potato *1.* Throw (toss) the potato into the air and catch it with both hands. *2.* Peel (slice, stick the pin into) the potato. *3.* Wrap the potato in aluminum foil because you're going to bake it.

pound *1.* Pick up the hammer and pound (hammer, drive) the nail into the board. *2.* Pound (bang) on the door (wall; your desk). *3.* Pick up (touch, draw, point to) an object that weighs less (more) than two pounds.

pour *1.* Pour some water from the pitcher into the glass. *2.* Pretend you're pouring some water on the teacher's head. *3.* Pick up the box of cereal *(empty container)* and pour some into the bowl. *4.* Draw a picture in which it's pouring (drizzling).

powder *1.* Pick up the box of soap powder *(empty container)* and pour some into the bowl (pail). *2.* Crush the aspirin until it forms a fine powder.

powerful *1.* Imitate (draw) a powerful (weak) animal.

practice *1.* Practice the commands on page 30 with your partner. *2.* Practice balancing the pencil (ruler) on the tip of your finger until you can do it.

praise Praise the student who carried out the command correctly (formulated a long command, came in first in the race) by saying, "very good."

pray *1.* Go (walk, swim, run) to the church *(pc),* fold your hands together, and pray. *2.* Touch (pull the nose of) a student who's at a place where people pray *(church pc).*

precede Write (shout, whisper, sing) the number that precedes (follows, comes before) ten.

prefer Write the names of two actors (actresses, books, films, fruits, sports, songs, singers) that you like. Now circle (underline, draw a rectangle around) the one you prefer.

prepare *1.* Go to the kitchen *(pc)* and pretend you're preparing dinner. *2.* Put the tea bag in the cup and pretend you're preparing a cup of tea. *3.* Pick up the jar of instant coffee *(empty container)* and pretend you're preparing (making) a cup of coffee.

present *1.* Write the name of a student who was present yesterday, but is absent today. *2.* When I call your name, stand up and say "present." *3.* Walk to Maria, hold the present behind your back, and give it to her.

present *1.* Draw a trophy, cut it out, and present it to the student who won the race. *2.* Present the flower to the girl who's wearing the yellow blouse.

president Write (print, sing) the name of the president of Brazil (France, Mexico, the United States).

press *1.* Press the Play (Pause, Rewind, Stop) button on your tape recorder. *2.* Press (squeeze) my hand. *3.* Press me against the wall (door). *4.* Pick up the iron and press (iron) my shirt (head; the towel, handkerchief).

pressure *1.* Squeeze my hand gently. Now apply some pressure. *2.* Drive the green car to the gas station *(pc)* and have the attendant check the pressure in your tires.

pretend *1.* Pretend (make believe) you're a dog (bird, cat, cow, horse, lion, monkey, sheep). *2.* Pretend you're sleeping (shaving, peeling a banana, putting on a pair of pants).

pretty *1.* Write the name of a pretty actress (singer). *2.* Hop (jump, run) to a student who is pretty (very) tall.

prevent Pedro, go out of the class. Carlos and Eduardo, prevent (stop, impede) him from coming back in.

price *1.* Touch (draw) an object whose price is over (under, less than, more than) five dollars. *2.* I'm going to show you some pictures cut out from magazine advertisements. Guess the price of each object.

priest *1.* Run (walk, jump, swim) to the priest *(pc)* and pray. *2.* Draw a church, cut it out, and take (carry) it to the priest *(pc)*. *3.* You're a priest. Put (place) your hands on Maria's head and bless her.

print *1.* Print (write, sign) your name (first name, last name, nickname). *2.* Print (sing) the name of the student who's at the bank (church, drugstore) *(pc's)*. *3.* Cut out (show us) an advertisement that's in big (small) print.

prison The boy wearing the mask is a thief. Take (push, carry) him to the prison (jail) *(pc)*.

prisoner Pedro, put on the badge. You're a policeman. Carlos is your prisoner. Take him to jail *(pc)*.

prize Give the prize *(e.g., a candy bar, cookie, etc.)* to the winner of the contest (race).

problem *1.* Put a simple (difficult, hard) math problem on the chalkboard. *2.* Solve the math problem I put on the board.

produce Write (shout, sing) the name of a company that produces computers (radios, cars, watches, televisions).

program Write (print, shout, whisper) the name of a program that's on television tonight (Monday evening, Saturday morning).

pronounce 1. Write a word in your native language and pronounce it with an American accent. 2. Pronounce the words on the chalkboard (on the cards I show you).

pronunciation Write a word (sentence) in your native language and say it with an American pronunciation.

propose Kneel in front of a female student who's wearing a necklace (bracelet, red skirt, blue blouse) and propose to her.

protect 1. Draw an object we use to protect ourselves from the rain. 2. Jump to the person who protects people *(policeman pc)*. 3. When I count to three, everyone is going to throw a paper ball at Pedro. Pedro, protect yourself with your notebook (book).

protractor 1. Pick up the protractor and measure the angle that you drew. 2. Use the protractor to draw a thirty-degree angle.

publish Open your history (English, math, geography) book and write the year it was published.

pull 1. Pull your (a friend's) nose (hair, left ear). 2. Pull (push) Maria to the door (window, chair, desk). 3. Push me down and then pull me up. *4.* Pull out (push in) the drawer. *5.* Pull (take) Maria aside and whisper something in her ear.

pulse Pretend you're a doctor (nurse) and feel (check) my pulse.

pump Shake hands with Pedro pumping his hand.

punch *1.* Punch (sock, hit) Pedro in the arm (shoulder). *2.* Punch (make) a hole in the paper with your finger (pencil, pen). *3.* Give me a punch in the arm.

punish Maria, pretend Pedro is your baby. When he sticks out his tongue (makes a face) at you, punish him by giving him a spanking (making him sit in the corner).

purchase *1.* Go to the department store *(pc)* and purchase (buy) a radio (watch, shirt). *(Use play money and magazine cutouts.)* *2.* Pick up (draw) an object that you can purchase (buy, get, find) at a hardware store (supermarket, drugstore, furniture store).

purse *1.* Hide (zip up, unzip, open, close) the purse. *2.* Put the pen (key, eraser) in Maria's purse. *3.* Empty the contents of the purse onto the table. *4.* Take Maria's purse, put the strap over your shoulder, and slowly walk (parade) around the class (desk).

push *1.* Push (pull) me to the desk. *2.* Push (shove) the desk against the wall. *3.* Push the pen (paper ball) off the desk with your nose. *4.* Push in the drawer that you just pulled out. *5.* Give me a big (gentle) push (shove).

put *1.* Put (stick) the candle (bar of soap, pack of cigarettes, pen, pencil) in your pocket. *2.* Put (place) the pen in (on, under, next to, beside) the glass.

put away *1.* Put your books away. *2.* Take out your wallet (driver's license; a credit card), show it to the class, and then put it away.

put down *1.* Pick up the candle (pen, pencil, eraser, notebook, book), show it to the class, and then put it down. *2.* Pick up and then put down the circle (square, red fish, blue car).

put on Put on the hat (tie, bracelet, watch, cap, necklace, scarf, wig, glove). Now take it (them) off.

put out *1.* Put (stick) out your hand. *2.* Light a match (the candle) and put (blow) it out. *3.* Put out the cigarette in the ashtray.

puzzle Take the jigsaw puzzle apart and then put it back together again.

pyramid *1.* Build (erect, construct, make) a pyramid with the blocks (spools, match boxes). *2.* Draw a pyramid. *3.* Write (tell us) the name of a country famous (noted) for its pyramids.

quantity *1.* Touch (point to) the glass that has a large (small) quantity of water in it. *2.* Pick up the box of cereal *(empty container)* and pretend you're pouring a large quantity into the bowl.

quarrel Stand in front of Maria and pretend you're quarreling (arguing) with her.

quarter *1.* Count the bottle caps (coins, paper balls, clips, pebbles) and give a quarter (third) of them to Maria. 2. Draw a large number of hearts (stars, doors, chairs) and then erase a quarter (two thirds, one half) of them.

queen *1.* Bow to (kneel in front of, shake hands with) the queen *(pc).* *2.* Write (spell) the name of a country that has (doesn't have) a queen (king, president).

question *1.* Draw a big (huge, tiny) question mark. *2.* Change (transform, convert) the statement on the chalkboard into a question.

quick *1.* Walk around (to) the desk (teacher, chair) at a quick (slow) pace. *2.* Swim (walk, run, hop) to the desk (chalkboard, window) quickly (slowly). *3.* Erase the chalkboard (draw ten circles, shake hands with everybody) as quickly as you can.

quiet *1.* When I count to four, I want everybody to become quiet (silent, noisy). *2.* Speak in a quiet (soft, loud) voice. *3.* When I raise my right hand, everyone will cry (hum, yell, sing). Then Maria will stand up and quiet the class. *4.* Please be quiet.

quit Run (hop, jump, swim) around the class (desk, teacher). When I ring the bell (raise my foot, sneeze, clap), you will quit (stop, cease).

rabbit *1.* Wiggle your nose like a rabbit. *2.* Draw a rabbit. *3.* Draw (pick up) something a rabbit likes to eat.

race *1.* Pedro, race Carlos to the door (window, fan). *2.* We're going to have a race to see who can walk (hop) backwards to the door (chalkboard) the fastest.

racket *1.* Pretend you have a tennis racket in your hand

and are playing tennis (serving a tennis ball). *2.* Make a racket by pounding on the table (stamping your feet, whistling, clapping).

radio *1.* Turn on (turn off, plug in, unplug) the radio. *2.* Run (swim) to the student who has the radio and buy it from him *(use play money).*

rag *1.* Wipe the table (desk, chalkboard; your left shoe) with the rag. *2.* Fold the rag in half (thirds). *3.* Shine Pedro's right shoe with the rag.

rain *1.* Draw a cloud over a house. It's raining. *2.* Draw an object that protects us from the rain. *3.* Pretend it's raining, pick up the umbrella, and walk around the class (teacher, desk).

rainbow *1.* Draw a rainbow, cut it out, and hold it over Maria's head. *2.* Draw a rainbow over a cloud (mountain, tree, house, church).

raise *1.* Raise your right hand (left foot; both hands, both feet; one of your hands). *2.* Count to ten. After each number, raise (lower) your voice a little. *3.* Raise (hold up) the can (book, notebook, pen, pencil, sponge, red fish).

raisin *1.* Drop a raisin into your mouth, chew it, and then swallow it. *2.* Put (place) two raisins on the plate (saucer) and serve them to Maria. *3.* Throw (toss) a raisin into the air and catch it in your mouth.

rake *1.* Draw some leaves on the floor (desk) in chalk, pick up the toy rake, and rake them up. *2.* Draw a man raking some leaves.

range Write (tell me) the name of a mountain range in Europe (Asia, North America, South America).

rank Consult the almanac and rank these cities by population: New York, Paris, Tokyo, London.

rapidly *1.* Walk (hop, swim) rapidly (slowly) to the door (desk, chalkboard, window). *2.* Count to ten (draw five circles, write your name) as rapidly (fast, quickly) as you can.

rare *1.* Draw (write the name of, imitate) an animal that's rare (common) in the city. *2.* Shake hands with (point to, pull the hair of) a student who rarely comes to class late (is rarely absent).

rate Rate the actors (actresses, films, singers, tv programs) I put on the chalkboard. Use the following classifications: excellent, good, fair, poor.

rattle *1.* Pretend Maria is a baby and give (hand) her the rattle. *2.* Walk (jump, hop) around the class shaking the rattle.

ray Draw the sun with many (several, a few) long (short) rays extending from it.

razor Pick up the razor and shave the student who has curly hair (long hair, wavy hair; a beard, mustache).

reach *1.* Hop (swim) around the class. When you reach (come to) your seat, clap (sneeze, cough) loudly and then sit down. *2.* Stretch (jump) and make a chalk mark as high as you can reach. *3.* Reach into the bag and take out six bottle caps (pebbles, coins).

183

read *1.* Open the book (magazine) to page 20 and read. *2.* Write a sentence on the chalkboard and then read it to the class. *3.* Silently read and perform the commands on your card. *4.* Read my lips and perform the command I'm mouthing. *5.* Read my palm.

ready As soon as you're ready (finished with the exercises), look up (raise your hands, put down your pencils).

real Write (sing, say) the name of a real (imaginary) person.

rear *1.* Stand (stoop, kneel) in the rear (back, front) of the room. *2.* Shake hands with (touch, toss the ball to) a student sitting (standing) in the rear (front) of the class.

receive *1.* Congratulate a student who received (got, earned) an "A" on the test. *2.* When Maria knocks on the door, open it and receive her with a smile (frown). *3.* Pedro, write Maria a note. Maria, when you receive it, cry (laugh, jump up and down).

reckless *1.* Drive the red car to the door (window). Pretend you're a reckless (cautious) driver. *2.* Drive the car (jeep, bus, truck) around the class recklessly (carefully).

recognize *1.* Look at this baby picture and see if you recognize who it is *(each student has brought a baby picture to class).* *2.* Close your eyes. Some students will speak to you disguising their voices. Try to recognize who is speaking.

record *1.* Look at me (the door) through the hole in the

184

record. *2.* Stick the pencil (toothpick, straw, string) through the hole in the record. *3.* See if you can break the class record for bouncing the ball.

record *1.* Turn on the tape recorder and record five commands. *2.* Record (mark) the points for your team.

rectangle *1.* Touch (point to, show me, pick up, put down) the big (small) rectangle. *2.* Draw a rectangle over (and, next to, under, inside) a square (triangle, circle).

rectangular Touch (pick up, draw, point to) an object that is rectangular (round, square, cylindrical, oval) in shape.

reduce *1.* Write a number, reduce it by half (a third), and then draw a circle (square) around (under) the new number. *2.* Draw many flowers (triangles, hearts, stars). Now reduce (increase) the number of flowers you drew by two.

reflect Use the mirror to reflect some light onto the chalkboard (ceiling; into my eyes).

refuse Maria, when Pedro invites you to dance, you will refuse by shaking your head (laughing, walking away, slapping him).

relax *1.* Breathe in, breathe out, relax. *2.* Squeeze my hand (shoulder, elbow). When I count to five, you will relax your grip.

release *1.* Blow up the balloon, release it, and watch it shrink (fly away). *2.* Hold Pedro tight. Now release him (let him go).

relief Pick up (touch, show us) something that gives (brings) you relief for a headache (cough) *(e.g., the aspirin, cough medicine).*

remain *1.* Stand up and remain (continue) standing until I tell you to sit down. *2.* Let's see who can remain perfectly still the longest. *3.* Draw six circles (stars) in a row. Erase two of them and draw a line through (over, under) the remaining ones.

remember *1.* Look at the list of words on the board for one minute. I will then erase them. Let's see who can remember and write the most words from the list. *2.* Congratulate (shake hands with) the student who remembered the greatest number of words.

remind Remind me to stop the class five minutes early today.

remove *1.* Remove the lid from the can (cap from the bottle, flower from Pedro's shirt, soap from the soap dish). *2.* Remove everything from your desk (pocket, purse).

repair Drive the green car to the man who repairs (fixes) cars *(mechanic pc).*

repeat *1.* Repeat my (your) name three (several, a few) times. *2.* Repeat the action you just performed.

replace *1.* Take a book (pen) from Maria's desk and replace it with one of your own. *2.* Pick up the eraser (a piece of chalk), use it, and then replace it where you found it. *3.* Draw a flower (circle). Now erase it and replace it with a house (happy face).

represent Draw a symbol that represents love (male, female, good luck, money).

require Write a sentence that requires a period (comma, question mark; an exclamation point).

rescue Maria, pretend you're drowning. Pedro, swim to her and rescue her.

resemble Everybody, draw a picture of Pedro. Now let's vote and choose the picture (drawing) that most resembles (looks like) him.

resist *1.* Pedro, pull (push) Carlos to the door (chalkboard, window, desk). Carlos, resist. *2.* Pedro, become serious. Maria, make funny (crazy) faces and try to make him laugh. Let's see how long he can resist laughing and remain serious.

respond I'm going to ask you some questions. Respond by nodding for "yes" and shaking your head for "no."

responsible Pedro, today you will be responsible for taking attendance (passing out papers, collecting the tests, erasing the chalkboard).

rest *1.* Take five coins out of the bag. Put one in your pocket and give the rest to Maria. *2.* Pinch one of the students in your group and slap the rest. *3.* Draw six clouds in a row. Erase two and draw a rectangle around the rest. *4.* Do some jumping jacks. Now rest.

restaurant *1.* Accompany (take) Maria to the restaurant *(pc).* *2.* Write (whisper) the name of a restaurant that serves Mexican (Chinese, Japanese, Korean) food.

return *1.* Pick up the eraser, use it, and return it to its place. *2.* Stand up, pull my nose (hair, ears), and then return (go back) to your seat. *3.* Take the book (notebook, pen, pencil) from Pedro, show it to the class, and then return it to him.

reverse *1.* Say the alphabet in reverse order. *2.* Draw a picture of someone in the class and on the reverse side write the name of the person you drew.

revive Maria, faint. Pedro, gently slap her face to revive her.

reward *1.* Reward the winner of the race with a cookie (raisin, handshake, pat on the back). *2.* Give the reward to the student who won the race.

rewind *1.* Unwind some thread from the spool and then rewind it. *2.* Press the Rewind button and rewind the tape in the tape recorder.

rhyme *1.* You will hear pairs of words. If the two words you hear rhyme, you will nod (clap). If they don't rhyme, shake your head. *2.* For each word I say, you will write a word that rhymes with it.

ribbon *1.* Tie the ribbon (yarn) in your (my) hair. *2.* Wrap the ribbon (string) around the pencil (your thumb). *3.* Measure the blue ribbon. *4.* Cut a piece of string the same length as the red ribbon. *5.* Show us (hand me) the longer (shorter) ribbon.

rice *1.* Write the name of a country where the people eat a lot of rice. *2.* Pick up the box of rice *(empty container)* and pour some rice into the pan.

rich *1.* Go (walk, run, hop, swim) to the rich man *(cc-9)* and borrow (beg for) some money *(play money).* *2.* Write (whisper) the name of a famous rich person.

ride *1.* Draw a man riding a camel (horse, bicycle). *2.* Pedro, give Carlos a ride on your back to the door (window, desk, chalkboard).

rifle Aim the rifle at Pedro, pull the trigger, and say "bang." Pedro, fall down and pretend you're dead.

right *1.* Raise your right (left) hand (foot). *2.* Sit on my right. *3.* Move over one seat to your right. *4.* Turn right (left, around, about). *5.* Maria, open the door. *(Wait for her to perform the action.)* Class, if that's right, applaud. If it's wrong, cry.

rigid Stand (sit) in a rigid (relaxed) position.

ring *1.* Hop around the class ringing the bell. *2.* Pick up the phone and give Maria a ring. Pedro, make the sound of the phone ringing. *3.* Take off your ring (wedding band). *4.* The students in the first row will now form (make, stand in) a ring around Maria.

rinse Maria, pour some water on Pedro's hands so that he can wash them. *(Pedro washes his hands over the pail or at the sink.)* Now pour some water so that he can rinse his hands.

rip *1.* Rip (tear, cut) open the envelope. *2.* Rip (tear) a sheet of paper into small pieces. *3.* Draw a picture of a sad face (fat man, cat) and then rip it up.

rise *1.* Count to ten. After each number, I want your voice to rise (go up, go down) a little. *2.* When Maria walks in the door, everybody will rise (stand up). *3.* Point to (kick) the student who rises (gets up) at 6:30 *(student-made cc).*

river *1.* Draw a river with a boat (fish, canoe, man swimming) in it. *2.* Draw a bridge across the river you just drew. *3.* Write the name of a river that begins with the letter "m." *4.* Write the name of a river in France (England, Brazil).

road *1.* Pick up the chalk and draw a road with several sharp (wide) curves on the teacher's desk. *2.* Drive the blue car along the road you drew.

roar Roar like (as if you were) a lion.

rob Pedro, put on the mask, pick up the gun, and rob the bank (supermarket, drugstore, hardware store) *(pc's).*

robot Walk around the class like (as if you were, imitating) a robot.

rock *1.* Put (place) the rock in the wastebasket (top drawer, bottom drawer). *2.* Tie the string around the rock. *3.* Toss the rock into the air and catch it with your right hand. *4.* Put the doll in your arms and rock it to sleep.

rocket *1.* Draw a rocket, cut it out, and fly it to the desk (chalkboard, window, door). *2.* Draw a rocket going (flying, traveling) to the moon (sun).

roll *1.* Roll the ball (coin, orange) to Maria. *2.* Roll the clay into a ball (cylinder). *3.* Tear some toilet paper from the roll. *4.* Call the roll for me today.

roll up Roll up your sleeves.

romantic Sing (hum, whistle) a romantic (sad, happy, children's, patriotic) song.

roof *1.* Draw a boy (girl, fat man, cat) standing (sitting) on the roof of a house (church). *2.* Draw a house and then erase the roof (floor, door, window).

room *1.* Swim (run, jump) around the room. *2.* I want you three students to sit on the desk. Now move over and make room for Pedro. *3.* Put (write) our room number on the chalkboard and draw a circle (triangle) around (under) it.

root   *1.* Draw a tree (flower) showing the roots underground. *2.* Underline the roots of the words you see on the chalkboard. *3.* We're going to have a contest. Root for your team.

rope *1.* Tie the rope around your waist. *2.* Tie Pedro's feet together with the rope. *3.* Coil (tie a knot in, extend) the rope. *4.* Hold the rope by an end (both ends, the middle). *5.* Pedro and Carlos, stretch the rope tight. Maria, jump over the rope.

rough *1.* Pick up (touch, show us) a rough (smooth) object. *2.* Draw a boat in a rough (calm) sea. *3.* Put a rough (easy) math problem on the chalkboard. *4.* Give me a rough (gentle) shove.

round *1.* Touch a round (cylindrical, rectangular) object. *2.* Draw a man with a round (square, triangular, oval) face. *3.* Gather round the teacher's desk. *4.* Let's sing the song as a round. *5.* Give Maria a big round of applause.

row *1.* Draw five triangles (circles, hearts, squares) in a row (column). *2.* Draw a row of seven hats (stars, clouds). *3.* Sit in the first (last) row. *4.* Pull the hair (nose) of a student who's sitting in the second row. *5.* Pretend you're rowing a boat.

rub *1.* Rub your hands together (the paper with your thumb). *2.* Rub your nose (forehead, chin, cheek, belly).

rubber Touch (hold up, show the class) something made of rubber (cotton, plastic, wood, metal, paper, glass).

rubber band *1.* Stretch (snap) the rubber band. *2.* Set (place) the paper cup on the edge of the desk and try to shoot it off with the rubber band. *3.* Band the toothpicks (pencils, pens, rods) together with the rubber band.

rubbish Empty the rubbish (trash) from the wastebasket into the large paper bag.

rug Draw a rug with a geometric design and a dark (light) border.

rule Write (sing, whisper) the name of the person who rules Spain, (France, Germany, Brazil).

ruler *1.* Pick up the ruler and measure the candle (teacher's nose). *2.* Stick the ruler in Pedro's pocket. *3.* Balance the ruler on your finger. *4.* Hit Maria on the elbow with the ruler. *5.* Write the name of the current (a past) ruler of Spain.

run Run (walk, hop, jump, limp, skip, swim) to (around) the desk (door, fan, teacher, student wearing the yellow skirt).

rush *1.* Rush (speed, hurry) to the door (desk, chalkboard, window, teacher). *2.* Draw some (many) circles (hearts, triangles, hats). Rush (hurry, take your time).

rusty Pedro, pretend your arm is made of metal and it's rusty. Bend it making a creaking sound. Maria, pick up the oil can *(empty container)* and oil his arm.

sack *1.* Unfold the sack and put it over your head *(use a large grocery bag).* *2.* Put some objects in the sack (bag) and then take them out. As you remove each object, tell the class its name.

sad *1.* Pretend you're sad (happy, angry, surprised, tired). *2.* Draw a big (small, huge) sad (happy) face with long hair (short hair, pointed ears, three eyes; a beard, mustache, long nose).

safety pin *1.* Pin the handkerchief to your sleeve. *2.* Blow up the balloon and pop it with the safety pin. *3.* Fasten (attach) the cloth rectangle (triangle) to the back of Pedro's shirt with the safety pin.

sail *1.* Draw a sailboat, cut it out, and sail it around the class (teacher, desk). *2.* Maria, sail the boat you drew and cut out. Pedro, stand in back of her and pretend you're the wind.

sailor *1.* Draw a ship, cut it out, and navigate (pilot) it to the sailor *(pc).* *2.* Draw an object you associate with sailors.

salad You're going to make a salad. Pretend you're slicing the cucumber and the tomato.

salesman Go to the clothing store (department store)

(pc's), talk to a salesman, and buy something *(use paper money and magazine cutouts).*

salt *1.* Pick up the saltshaker and salt (sprinkle some salt on) the corn (food on your plate; Maria's head). *2.* Put some salt on the back of your hand and taste it.

saltshaker *1.* Put (set, place) the saltshaker next to the plate (glass, cup, fork). *2.* Lay the saltshaker on its side. *3.* Cover the saltshaker with the towel (cloth, handkerchief, napkin). *4.* Put the saltshaker in your pocket (purse).

salute 1. Stand in front of the student wearing the tie (hat, cap, beard, mustache, blue shirt) and salute him. *2.* Run (hop, swim, skip) to the soldier *(pc)* and salute him.

same *1.* Do the same thing I do. *2.* Touch two students who are wearing the same color shirts. *3.* Draw a big circle and write a word inside it. Now write the same (a different) word under the circle. *4.* Hit the same student Pedro is hitting.

sand *1.* Walk (run, limp, skip) to a place where you can see sand *(beach pc). 2.* Pretend you're walking on the beach and the hot sand is burning your feet. *3.* Pick up the sandpaper and sand the board (teacher's head; Pedro's elbow).

sandpaper *1.* Feel (touch) the rough (smooth) side (surface) of the sandpaper. *2.* Sand the board (teacher's nose) with the sandpaper.

sandwich *1.* Cut out a sandwich from two pieces of paper and pretend you're eating it. *2.* Draw a house sandwiched between two tall buildings (trees, churches).

saucer *1.* Put the cup of coffee on the saucer and serve it to Maria. *2.* Drop the saucer into the bag (wastebasket; your purse). *3.* Spin (cover the cup with) the saucer. *4.* Roll (slide, hand, toss) the saucer to Pedro.

save *1.* Maria, pretend you're drowning. Pedro, save her. *2.* Pedro, drive the red car as if you were going to run over Maria. Carlos, save her by pulling her out of the path (way) of the car.

saw *1.* Touch the blade (handle) of the saw. *2.* Pick up the saw and saw my arm (neck, wrist; the table, door, teacher's leg).

say *1.* Do what I say. *2.* Say (sing, whisper, shout) hello to the teacher (student who has the red fish). *3.* If you know how to say "table" in Spanish, go to the chalkboard and write it in big (small, huge, tiny) letters.

scale *1.* Draw a man weighing a fish on a scale. *2.* Draw a man scaling (climbing) a mountain. *3.* Sing (hum, whistle) the scale. *4.* Draw a fish with big (small) scales. *5.* Pick up the knife and pretend you're scaling the yellow fish.

scan Scan this page and find (underline, circle) a word that begins (ends) with the letter "b" (that has five letters).

scar Draw a man with a scar on his chin (forehead, left cheek).

scare *1.* Pretend you're a lion (bull, dog, monster) and scare Maria. Maria, scream and faint (run away). *2.*

195

Creep (sneak) up behind Maria and give her a scare.

scarf *1.* Wrap the scarf around your neck. *2.* Cover my eyes (head, left hand, shoulder, knee) with the scarf.

scatter *1.* Scatter the papers (paper balls, clips, bottle caps, coins, books, notebooks) on the table. *2.* I want the students in the first two rows to gather in the center of the class and scatter when I count to three (clap my hands).

scene Draw a scene (picture) of some people at the beach (park).

school *1.* Write the name of our school in big (small) letters. *2.* Swim (hop, jump, run) to the student who's at school *(pc)*.

scientist *1.* Pull the hair (nose, ears, foot) of the scientist *(pc)*. *2.* Write (whisper, sing) the name of a famous scientist.

scissors *1.* Pick up the scissors and cut my (your, our) hair. *2.* Use the scissors to cut the string (thread, yarn, paper). *3.* Draw a scissors between two hearts (stars, happy faces, doors, fans).

score *1.* Keep score for this contest (game). *2.* Congratulate the members of the team that has the highest score. *3.* The team that just scored (failed to score) a point will now clap (cry).

scramble *1.* Pretend you're making scrambled eggs. *2.* Write a sentence. Now rewrite the sentence scrambling the order of the words. Give Maria the sentence with the scrambled words. Maria, see if you can produce the original sentence.

scrap Write your name (nickname, birth date) on a scrap (slip, piece) of paper.

scrape Flatten some clay on the teacher's desk and then scrape it off.

scratch *1.* Scratch your head (back, chin, belly) with your hand (the ruler, a pencil). *2.* Pretend you've been bitten by a mosquito. Scratch yourself.

scream *1.* Pretend you're drowning and scream (cry out) for help. *2.* When Maria hits you on the arm (back, head, knee), you will scream (cry, laugh, make an angry face).

screw *1.* Pick up the screw and show it to the class. *2.* Tighten (loosen) a screw with the screwdriver. *3.* Screw the lid on the jar.

scribble Scribble your mother's (father's, teacher's) name on a slip (scrap, piece) of paper.

scrub *1.* Pick up the Brillo pad and scrub the dish (pan, pot, plate, knife, fork). *2.* Pretend you're scrubbing the floor.

scrub brush Pick up the scrub brush and scrub the floor (teacher's head).

seal *1.* Put (insert) the letter (postcard, drawing) in an envelope, seal the envelope, and deliver (give) it to Maria. *2.* Clap your hands and bark like a seal.

search *1.* Pretend you're a policeman and search Pedro.

2. Go out of the room. When I call you back in, search the room for the piece of chalk I hid.

season *1.* Pick up the salt and the pepper and season the food *(magazine cutouts)* on your plate. *2.* Write the name of the season in which it snows (in which you go to the beach).

seat *1.* Walk (run, hop, swim) to the door (window, desk, fan) and then return (go back) to your seat. *2.* Count (touch) the seats in this row. *3.* Take a seat next to (in front of) Maria. *4.* Seat yourself behind (beside) Pedro.

second *1.* Jump (sing, cry) for ten seconds. *2.* Tell me how many seconds I hopped. *3.* Draw a row of seven circles and erase the second one. *4.* Slap the second student from the left in the last row. *5.* Kick the student who finished second (last) in the race.

secretary *1.* Take (carry) the pen (pencil, book, notebook) to the secretary *(pc)*. *2.* Pretend you are a secretary and are typing.

see *1.* Imitate an animal that can see in the dark. *2.* Hold the picture card so that everybody (nobody) can see it. *3.* Draw something you see in the sky. *4.* Go see what Maria drew on her paper. *5.* See if you can balance a book on your head.

seed *1.* Count the seeds. *2.* Drop a few (many) seeds into the cup (glass, bowl). *3.* Draw a slice of watermelon with many seeds. *4.* Scatter the seeds on the table.

seem Touch the nose (forehead, chin, cheek) of a student who seems (appears, looks) happy (sad, tired, sleepy, afraid, nervous).

seize *1.* Seize Maria by the arm (elbow, wrist). *2.* Pedro, carry the ball. Carlos, run after him and seize (grab, take) the ball from him.

seldom *1.* Go to the map and touch a place where it seldom (rarely, often, frequently) rains (snows). *2.* Shake hands with (wave to) a student who is seldom absent (late).

sell *1.* Write the name of a store that sells furniture (shoes, radios, notebooks, watches, shirts). *2.* Draw (touch, pick up) an object that sells for more (less) than fifty dollars.

send *1.* Write a note to Maria, fold it twice, and send it to her by throwing it (sliding it along the floor). *2.* Pedro, send Maria (tell Maria to go) to the door (window, desk, chalkboard).

sentence *1.* Write a sentence that begins with the word *there* and ends with the word *desk*. *2.* Count (number) the sentences in the first paragraph.

separate *1.* Separate the geometric figures by size (color, shape). *2.* Pedro and Carlos, pretend you're fighting. Roberto, separate them.

separate Divide the class into four groups. Put (place) Maria and Pedro in separate (different) groups.

series *1.* Give a series of commands to Pedro. *2.* Draw a series of circles (hats, hearts, squares, stars).

serve *1.* Serve Maria a banana (cup of coffee, glass of water, candy bar, cookie). *2.* Pretend you're playing tennis and serve the paper ball using your hand as a

199

racket. *3.* Pull the nose of the man who serves food in a restaurant *(waiter pc)*.

set *1.* Set (place, put) the book (eraser, notebook, pen) on the floor (desk). *2.* Set the table. *3.* Set up (build, construct) a tower with the blocks (spools). *4.* Congratulate the student who set the class record for jumping to the door backwards.

several *1.* Hit several (a few, many) students on the head with the bottle (book, newspaper, magazine). *2.* Draw sever

sew *1.* Pretend you're sewing. *2.* Pick up the needle and the thread and sew a button to the handkerchief (to Pedro's sleeve).

shade *1.* Shade your eyes with your hand. *2.* Draw a girl (boy, man) standing in the shade of a tree. *3.* Touch (point to) something that's a light (dark) shade of blue.

shade in Shade in the circle (triangle, heart, square) that you drew next to (inside, under, over) the rectangle.

shake *1.* Shake your head (hands, foot, feet, body, teacher). *2.* Shake some salt (pepper) onto the food *(magazine cutouts)* on your plate. *3.* Hop (jump, run) around the class shaking the can (box of matches).

shake hands Shake hands with the student sitting (standing) next to (in front of, in back of, behind) the desk (teacher, chair).

shallow Draw a man (woman) standing (swimming) in some shallow (deep) water.

shampoo *1.* Pick up the tube of shampoo *(empty container)*, remove the cap, pour (squeeze) some shampoo onto your hair, and pretend you're washing (shampooing) your hair. *2.* Write the name of a brand of shampoo.

shape *1.* Draw (pick up) two objects that have different shapes (the same shape). *2.* Touch (draw) something that has a round (oval, rectangular, cylindrical) shape. *3.* Shape the clay into a ball (rocket, snake, ring).

share Pedro, share your book with Maria. She forgot to bring hers today.

shark Draw a man swimming in a lake (river) with a big shark (whale) behind him.

sharp *1.* Touch (pick up, show us) the sharp (dull) pencil. *2.* Feel the knife to see if it's sharp or dull. *3.* Draw a road with a sharp (wide) curve.

sharpen *1.* Insert (stick) the pencil in the sharpener and sharpen it. *2.* Pretend you're sharpening the knife.

shatter Pick up the hammer (rock) and shatter (smash) the pencil.

shave *1.* Pick up the razor and shave. *2.* Jump (hop, swim) to Pedro and shave him quickly (slowly). *3.* Drive your car to the barber *(pc)* and get a shave.

shaving lotion *1.* After you shave, uncap the shaving lotion *(empty container)* and then put (slap, splash) some on your face. *2.* Smell the shaving lotion.

sheep Imitate (pretend you are) a sheep.

sheet *1.* Give (hand) me a sheet of paper. *2.* Tear (rip) out a sheet of paper from your notebook. *3.* Take out a sheet of paper and draw a happy face (sad face, cat, fat man wearing a narrow tie).

shelf Draw a bookcase with a clock (lamp, vase, happy face) on the top (bottom, middle) shelf.

shell *1.* Draw an animal that has (lives in) a shell. *2.* Crack the nut and give me a piece of the shell.

shield *1.* Draw a man holding a shield. *2.* When Maria throws the paper ball at you, use your notebook (book) as a shield. *3.* Draw sometning that shields your head from the sun. *4.* Draw the sun on the chalkboard and shield your eyes with your hand (arm).

shift Stand with your weight on your right (left) foot. Now shift (transfer) your weight to your other foot.

shin *1.* Walk (swim, run, hop, jump) to Pedro and kick him in the shin (ankle, foot). *2.* Touch (point to, tap) your shin (chin, knee).

shine *1.* Pretend you're shining your shoes. *2.* Draw a picture with the sun shining brightly (dimly). *3.* Shine the flashlight on the ceiling (door, chalkboard, wall; into my eyes).

ship *1.* Draw a ship in a river (lake). *2.* Travel (go) by ship (canoe, car, boat) to the door (window, desk, teacher).

shirt *1.* Stand in front of (behind, next to) a student who's wearing a shirt with long (short) sleeves. *2.* Count (touch) the buttons on my shirt. *3.* Smile (wink, frown) at a student who's wearing a shirt which is the same color as Pedro's.

shiver You're very cold, so shiver.

shock *1.* Touch the plug (wire, socket) and pretend you got (received) a big shock. *2.* Sit with a shocked (surprised, happy, sad) look on your face.

shoe *1.* Touch (take off, shine, polish, unlace) one of your shoes. *2.* Write the size of your shoes on a slip of paper, fold it, and put it in Maria's purse (wallet). *3.* Wipe (clean) your shoe with a napkin (the rag).

shoelace *1.* Tie my shoelaces together. *2.* Unlace one of your shoes and measure the shoelace.

shoot *1.* Pick up the gun (rifle, shotgun) and shoot Maria. *2.* Pick up the camera and shoot (snap, take) my picture. *3.* Shoot a rubber band at the paper cup you set (placed) on the edge of the desk and try to knock it off.

shore Draw a beach with a boat (canoe, ship, shark, whale) off shore.

short *1.* Draw a short (long) vertical line. *2.* Hand me the shorter (longer) rod. *3.* Draw a short man next to a tall woman. *4.* Kick the shortest student in the class. *5.* Draw a man with short hair (legs, arms; a long nose, neck).

shorten *1.* Draw a long horizontal (vertical, diagonal, curved) line. Now pick up the eraser and shorten it. *2.* Cut a long piece of string (yarn, thread) and then shorten it.

shorts Draw a tall (fat, thin) boy wearing shorts.

shoulder *1.* Put (place, lay) your right hand on my left shoulder. *2.* Touch (pinch, hit) both of my shoulders. *3.* Draw a man with a cat sitting (girl standing) on his shoulder.

shout *1.* When I count to three, everybody will shout (whisper, sing, say) the teacher's name. *2.* Shout hello to the student who just came (walked) in.

shove *1.* Look at the five students who are blocking the door. Shove (push, pull) them away from the door. *2.* Shove (push) the desk against the wall. *3.* Give me a big (gentle) shove.

shovel *1.* Pick up the shovel and pretend you're digging a hole. *2.* Draw a man holding a shovel in one hand and a rake (pail) in the other.

show *1.* Show the blue fish to the class. *2.* Show me a hand (foot). *3.* Show the class how to make a paper airplane (how to eat with chopsticks). *4.* Show Maria to the door (to her seat). *5.* Draw a clock showing seven thirty.

shower *1.* Pretend you're taking a shower. *2.* Draw a man taking a shower. *3.* Shower Maria with paper balls.

shrink Blow up the balloon, release it (let it go), and watch it shrink.

shrug Stand (sit) in front of (beside, far from) the student who has the blue fish and shrug your shoulders.

shuffle *1.* Shuffle the cards. Now deal five cards to the student sitting on your left. *2*. Walk across the class shuffling your feet.

shut   Shut (close, open) the door (window, drawer; your eyes, mouth, book).

sick   *1*. You're sick. Go see the doctor *(pc)*. *2*. Pedro's very sick. Paulo and Roberto, carry him to the hospital *(pc)*.

side   *1*. Touch the four sides of the square. *2*. Draw a heart on both sides of your paper. *3*. Skip to a student who's sitting on the other side of the class. *4*. Maria will clean one side of the chalkboard and Pedro will clean the other.

sideburns   *1*. Draw a man with sideburns (a long beard, a big mustache). *2*. Touch (point to) the nose (neck, ears, head) of a student who has sideburns.

sideways   *1*. Turn sideways (around, left, right, about). *2*. Enter the class (come in, walk through the door) sideways (backwards).

sigh   *1*. Stand next to (in back of, in front of) the teacher (desk, chair) and sigh (groan, cry, laugh, frown, smile). *2*. Look at Maria and give a big sigh.

sight   Maria, go out of the room and then appear in the door or the window. When she comes into sight, everyone will clap (whistle, cry, stand up).

sign   *1*. Sign (print) your name on the dotted line Maria drew. *2*. Pretend you're a policeman directing traffic and make a sign for the cars to stop. *3*. Make a "No Smoking" sign and hang it on the wall.

signal When you finish (get done with) the exercises on page 10, signal by putting down your pencils (looking up, smiling, closing your books).

silence When Maria starts talking (singing, humming, laughing, crying), silence her by putting your finger to your mouth and saying "hush" (by covering her mouth with your hands).

silent I want everybody to make a lot of noise by laughing (crying, humming, singing) loudly. When I raise my hand (stand up, clap twice, point to my nose), you will become silent immediately (at once).

silk Touch (handle, finger, feel) something made of silk (cloth, cotton, plastic, rubber, metal).

silly *1.* Make a silly (funny, sad, surprised) face. *2.* Give Maria a silly (crazy) command.

silver Touch (pick up) something made of silver (gold, plastic, wood, cloth).

simple *1.* Give a simple (hard, difficult) command to Pedro. *2.* Put a simple (an easy) math problem on the chalkboard.

since *1.* Pinch a student who's been living in Paris since 1965 *(cc-11)*. *2.* Point to the student who's been standing (sitting) in the corner since our class began (since 9:30). *3.* Touch a student who can't write since he's sitting on his hands.

sing *1.* Sing (hum) a song by the Beatles. *2.* Sing a sad (silly, romantic, patriotic, children's) song. *3.* Stand in front of the class and sing a song with Maria.

singer *1.* You're a famous singer. Pretend the pencil (pen) is a microphone. *2.* Write (whisper, shout) the name of your favorite singer. *3.* Pull the nose (hair, ears) of two students who have the same favorite singer *(student-made cc).*

single Wave to (shake hands with, pull the hair of) a student who is single (married, engaged).

single file *1.* Form (get into, stand in) a single (double) file line behind the teacher (desk; Maria). *2.* March (jump, hop, run) around the class (desk) single file.

sink *1.* Draw a canoe (ship, boat) sinking. *2.* Draw the sun sinking in the sky. *3.* Draw (cut out) a picture of a kitchen sink and show it to the class.

siren Maria, make the sound of a siren as (while) Pedro drives (rushes, speeds) the ambulance around the class.

sister *1.* Write your sister's name and draw a circle (triangle, rectangle, square) around (under, over) it. *2.* Draw a family with two children, a boy and a girl. The boy's sister is taller (shorter) than he is.

sit *1.* Sit down. *2.* Sit next to (in back of, beside, in front of, to the left of) the desk (teacher, fan). *3.* Lay your head on your desk (slump over on your desk). Now sit up straight.

size *1.* Touch (point to) two objects that are approximately (about) the same size. *2.* Draw two triangles (circles, hearts, flowers) the same size. Now draw two circles of different sizes. *3.* Write the size of your shoes (shirt).

skip *1.* Skip (hop, jump, run, swim, walk) to the window (door, teacher, desk). *2.* Write (say) the numbers from one to thirty, but skip any number with a five or a multiple of five. *3.* Touch everyone in the class, but skip anyone wearing glasses.

skirt *1.* Give (offer) the flower to the girl wearing the light blue skirt. *2.* Draw a girl wearing a striped (checked) skirt (blouse).

sky *1.* Point to the sky (ground). *2.* Draw the sun (moon; an airplane; a cloud, bird) in the sky. *3.* Draw (imitate) an animal you see in the sky.

slam *1.* Slam your book shut. *2.* Slam (bang) your fist on the table. *3.* Pretend you're slamming the door.

slap *1.* Slap Pedro with your hand (the glove). *2.* Slap some shaving lotion *(empty container)* on your face.

slave You're Pedro's slave. When he claps twice, you will bow and say "Yes, master?"

sleep *1.* Put your head down, pretend you're sleeping, and snore loudly. *2.* Maria's sleeping. Shake her and wake her up. *3.* Draw a clock showing the time you go to sleep.

sleepy Yawn. You're sleepy.

sleeve *1.* Touch (point to, wave to) a student who's wearing a shirt with long (short) sleeves. *2.* Measure the sleeve on Pedro's shirt. *3.* Stand in back of (beside) Pedro and pull (tug on) one of his sleeves. *4.* Roll up your right sleeve.

slice *1.* Draw a cake and pretend you're slicing it. *2.* Cut a slice of the candle (banana, potato, carrot) and give it to me.

slide *1.* Slide the coin (bottle cap, pencil, pen, ruler) along the floor to Maria. *2.* Write a note to Pedro, fold it, and slide it to him.

slight *1.* Walk to the door with a slight (heavy) limp. *2.* Speak your native language with a slight (heavy) American accent. *3.* Sneeze (cough) as if you had a slight (bad) cold. *4.* Draw two trees. Make the one on the left slightly (much) taller (shorter).

slip *1.* Everyone, write your name on a slip of paper and put it in the hat. The person whose name is written on the slip Pedro chooses will perform the next command. *2.* Draw a banana peel on the floor in yellow chalk. Now walk and slip (trip) on it.

slope *1.* Draw a hill with a gentle (steep) slope. *2.* Pretend you're driving the blue car up (down) a steep slope.

slow *1.* Run to the window (comb your hair, brush your teeth, sit down, stand up) in slow motion. *2.* Draw some circles (hearts, hats, triangles, squares) slowly (quickly). *3.* Erase the chalkboard slowly (quickly, as fast as you can).

small *1.* Touch (pick up) the small (big, large) triangle. *2.* Touch (show the class) a small object. *3.* Draw a small (tiny, huge) house (cat, car, airplane, turtle). *4.* Print your first (last, middle) name in small letters.

smash *1.* Smash (shatter) the pencil with the hammer (rock). *2.* Smash the car into the wall (door). *3.* Smash the paper cup (tin can) by stepping on it.

smell *1.* Smell the soap (shaving lotion, perfume, onion). *2.* Touch the part of your face that you smell with. *3.* Draw a flower and smell it.

smile *1.* Smile (frown, wink, grin) at the teacher. *2.* Go out and come back in smiling (crying, laughing, humming, singing).

smoke *1.* Pretend you're smoking the cigarette (cigar, pipe). *2.* Draw a cat (fat man, tall woman, fish) smoking a cigarette (pipe). *3.* Draw a house with smoke coming out of the chimney.

smooth *1.* Touch something that has a smooth (rough) surface. *2.* Fly the airplane and pretend it's a smooth (rough) flight. *3.* Crumple a sheet of paper and then smooth it out.

snake *1.* Draw a snake wrapped (coiled) around a tree (tall man, flagpole). *2.* Move the rope as if it were a snake and have it bite Maria.

snap *1.* Snap your fingers. *2.* Break the pencil in half and listen to it snap. *3.* Shut (close) your book with a snap. *4.* Snap the lock shut. *5.* Pretend you're a dog and snap at my arm. *6.* Pick up the camera and snap (take) my picture.

sneeze *1.* Smell the pepper and sneeze loudly (softly). *2.* Pretend you're trying to hold back a sneeze. *3.* Walk (run, hop, jump) around the class sneezing (coughing, sighing, humming).

snore Lay (rest) your head on your desk, pretend you're

sleeping, and snore loudly (softly).

so *1.* I think Frank Sinatra is a great singer. If you think so too, clap. *2.* Are you ready to begin? If so, stand up (nod). If not, cry (shake your head). *3.* Pick up an object that's so big that it won't fit in your pocket.

so that *1.* Hold the flash card (picture; your drawing) so that everyone (nobody) can see it. *2.* Write a word (sentence) on the chalkboard with letters that are so small that the students sitting in the back of the class can't read it.

soak up Spill (pour, sprinkle) some water on the desk (floor) and soak it up with the sponge.

soap *1.* Remove (take) the soap from the soap dish and smell it. *2.* Cut a slice (piece) of the soap. *3.* Throw (toss) the bar of soap into the air and catch it with your right hand. *4.* Soap your hands, rinse them off, and dry them on the towel (diaper).

soap dish *1.* Take the soap out of the soap dish. *2.* Put the coin (pebble, clip, eraser, piece of chalk) in the soap dish.

soap powder Pick up the box of soap powder *(empty container)* and pour a little (a lot) on the teacher's head.

soccer *1.* Pretend you're playing soccer. *2.* Write the name of a famous soccer player.

sock *1.* Fasten the clothespin to Pedro's sock. *2.* Swim (hop, skip, jump) to a student who's wearing blue socks. *3.* Stick your hand into the sock and pretend it's a puppet. *4.* Sock (hit) Pedro on the arm. *5.* Give me a sock on the arm.

soft *1.* Touch (feel, pick up) a soft (hard) object. *2.* Say hello to Maria in a soft (loud, harsh, sweet) voice. *3.* Give Maria a short (long) command. Speak softly (in a loud voice).

soft drink Serve (offer) a soft drink *(empty container)* to the student sitting next to (in back of, in front of) a student whose name begins (ends) with the third letter of the alphabet.

soldier *1.* Stand in front of the soldier *(pc)* and salute him. *2.* I want the students in the second row to stand up. Now pretend you're soldiers, form a double column, and march to the door (window, desk).

solid *1.* Pick up (show the class) an object that's solid (hollow) *(e.g., a pencil, straw).* *2.* Touch something that is (isn't) a solid color.

solution Make a solution by dissolving some salt in a glass (cup) of water.

solve Solve the math problem I put on the chalkboard.

some *1.* Draw some (many, a lot of, a few) circles (flowers, chairs, eyes, hearts, hats, doors). *2.* Shake hands with some (all, most) of the students in the first two rows. *3.* Pour some (a lot of, a little bit of) water into the glass (cup, bowl).

somebody Pull the nose (ear, ears, hair) of somebody who's wearing a beard (necklace, watch, bracelet; glasses).

someone *1.* Shake someone who was born in the same month as you *(student-made cc).* *2.* Touch someone who is (isn't) wearing something green. *3.* If there's someone sitting behind Maria, sneeze. But if nobody's sitting there, then point to the ceiling.

something *1.* Point to (touch, hold up) something blue. *2.* Touch (show me) something made of wood (metal, leather, glass, plastic, paper). *3.* If there's something (nothing) on the teacher's desk, write your name (phone number, address) on the chalkboard.

somewhat Draw a triangle (circle, heart, flower, happy face). Next to it draw another one that is somewhat (slightly, much, considerably) bigger (smaller).

somewhere Stand (sit, stoop) somewhere where Maria can (can't) see (touch, hit) you.

son *1.* Tell the class your son's name. *2.* Draw a picture of a family. It has two sons and one daughter.

song *1.* Sing (hum, whistle) a song by the Beatles. *2.* Sing a romantic (sad, happy, silly, patriotic) song. *3.* Sing a song that has the word *love* in it.

soon *1.* Draw a heart (fat man, happy face, cat, flower). Do (don't do) it soon. *2.* If our class will soon be over, cry (laugh, put your head on your desk). If not, touch your nose (ear, knee).

sore You hurt your arm (head, elbow, knee, back). It feels sore. Hold it and groan.

sort *1.* Sort the geometric figures by color (size, shape). *2.* Sort the students in the class into groups according to their favorite singers (dishes). *3.* Pick up the deck of cards and sort the cards by suits. *4.* Draw two sorts (kinds) of flowers (cars).

sound *1.* Make a sound like a car (train, bee, bomb, cat, dog). *2.* Close your eyes, listen to the sounds, and tell me what you hear *(teacher opens the door, drops a coin on the floor, etc.).* *3.* Write two words that sound (look) alike.

soup *1.* Pick up the can (package) of soup *(empty containers),* pour the contents into the pan, and heat it over the stove. *2.* Stir the soup in your bowl with the spoon (knife; your finger). *3.* Your soup is very hot. Blow on it to cool it.

sour Touch (pick up, show me) a sour fruit *(e.g., the lemon).*

south *1.* Face south (north, east, west). *2.* Write the name of a city that's south of here.

space *1.* Write a sentence leaving no (very little, hardly any, a lot of) space between the words. *2.* Draw the earth and a rocket in space going (traveling) to the moon (sun). *3.* Draw a row of ten triangles (hearts, eyes, chairs). Space them one inch apart.

spade Pick up the spade, go to the garden *(pc),* and plant the flower.

speak *1.* Wave to (shave, smile at, stare at) the student who speaks French *(cc-5).* *2.* Speak in a high (low, soft, loud, sweet, harsh) voice. *3.* Speak up so that everybody can hear you.

speed *1.* Speed (rush) the ambulance to the hospital *(pc).* *2.* Drive the red car around the class (teacher, desk) at a high (low) speed.

spell *1.* Spell the word "cat" (your last name, my name). *2.* Correct the word that isn't spelled correctly (that's spelled wrong).

spend *1.* Run to the student who plans to spend her vacation in Mexico *(cc-4)*. *2.* Spend the next five minutes working in pairs. *3.* Go to the supermarket (drugstore, department store) *(pc's)* and spend twenty dollars *(use play money and magazine cutouts)*.

spider *1.* Draw a spider. *2.* When you see the rubber spider on your desk, you will faint (scream, run away).

spill *1.* Spill (pour, sprinkle) some water on the table (floor). Now dry it up with the sponge (paper towels). *2.* Fill the glass (cup) with small paper balls. Now spill the balls onto the table.

spin *1.* Spin (turn, whirl) around until you feel dizzy. *2.* Spin the bottle (ball, coin, lid of the can). *3.* Wind up the top *(child's toy)* and spin it.

spiral Draw a spiral (straight, crooked, wavy, curved, diagonal) line.

splash Fill the glass (bowl, cup) with water and splash (sprinkle) some water on the teacher (door, wall, chalkboard).

split Split (divide) the bottle caps (coins, cards, students) into four groups.

sponge *1.* Squeeze the sponge. *2.* Hit me on the head (shoulder, back, neck, ear) with the sponge. *3.* Throw

215

(hand, toss) the sponge (ball) to Maria. *4.* Pour (spill, splash) a little bit of water on the table (floor) and soak (wipe) it up with the sponge.

spool *1.* Roll (throw, toss, hand) me the spool. *2.* Make (build, construct) a tower (pyramid) with the spools (blocks). *3.* Wind (wrap) the string (yarn, thread) around the red spool.

spoon *1.* Stir the water in the glass (cup, bowl) with the spoon (with your finger). *2.* Make a small paper ball, put it in the spoon, and fling (hurl) it across the room. *3.* Pretend you're putting a spoonful of sugar in the cup of coffee.

spot *1.* Draw a man with a spot on his tie (shirt). *2.* I'm going to show you two similar drawings. See if you can spot (find) the five differences between them. *3.* Stand (stoop) in a spot (place) where Maria can (can't) see you.

spread *1.* Spread your fingers. *2.* Spread the newspaper on the floor (desk). *3.* Put some glue on your finger, spread it on the heart (circle, triangle) you cut out, and glue it to the upper right-hand corner of the envelope.

spring *1.* Write the name of a spring month. *2.* Jump (run, hop) to a student holding a spring (winter) month *(cc-2).* *3.* Spring (leap) into the air. *4.* Draw a boy using springs on his shoes to jump into the air.

sprinkle *1.* Sprinkle some salt (pepper) on the food *(magazine cutouts)* on your plate. *2.* Dip your fingers into the water in the bowl (glass) and sprinkle (drip) some water on my head.

square *1.* Show the big yellow square to the class. *2.* Draw a square inside a circle. *3.* Square the number four and draw a heart around the result. *4.* Draw a girl with square eyes (a car with square tires). *5.* Look at me square (directly) in the eyes.

squash Squash the paper cup by stepping (sitting, jumping, putting a heavy book) on it.

squat Squat in front of (next to, behind) the desk (door, fan).

squeeze *1.* Squeeze my hand (foot, shoulder, nose; the sponge). *2.* Draw a big circle (square) on the floor in chalk. Now let's see how many people we can squeeze (pack) into it.

squirt Fill the squirt gun (syringe) with water and squirt Maria.

stab Pick up the cardboard (rubber) knife and stab Pedro.

stack *1.* Stack the spools (match boxes, coins). *2.* Make a stack (pile) of books (notebooks, purses) on the teacher's desk.

stadium Throw (kick, roll, toss) the ball to the student who's at the stadium *(pc)*.

stagger Pretend you're drunk and stagger to the door (window, desk, chalkboard).

stairs *1.* Pretend you're walking up a stairs. *2.* Draw a man (woman) going up (down) a flight of stairs.

stamp *1.* Glue (paste, fix) the stamp to the upper right (left) hand corner of the envelope. *2.* Wet the stamp and stick it to your (my) forehead. *3.* Pick up the stamp, ink it on the pad, and stamp your book (notebook, hand). *4.* Stamp your feet.

stand *1.* Stand up and laugh (cry, breathe in, sigh, stretch). *2.* Stand at (near) the door (window, chalkboard, desk). *3.* Stand on (in front of, in back of, next to, beside, behind) the chair (desk). *4.* Stand on my feet.

staple Staple (clip) two pieces (sheets, slips) of paper together.

star *1.* Draw a star over (under, beside) a cloud (butterfly, circle, happy face). *2.* Write (shout) the name of a famous movie star. *3.* Write the name of a television program and under it write the name of the actor or actress who stars in it.

stare *1.* Stare at Maria without blinking (smiling, laughing). *2.* When the next student comes in the class, don't say anything. Just stare at him or her.

start *1.* Write a word that starts (begins) with the third letter of the alphabet. *2.* Start to sing (hum, whistle) a song, stop, and then begin again. *3.* Count to ten slowly (quickly). Start when I raise (lower) my right (left) hand (foot).

state *1.* Stand up and state (say, whisper, sing) your name. *2.* Write (spell, shout) the name of the state (city, country) you were born in. *3.* Go to the map and touch the state that's to the south of Ohio.

statement Write (make) a statement and then change it to a question.

statue *1.* Pretend (make believe) you're a statue. *2.* When I face the chalkboard, everybody will move (walk) around the room. But when I turn around, you will freeze like a statue.

stay *1.* Stay (remain) seated until I tell (command, request, ask, order) you to stand up. *2.* Stay where you are.

steady Extend your hands and hold them steady.

steal *1.* Pretend you're a thief and steal Pedro's wallet. *2.* When Maria turns to talk to Rosa, Pedro will sneak (tiptoe) up to her desk and steal her purse (pencil, notebook, eraser).

steam *1.* Draw a kettle with steam coming out of the spout. *2.* Draw a steaming cup of coffee.

steel Touch (point to, pick up) something made of steel (paper, wax, cloth, plastic, wood, metal).

steep *1.* Draw a tall (fat, thin) man climbing a steep hill. *2.* Draw a hill with a steep (gentle) slope.

stem *1.* Pick up the flower by the stem. *2.* Draw a flower with a long (short) stem.

step *1.* Take (advance, walk) three giant (tiny, big) steps forward. *2.* Step out the door. Now come back in. *3.* Step into (out of) the circle you drew on the floor. *4.* Stand on the chair. Now step down. *5.* Step over the wastebasket (chair, book; Pedro).

stick *1.* Touch (point to) the door with the stick. *2.* Pick up the longer (shorter, heavier, lighter, thicker, thinner)

219

stick. *3.* Stick the pin into the potato. *4.* Stick up your hands (out your tongue). *5.* Use some tape to stick the picture to the wall.

stiff Pick up (show the class) something that is stiff (rigid, flexible, breakable).

still *1.* Remain (keep) perfectly still without moving. *2.* Point to the student who's still (no longer) jumping (walking, crying, sneezing, clapping).

sting Pretend you're a bee and sting the student who's sitting behind (to the left of, in front of, far from) Maria.

stir *1.* Pick up the spoon (knife) and stir the water in the glass (bowl, cup). *2.* Put many coins (small paper balls) in the glass and stir them with the pencil.

stomach *1.* Put (place) one hand on your stomach and the other on your head. Now switch. *2.* Hold your stomach and groan because you have a stomachache.

stone *1.* Throw (toss) the stone into the air and catch it. *2.* Carry the stone around the class on the back (in the palm) of your hand. *3.* Put (place) the stone in the wastebasket (in your pocket, on the edge of the desk).

stool *1.* Draw a girl (fat man, big cat) standing on a tall (short) stool. *2.* Draw a series of six stools in a row (column).

stoop Stoop behind (in front of, in back of, next to) the desk (teacher, fan, student who's wearing a red blouse).

stop *1.* Jump up and down until I say (tell you) to stop. *2.* Run (hop) around the class and stop in front of someone who's wearing glasses. *3.* Make a lot of noise. When I raise my hand you will stop. *4.* When Pedro tries to leave, you will stop him.

store Go to the store *(supermarket pc)* and buy some milk (soup, meat, fruit). *(Use play money and magazine cutouts.)*

story *1.* Write the name of a children's story. *2.* Draw a building that has five stories.

stove *1.* Put the fried egg in the frying pan and put the pan on the stove. *2.* Draw a woman at a stove cooking.

straight *1.* Draw a straight (curved, crooked, wavy, broken) line. *2.* Walk in a straight (crooked, curved) line to the door. *3.* Go (run) straight to the window. *4.* Slump over. Now sit up straight. *5.* Walk (go) straight ahead six small (big) steps.

straighten *1.* Bend your arm (leg; the wire) and then straighten it. *2.* Straighten Pedro's collar. *3.* The desk is messy. Straighten it up so that it's neat. *4.* Draw a line that's slightly crooked and then straighten it.

strange *1.* Use your imagination and draw a very strange animal. *2.* Circle (underline) any strange (new, unfamiliar) words in the text (reading passage, dialogue). *3.* Act (perform a familiar action) in a strange manner (way).

strap *1.* Grab (grasp, take hold of) the strap of Maria's purse and swing it around over your head. *2.* Draw a woman carrying a purse with a long strap.

straw *1.* Drink (sip) some water (soda pop) with the straw. *2.* Cut the straw in half (in thirds). *3.* Tie a knot in the straw. *4.* Measure (bend) the straw.

street *1.* Hop (swim, run) to a student who lives on a street that begins with the letter "s" *(student-made cc).* *2.* Draw a wide street on the floor in chalk. Cross the street, but first look both ways to see if any cars are coming.

stretch *1.* Everybody, stand up and stretch. *2.* Stretch the balloon (rubber band). *3.* Stretch your neck to look over the shoulder of the student sitting in front of you. *4.* Take hold of the rope and stretch it tight.

strike *1.* Strike (hit) Pedro with the sponge (notebook, book, bottle, purse, ruler). *2.* Strike a match and light the candle.

strike out Strike out (cross out, eliminate, erase) the third word in the sentence Maria wrote (put) on the chalkboard.

string *1.* Cut the string into three equal (unequal) lengths (pieces). *2.* Tie (wrap, wind) a piece of string (yarn) around your finger (thumb, wrist). *3.* Tie the string to the key (pencil, candle) and swing it around over your head.

strip Tear (cut) the paper into strips (pieces).

stripe *1.* Draw a flag with seven wide (narrow) stripes. *2.* Draw a girl (woman) wearing a striped (checked) blouse (skirt, dress). *3.* Put on the striped (checked) tie.

stroke *1.* Swim around the class (desk, teacher) with short (long) strokes. *2.* Pretend Maria is a cat and stroke (pat) her head.

strong *1.* Draw a strong (weak) man. *2.* Pretend you're walking against a strong wind (swimming against a strong current).

student *1.* Touch (pull the hair of, wink at, shake hands with) all (several of) the students in the first row. *2.* Write (shout, sing, whisper) the name of a student who's absent (present) today. *3.* Count the students who use glasses.

study *1.* Swim (run) to the student who studies at Harvard *(cc-13)*. *2.* Pull the nose (hair, ears) of a student who's studying to be a doctor *(pc's)*. *3.* Throw the paper ball to the student who's studying engineering *(cc-6)*. *4.* Study the exercises on page 10.

stuff *1.* Take all the stuff off of your desk and put it on the floor. *2.* Stuff the paper balls (crumpled paper) into the bag (sock, glass; Pedro's pocket).

subject *1.* Walk (hop, jump) to a student who's studying a subject that begins with the letter "h" *(cc-6)*. *2.* Point to a subject that you find difficult (easy, interesting, boring) *(cc-6)*. *3.* Underline the subject and the verb in this sentence.

submarine *1.* Draw a submarine, cut it out, and pilot (navigate) it to the door (window, desk, chalkboard). *2.* Draw a submarine surrounded by fish.

subtract *1.* Subtract (take) seven from ten and draw a box around the result. *2.* Write the number which when subtracted from twenty leaves twelve.

suck *1.* Suck in some air (your breath). *2.* Put a mint (piece of candy) in your mouth and suck on it. *3.* Pour some water into the glass and suck it through the straw. *4.* Pretend you're a baby and suck your thumb.

sudden *1.* Drive the car (jeep, truck, bus) around the class and come to a sudden stop (make a sudden turn). *2.* Jump (hop, run, swim) around the class and then suddenly stop (reverse your direction).

sugar *1.* Remove the lid from the sugar bowl (empty container) and put a spoonful of sugar in your coffee (tea). *2.* Touch something that is the same color as sugar.

suitcase *1.* Draw a suitcase, cut it out, and walk to the hotel *(pc)*. *2.* Draw a man carrying a heavy suitcase.

sum *1.* Add the numbers seven and two, and draw a box (circle) around the sum. *2.* Write two numbers whose sum equals (is more than, is less than) thirty. *3.* Pick up the play money and give Maria a sum of money equal to that which you gave Pedro.

summer Hold up (show the class) a summer (winter, spring, fall) month *(cc-2)*.

sun *1.* Draw the sun in the sky over a tree (house, church, cloud, bird). *2.* Put your hand (arm) to your forehead to shade your eyes from the bright sun you drew on the chalkboard.

sunglasses *1.* Put on (take off) the sunglasses. *2.* Put on the sunglasses and walk around the class like (as if you were) a famous movie star.

sunny Draw a picture showing a sunny (cloudy, rainy) day.

supermarket *1.* Drive your car to the supermarket *(pc)* and buy some groceries *(use play money and magazine cutouts).* *2.* Write the name of the supermarket where you do your shopping.

support Draw a house (building, church) supported by four columns (pillars).

surf *1.* Pretend you're surfing. *2.* Draw a boy surfing.

surface Touch the surface of the table (chair, desk, chalkboard).

surname *1.* Write your full name and draw a circle (rectangle, triangle) around (under, over) your surname. *2.* Touch the wrist (nose, elbow) of a student whose surname has six letters.

surprise *1.* Sit with a surprised look on your face. *2.* Draw a picture of a man who is surprised (happy, sad, angry).

surround *1.* Everybody, surround Maria and touch her head (pat her on the back, shake her). *2.* Draw the moon surrounded by clouds (stars, small circles, many hearts).

suspend *1.* Tie (attach) the string to the pail (cup, purse). Now suspend it. *2.* Begin to draw a happy face (sad face, fat man), suspend your work while Pedro jumps (hops, swims) around the class, and then finish it.

225

swallow Pretend you're eating the banana (candy bar, apple). Bite into it, chew it slowly, and then swallow it.

swat Pretend there's a mosquito on your arm and swat it with your hand (the newspaper).

sway Sway back and forth.

sweat *1.* Do some exercises and then wipe the sweat off of your forehead with the handkerchief (napkin, towel, back of your hand). *2.* Draw a man in the desert with sweat dripping from his forehead.

sweep *1.* Pick up the broom and sweep the floor in front of (in back of, next to) the desk. *2.* Draw a short woman (tall man) sweeping the floor.

swim *1.* Swim (hop, run, skip, limp) to (around) the desk (teacher, chair, student standing in the corner). *2.* Draw a man swimming in a lake (river). There's a shark swimming behind him.

swing *1.* Swing your arms (the door) back and forth. *2.* Tie the string to the cup (candle) and swing it around over your head.

switch *1.* Put one hand on your head (ear, nose, chin, forehead) and the other on your belly (back, knee, elbow). Now switch. *2.* Switch places with Maria. *3.* Switch on (off) the lights (fan, radio, television). *4.* Touch (point to) the light switch.

sword *1.* Attack Pedro with the sword. *2.* Draw a man holding a sword in one hand and a shield in the other.

syringe *1.* Pretend you're a nurse (doctor), pick up the syringe, and give the student who's at the hospital *(pc)* a shot in the arm. *2.* Fill the syringe with water and squirt the teacher.

table *1.* Set the table. *2.* Put (set, place) the book (notebook, pen) on (under) the table. *3.* Stand behind (in front of, next to) the table. *4.* Sit on the table and clap (cry, snore, point to the ceiling). *5.* Open your books to the table of contents.

tablet *1.* Tear a sheet of paper out of the tablet and draw a happy face (sad face) on it. *2.* Hit me on the shoulder (head) with the tablet. *3.* Roll the tablet into a cylinder. *4.* Crush an aspirin tablet with your thumb.

tack *1.* Draw a picture of your teacher and tack it to the door (back wall). *2.* Push in (remove) the tack. *3.* Pretend you just sat on a tack.

tail *1.* Draw a cat (dog, pig) with a long tail. *2.* Draw a fat man (woman) sitting (standing) on the tail of an airplane.

take *1.* Take a book from Maria's desk. *2.* Take two from ten. *3.* Take a drink of water. *4.* Take a seat behind Pedro. *5.* Pick up the camera and take my picture. *6.* Draw some circles. Take your time. Now hurry. *7.* Take a look at the picture Maria drew.

take off Take off your hat (tie, ring, earring, necklace, shoe, bracelet, watch). Now put it back on.

take out Take out your books (notebooks; a sheet of paper).

talk Talk to Maria in your native language in a loud (soft, harsh) voice.

tall *1.* Draw a tall girl (boy, woman, building). *2.* Pedro, stand Carlos and Roberto back to back and pull the hair (nose, ear, ears) of the taller (shorter) of the two. *3.* Draw two men (trees). Make the one on the left (right) taller.

tank *1.* Drive the tank to the window (door, desk, teacher). *2.* Drive your car to the gas station *(pc)* and fill the tank with gas.

tap *1.* Tap (hit) Maria on the back (head, shoulder, elbow, ear). *2.* Tap your feet to the music.

tape *1.* Seal the envelope with some tape. *2.* Tape your (my) mouth shut. *3.* Use the tape to attach the picture you drew to the wall. *4.* Pick up the microphone, tape five commands, and then play them back for the class.

tape measure *1.* Pick up the tape measure and measure Pedro's waist (arm, head, foot). *2.* Wind the tape measure around the pencil (your wrist).

tape recorder *1.* Insert the tape in the tape recorder and play it. *2.* Plug in (unplug) the tape recorder and press the Play (Fast Forward, Rewind, Pause) button.

target Throw the sponge (paper ball, eraser) at the target you drew on the chalkboard.

taste *1.* Cut a slice of the apple (banana) and taste it. *2.* Taste the cookie and if you like it, take another bite. *3.* Pour some salt on the back of your hand and taste it. *4.* Take some medicine *(empty container)*. It tastes terrible, so make a face.

tea *1.* Put the tea bag in the cup, pick up the kettle, pour some water into the cup, and make yourself a cup of tea. *2.* Put the tea bag in the cup and serve it to Maria.

teach *1.* Swim (run, walk, hop) to someone who teaches history *(cc-6)*. *2.* Pretend you're teaching Maria how to swim (play tennis).

teacher *1.* Say (whisper, sing, shout) hello to the teacher. *2.* Everybody, hold (join) hands and walk (jump, hop) around the teacher. *3.* Write your teacher's name and draw a circle around (next to) it.

team *1.* Write the name of a soccer (baseball, football, basketball, hockey) team. *2.* For this contest we're going to divide the class into two teams. *3.* Congratulate (shake hands with) the students on the team that won the contest.

tear *1.* Tear (rip, cut) the paper in half (into small pieces). *2.* Tear out a sheet of paper from your notebook. *3.* Tear open the envelope that Pedro handed you. *4.* Tear up a sheet of paper.

tear Draw a sad face (fat man, tall woman) with tears running down its (his, her) face.

teeth *1.* Pick up the toothbrush and brush your teeth. *2.* Touch (point to) your teeth. *3.* Draw a happy (sad) face with four teeth. *4.* Draw a fish with pointed teeth.

telephone *1.* Write your telephone number on a slip of paper and hand it to a student whose name has six letters. *2.* Run to the student whose telephone number is 253-27-29 *(student-made cc)*. *3.* Pick up the receiver and dial Maria's number.

telescope *1.* Look at me through the telescope. *2.* Roll up the paper into a cylinder, pretend it's a telescope, and look at the moon (star, sun) that Maria drew on the chalkboard.

television *1.* Turn on (off) the television you drew. *2.* Write (whisper) the name of a program that's on television Monday evening. *3.* Smile (frown, grin) at a student who likes to watch a television program that you like (don't like) *(student-made cc)*.

tell *1.* Tell the class your first name (nickname; favorite singer, actor, song, movie, sport). *2.* Tell (order, command) Pedro to stand up (sit down, jump to the door, take off his watch, draw a triangle).

temperature *1.* Write the temperature at which water boils (freezes). *2.* Feel my forehead to see if I have a temperature. *3.* On the map touch a place where the temperature is usually (always, never) low (high).

tennis *1.* Pretend you're playing tennis. *2.* Make a paper ball, pretend it's a tennis ball, toss it into the air, pretend your hand is a racket, and serve the ball. *3.* Bounce (squeeze, toss me) the tennis ball.

tennis shoes Swim to a student who's wearing tennis shoes and unlace them (tie the laces together).

test *1.* Congratulate the student who got (earned, received) an "A" on the test. *2.* If you think the test was easy (hard), raise your hand (shake your body). *3.* The time is up. Turn (hand) in your tests.

than *1.* Smile at (point to, swim around) a student who's shorter (taller, older, younger) than you. *2.* Run (hop, jump) to a student who has more (less) than fifty dollars *(cc-9)*. *3.* Throw the eraser to someone. Throw it to anyone other than Pedro.

that *1.* Hand the book to this student over here and throw the eraser to that student over there. *2.* Pick up the notebook that's on the floor. *3.* Run to the door. After (before) that, touch your nose. *4.* Do everything that I do exactly as I do it. *5.* If you think that Frank Sinatra is a good singer, wave to Maria.

then *1.* Jump (swim, run) to the door (desk) and then pretend you're a dog (cat, cow). *2.* If Maria's wearing something red, then you will give her the flower. *3.* In one minute you will stand up (cry). Until then, put your head on your desk.

there *1.* If there's a book (pencil) on the desk, scratch your nose (back). If not, sing a song. *2.* There's a pen (ruler, flower) on the table. Pick it up and show it to the class. *3.* Throw the ball (eraser) to the student standing over there.

thermometer Pretend the pencil is a thermometer, stick it under Pedro's arm, remove it, read it, and put his temperature on the chalkboard.

these Whisper (sing, shout, say) hello to these students over here and wave to (smile at, frown at) those students over there.

thick *1.* Pick up (show me, open, close) the thick (thin) book (magazine). *2.* Touch my nose (ear, knee) with the thicker (thinner) stick. *3.* Speak your native language

231

with a thick (heavy, slight) American accent.

thicken Draw a thin horizontal (diagonal, vertical) line and then thicken it.

thief Pretend you're a thief and steal (take) Maria's purse (pen, notebook, book) while she's not looking (paying attention).

thigh Touch (point to, hit, slap) your thigh.

thin *1.* Draw a thin (fat, tall, short, weak, strong, muscular, skinny) man. *2.* Touch (pick up, show me, point to) the thin (thick) book (magazine).

thing *1.* Take the things off of your desk and put them on the floor under (beside) the table. *2.* Pick up (show the class) a thing that's used to cut (serve, tie, write, measure). *3.* Touch the thing (object) that's between the can and the candle.

think *1.* If you think that maria will win the race, raise your hand. *2.* Jump (swim) to the student who thinks that _____ is a good singer (author, actor, actress, tv show, movie) *(student-made cc).* *3.* Try to guess the number I'm thinking of.

third *1.* Sit on the third student from the right in the last row. *2.* Hit one third of your classmates. *3.* Draw a square and divide it in thirds. *4.* Erase a third of the hearts you drew. *5.* Write the third letter of the alphabet and circle it.

thirsty You're thirsty. Pour yourself a glass of water and drink it slowly (quickly).

thread *1.* Cut (break) off a piece of the thread. *2.* Wet the thread and thread the needle. *3.* Unwind some thread from the spool. *4.* Wrap some thread around your finger. *5.* Tie Maria's fingers together with the thread.

threaten Pick up the knife (gun, hammer, bat, bottle) and threaten the teacher.

throat *1.* Touch (point to) your throat. *2.* Clear your throat and then cough.

through *1.* Look at me through the cylinder. *2.* Stick the pencil (your finger, a match) through the hole you made in the paper. *3.* When you're through with this exercise, raise your hands (clap, put down your pencils).

throw *1.* Throw (toss, hand) the ball (sponge, book, eraser) to Maria. *2.* Let's see who can throw the paper ball the farthest.

throw away Crumple up a piece of paper and throw it away.

thumb *1.* Hit your thumb with the hammer and cry. *2.* Tie my thumbs together with the string (yarn). *3.* Touch your chin (knee, elbow) with a thumb (finger). *4.* Extend your left hand, fingers closed and thumb up. *5.* Pretend you're thumbing a ride.

thumbtack *1.* Shake the box of thumbtacks. *2.* Take out a thumbtack and fasten the picture you drew of your teacher to the door (bulletin board).

ticket *1.* Maria is a famous singer. Pedro, pick up the play money, go to Carlos, and buy a ticket for her show. *2.*

233

Maria, drive the car around the class very fast. Pedro, you're a policeman. Give her a ticket for speeding.

tickle Stand in back of Pedro and tickle him.

tidy *1.* Arrange the objects on the desk so that it is tidy (messy). *2.* Tidy up the teacher's desk.

tie *1.* Tie the rope (yarn, string) around Pedro's waist (to the doorknob). *2.* Tie my hands (feet) together. *3.* Tie (untie) your shoes. *4.* Put on (take off) the striped (checked, wide, narrow) tie. *5.* Maria tied the score for her team. Congratulate her.

tight *1.* Tie a tight (loose) knot in the end of the rope. *2.* Take a tight (loose) hold of Pedro's arm (elbow). *3.* Screw the lid on the jar tight. *4.* We're going to have a tug of war. Hold on tight to your end of the rope.

tighten *1.* Tighten (loosen) the lid on the jar (nut on the bolt). *2.* Tighten your grip on my arm. *3.* Pick up the wrench and pretend you're tightening Pedro's nose.

till Run (swim, walk, skip) around the class till I say (tell you) to stop (sit down, rest).

tilt *1.* Tilt your head to one side. *2.* Tilt the hat that Maria's wearing.

time *1.* Draw a clock showing the time you get up. *2.* Cry for a short (long) time. *3.* Sneeze (cough, jump) three (many, several) times. *4.* Pedro's going to hop to the door. Time him. *5.* Write the result of ten times seven. *6.* Touch the student who drew two times as many circles as you did.

tin *1.* Pick up (show the class, crush) a tin can. *2.* Touch something made of tin (aluminum, wood, plastic, rubber).

tiny *1.* Write your name in tiny (big, small, huge, enormous) letters. *2.* Draw some (many, a few) tiny circles (hearts, hats, doors, chairs).

tip *1.* Stand in front of us and tip your hat. *2.* Set the bottle (candle) on the desk and then tip it over. *3.* Touch the tip of the knife (pen, pencil; your nose). *4.* Give the waiter *(pc)* a big tip *(use play money)*.

tiptoe *1.* Tiptoe to the door (window, teacher, chalkboard). *2.* Walk (run) around the class (desk, chair) on your tiptoes (heels). *3.* Stand on your tiptoes and make a chalk mark as high as you can reach.

tire *1.* Draw a car with square (big, small, huge) tires. *2.* Spin the tires on the toy car.

tired *1.* Point to (wink at) the student who's tired because she ran (hopped, jumped) to the door (window, fan, desk). *2.* Pull the nose (hair) of a student who isn't (shouldn't be) tired because she has been seated since the beginning of our class.

tissue *1.* Take a piece of tissue and blow your nose. *2.* Wipe the table (your glasses) with a piece of tissue.

title *1.* Write the title of a book (movie, poem, play, song). *2.* Draw a picture and give it a title.

to *1.* Run to (around) the chair (fan, desk, teacher). *2.* Give (show, offer, hand, throw) the flower (candy bar, sponge, apple) to Maria. *3.* Take two steps to your right.

4. Set the clock to five to ten.

today *1.* Shout (whisper, sing) the name of a student who is (isn't) absent today. *2.* Open your books to today's lesson. *3.* If today's Monday, cry (sneeze, cough, sigh). If not, stoop (pull your nose, touch your right foot).

toe *1.* Touch your toes without bending your knees. *2.* Step (stand) on my toes. *3.* Draw a foot with long (curved, short) toes.

together **1.** Tie Pedro's shoelaces (hands, feet) together. *2.* When I count to three, Pedro and Maria will sing a song together. *3.* I want everybody to stand up all together.

tomato *1.* Pretend you're slicing the tomato and the cucumber to make a salad. *2.* Touch something that is the color of a tomato.

tomorrow *1.* Tell me the name of a program that's on tv tomorrow evening. *2.* If tomorrow's Sunday, sing a song (recite a poem). If not, cry (hop around the class, kiss your hand).

tongue *1.* Stick out (touch the tip of) your tongue. *2.* Pretend you're a dog panting with your tongue hanging out of your mouth.

tonight Write the name of a program that's on tv tonight.

too 1. Pedro was born in May *(student-made cc)*. If Maria was born in May too, give her the flower (orange, eraser, keys). 2. Touch (draw) an object that's too heavy to pick up. 3. Draw some circles (stars, doors). You drew too many. Erase some.

236

tool Draw (pick up) a tool that's used to cut (measure, drive a screw, hit a nail).

tooth *1.* Touch a tooth. *2.* Draw a happy (sad) face with one big (small, pointed) tooth.

toothache *1.* Hold your jaw and groan as if you had a toothache. *2.* You have a toothache. Go to the dentist *(pc)*.

toothbrush *1.* Pick up the toothbrush and brush your teeth. *2.* Draw a man holding a toothbrush near his mouth. *3.* Dip the toothbrush in the water and fling some water at the teacher.

toothpaste *1.* Squeeze some toothpaste *(empty container)* onto the toothbrush and brush your teeth. *2.* Write (print) the name of a brand of toothpaste.

toothpick *1.* Stick (insert) a toothpick into the sponge (potato). *2.* Break the toothpick in half. *3.* Form (make) a rectangle (triangle, square) with the toothpicks. *4.* Walk around the class shaking the box of toothpicks.

top *1.* Spin the top *(child's toy)*. *2.* Draw a house on the top of a hill (mountain). *3.* Write the name of one of your country's top singers (actors, actresses). 4. Jump (hop, walk) to a student whose height (weight) tops Pedro's.

toss *1.* Toss the ball around the class. *2.* Toss (throw, roll, bounce) the ball to Pedro. *3.* Bend (form) the wire into a ring and toss it around the pencil Pedro's holding up. *4.* Toss a coin into the air and call it Heads or Tails.

total *1.* Count the males in the class. Count the females. Now write the total number of students. *2.* Take down the numbers I call out, add them up, and then draw a circle (triangle) around the total.

touch *1.* Touch one (both) of your ears (eyes, feet, cheeks, knees). *2.* Touch your nose (hair, chin, forehead, hip) with your thumb (ruler, pencil). *3.* When you feel the touch of my hand on your shoulder (neck), stamp your feet (sing a song).

tough *1.* Touch (pick up) something tough (soft). *2.* Pretend you're chewing a tough piece of meat. *3.* Put a tough (an easy) math problem on the chalkboard.

towards *1.* Walk (run, jump) towards the door (desk, fan, window). *2.* Stand with your back towards the door (teacher, chalkboard). *3.* Towards the end of the class, stand up and turn around three times.

towel *1.* Dry your hands (face) on the towel. *2.* Cover the book with the towel. *3.* Fold the towel into a triangle. *4.* Snap the teacher with the towel. *5.* Wet the towel and wring it out. *6.* Tear off a paper towel and wipe up the water you spilled.

tower *1.* Build (construct, make, set up) a tower with the blocks (spools, match boxes). *2.* Write the name of a famous tower in France. *3.* Draw a skyscraper towering over a low building.

toy *1.* Pick up (draw, show me) a toy that boys (girls) like to play with. *2.* Drive the toy car to the window (door, desk).

trace *1.* Draw a picture with heavy (thick) lines. Now put this picture under another sheet of paper and trace it. *2.* Trace a triangle in the air with your nose (finger).

trade *1.* Trade an object on your desk for one on Pedro's. *2.* Trade seats (places) with Maria. *3.* Trade papers with a friend and correct each other's paper.

traffic *1.* Write the name of a street that has little (a great deal of) traffic. *2.* Pretend you're a policeman directing traffic.

train *1.* Draw a train, cut it out, and drive it to the door. *2.* Everybody, line up single file. Now put your hands on the waist of the person who is in front of you, pretend you're a train, and move around the class saying "chu, chu."

transfer *1.* Transfer the books (notebooks, objects) from Pedro's desk to yours. *2.* Put three coins (bottle caps) in your pocket. Now transfer them to another pocket. *3.* Stand with your weight on your left foot. Now transfer your weight to your right foot.

translate Translate these commands (sentences, words) into your native language.

transparent Touch (point to, pick up) something that is (isn't) transparent.

trash Spread out the newspaper on the floor. Empty the trash from the wastebasket onto the newspaper. Roll up the trash in the newspaper and put it back in the wastebasket.

travel *1.* Pick up the car (boat, airplane, train) and travel to the door (window, desk, chalkboard). *2.* Swim (jump, hop, run) to the student who traveled (is going to travel, would like to travel) to Spain *(cc-4)*.

tray *1.* Put the glass of water (cookie, cup of coffee, banana) on the tray and serve it to Pedro. *2.* Cover the glass (bowl, cup) with the tray. *3.* Hold the tray with one hand (with both hands).

tree *1.* Open the door (look out the window) and point to a tree. *2.* Draw a man (boy, girl, cat, house) next to a tall tree. *3.* Draw an arrow through (pointing to) a tree.

tremble When Maria points the gun (rifle) at you, you will tremble (shake).

triangle *1.* Draw a triangle with broken (dotted) lines. *2.* Put the small green triangle next to the big brown square. *3.* Fold the towel (handkerchief, napkin) into a triangle. *4.* Draw a happy (sad) face with triangles for its eyes.

triangular Draw a man (woman, boy, girl) with a triangular (round, square, rectangular) head.

trick *1.* Watch me. I'm going to perform (do) a magic trick. *2.* Do what I say and not what I do. Be careful. I will try to trick you.

trim Pick up the scissors and pretend you're trimming your hair (beard, mustache).

trip *1.* Pull the nose (hair, ear, ears) of the student who took a trip to Japan last year *(cc-4)*. *2.* Pedro, extend your feet into the aisle. Maria, walk down the aisle and trip over his feet.

triple *1.* Write a number and then triple it. *2.* Write the number that's triple the number of students who are present in (absent from) class today. Draw triple the number of circles (hearts, stars) that I drew.

trophy Draw a trophy, cut it out, and give (present) it to the student who won (came in first in) the race.

trousers *1.* Throw the ball (eraser, sponge) to the student who's wearing brown trousers. *2.* Pretend you're putting on a pair of trousers (pants).

truck *1.* Drive the truck around the class (desk, teacher, chair). *2.* Draw a truck in front of (in back of) a bus (car).

true *1.* If what I say is true, clap your hands (laugh, whistle, breathe in). If it's false, stamp your feet (stand up, wave, cry). *2.* If it's true that today's (tomorrow's, yesterday was) Monday, run to the door (window). If not, touch your nose (chin).

trunk *1.* Draw a man carrying a trunk on his head. *2.* Pretend you're an elephant and use your hands to represent the trunk. *3.* Draw a tree with two trunks.

truth I'm going to write a number on a slip of paper and then say the number I wrote. If you think I'm telling the truth, stand up (clap, sneeze). If you think I'm lying, point to the ceiling (door, floor).

try *1.* Toss the ball into the air and try to clap four times before you catch it. *2.* Set the candle on the floor, stand back, roll the ball, and try to knock it over. *3.* Make a paper ball and try to toss it into the wastebasket. You have three trys.

tube Squeeze (remove the cap from) the tube of toothpaste (shampoo, shaving cream) *(empty containers)*.

tuck in Pull out your shirt and then tuck it in.

tug *1.* Tug on my sleeve (ear, shirt, collar, belt). *2.* Pedro and Carlos, each of you take hold of an end of the rope. Now tug and try to pull the rope out of each other's hands.

tunnel *1.* Rip (tear) out a sheet of paper from your notebook and make a tunnel by folding the paper in half and setting it on the desk. *2.* Draw a train (car) going into a tunnel.

turn *1.* Turn around quickly (slowly, twice). *2.* Turn the teacher (chair) around. *3.* Turn the page in your book (notebook). *4.* Turn to page 10 and read. *5.* Turn to Maria and say hello. *6.* Turn the door knob. *7.* Drive the car and make a sudden turn.

turn in Turn (hand) in your homework (exercises, tests).

turn off Turn off the lights (television, radio, water, fan).

turn on Turn on the lights (radio, fan, television).

turn up *1.* Turn up the volume on the radio (television, tape recorder) so that everybody can hear it. *2.* Pretend Pedro is a radio and turn up (down) the volume. His ear is the volume control.

twice *1.* Clap (sneeze, cough, walk around the desk) twice. *2.* Write the number that's twice ten. *3.* Kick the student who has twice as much money as Pedro *(cc-9)*. *4.* Throw the ball to the student who's twice as old as Maria *(cc-1)*.

twine *1.* Cut a piece of twine the same length as your arm. *2.* Tie Pedro's feet (hands) together with the twine.

twist *1.* Twist my arm (ear, foot, hand; the towel, handkerchief, napkin, rag). *2.* Twist open the lid of the jar. *3.* Twist the lid off the jar.

type Pretend you're typing a letter.

ugly Draw an ugly (a handsome) face.

umbrella *1.* Walk (parade, march) around the class holding the umbrella in your right (left) hand. *2.* Hold the umbrella over your (my) head. *3.* Draw a girl (man, woman) holding an umbrella. *4.* Open and then collapse the umbrella.

unable Pedro was unable to walk around the class balancing a book (balloon, paper cup) on his head. Put your arm around his shoulder and console him.

under *1.* Write a number that's under ten but over five. *2.* Put (place) the book under (on, next to) the chair. *3.* Draw a heart under (beside, over, inside) a circle. *4.* Pull the hair of a student who has under ten dollars *(cc-9).*

underline *1.* Underline the third word in the fourth sentence. *2.* Underline (erase) all the words that have three letters (begin with the letter "s"). *3.* Write your full name and then underline (cross out) your first (last, middle) name.

underneath *1.* Put (set, place) the eraser (pen, book) underneath (on top of) the table. *2.* Look underneath your desk (notebook, book). *3.* Draw a bird (bat, butterfly; an airplane) underneath (over, next to) a cloud (star; the moon).

understand *1.* Jump (skip, march) to the student who understands French *(cc-5)*. *2.* If you didn't understand the command, raise your hand (shake your head, sit down and cry). *3.* Pull the nose (hair) of the student who didn't understand the command.

university *1.* Jump to a student who studies at a university that begins with the letter "h" *(cc-13)*. *2.* Kick (pinch, slap) a student who attends (goes to) a university that was founded in 1636 *(cc-13)*.

unless *1.* Jump to the chalkboard (desk, window, door), unless today is (yesterday was) Monday. In that case, pull your nose (hair, left ear). *2.* Don't hit (kick, slap, pinch, smile at) Pedro unless he's sitting next to (in front of) Maria.

unplug Plug in (unplug) the radio (tape recorder, fan).

until *1.* Sing (jump, cry, dance, sneeze, cough) until I say (tell you) to stop. *2.* Don't sit down until I point to the ceiling (floor, door). *3.* Pull Pedro's hair (ears) until Maria finishes erasing the chalkboard.

up *1.* Look up (down). *2.* Speak up. I can't hear you. *3.* When you're ready, put up your hands. *4.* Lay your head down. Now sit (stand) up. *5.* Unbutton (button up) your shirt. *6.* Take down the numbers I call out and then add them up. *7.* Wake Maria up.

upper *1.* Draw a big rectangle (square). In the upper (lower) right (left) hand corner, draw a heart (hat, car, triangle, star). *2.* Tie the ribbon (string, yarn) around your upper (lower) arm.

upset *1.* Upset the bottle (candle, tower of spools). *2.* Hold your belly, make a face, and groan because you have an upset stomach. *3.* Look (act) upset (sad, happy, angry).

use Draw (touch, pick up) an object that has (doesn't have) a practical use.

use *1.* Draw (touch) an object that's used to cut (measure, write, erase, serve, dry). *2.* Use the car (bus, truck) to go (travel) to the door (window, desk). *3.* Draw a cat (happy face, house, tree). Use your right (left) hand.

useful Draw (pick up) an object that's useful (useless, dangerous, harmful).

usually *1.* Wave to (smile at, pull the nose of) a student who usually sits in the back (front) of the class. *2.* Run (swim, hop, jump) to a student who usually (hardly ever, never) has a big breakfast (watches tv, gets up early) *(student-made cc).*

vacation Wink (smile, frown) at the student who's going to Spain for her vacation *(cc-4).*

vase *1.* Put the flower in the vase. *2.* Pretend Pedro's pocket is a vase and put the flower in it. *3.* Draw a vase with many flowers in it.

veil Put on (take off) the veil.

vertical *1.* Draw a long (short) vertical (horizontal, curved, diagonal) line and write your name over (under, next to) it. *2.* Hold the pencil (ruler) under your nose (chin) in a vertical position. *3.* Draw a heart between two broken vertical lines.

very *1.* Draw a big circle (flower, car, bell, hat). Now next

245

to it draw a very big heart (star, triangle). *2.* Walk (spin around, draw some circles) fast (slowly, very fast, very slowly).

view *1.* Stand in front of Maria blocking her view. *2.* View (look at, examine, observe) the objects on the desk. Turn around and I will remove one. Now turn around again and tell me which one is missing.

visit *1.* Laugh at (point to, say hello to) the student who's going to visit a country in Europe *(cc-4)*. *2.* Maria's in the hospital *(pc)*. Pedro, visit her and take her some flowers.

voice Say hello to the class in a high (low, deep, soft, loud, sweet) voice.

volcano *1.* Draw a volcano with smoke coming out of it. *2.* Write the name of a famous volcano.

volume *1.* Turn up (down) the volume on the radio (tape recorder, television). *2.* Draw a cube, measure it, and calculate its volume.

volunteer *1.* Applaud the student who just volunteered for the next command. *2.* I need two volunteers. If you want to volunteer, stand up (raise your hand, sneeze loudly).

vote *1.* Indicate your vote for the student who made the best drawing by writing his or her name on a slip of paper. *2.* Hop (skip, run) to the student who got (obtained, received) the most (greatest number of) votes.

waist *1.* Tie the rope (string, twine) around my waist. *2.* Stand in a single file line and put your hands on the waist of the person who is in front of you. 3. Measure Pedro's waist.

wait *1.* You are going to stand up (point to the ceiling, touch your nose, walk around the desk). Wait until I count to five. *2.* Pedro and Maria, go to the chalkboard and draw a car (house, tree). Pedro, wait for Maria to finish before you begin.

waiter *1.* Hop (swim, jump, skip) to the waiter *(pc)*. *2.* Pretend you're a waiter. Put the towel over your arm, put the banana (cookie, candy bar) on the tray, and serve it to Maria.

waitress *1.* Pull the nose (ear, ears) of the waitress *(pc)*. *2.* Pretend you're a waitress and serve me a glass of water (glass of beer, cup of coffee).

wake up *1.* Toss the ball (sponge, coin, eraser) to the student who wakes up at 6:15 *(student-made cc)*. *2.* Pedro's sleeping. Wake him up by shaking him (pounding on his desk, blowing the whistle, dropping a book on the floor, imitating an alarm clock).

walk *1.* Walk around the class quickly (backwards, slowly, on your toes). *2.* Pedro is your dog. Tie the string around his neck and walk your dog. *3.* Walk Maria to the door. *4.* Write the name of a store (restaurant, hotel) that's a short walk from here.

wallet *1.* Show your wallet to the class. *2.* Sneak up behind Pedro and try to steal his wallet from his back pocket. *3.* Count the money in the wallet *(class prop with play money)*.

waltz *1.* Waltz around the class with maria. *2.* Dance a waltz (tango) with the student who's wearing the yellow blouse.

want Pedro, jump (hop, run, sing, cry). Maria, when you want him to stop jumping, stand up and tell him to stop.

war Write the names of two countries that fought against each other in World War II.

warm *1.* Feel my forehead to see if it's warm. *2.* Write the name of a city that has a warm (cold, hot, cool) climate. *3.* When Pedro walks in the class, give him a warm (cool) welcome.

wash *1.* Wash the cup (glass, knife, fork, saucer) in the pail. *2.* Draw a sink on the chalkboard and pretend you're washing your hands (face).

wastebasket *1.* Drop the book (eraser, paper ball, coin) into the wastebasket. *2.* Put your left foot in the wastebasket. *3.* Crumple up a sheet of paper and toss it into the wastebasket. *4.* Walk around the class with the wastebasket on your head.

watch *1.* Take off (put on) your watch. *2.* Smile at a student who's wearing a watch. *3.* Make a paper airplane, launch it, and watch it glide to the floor. *4.* Pinch a student who likes to watch a tv program you also like to watch *(student-made cc)*.

water *1.* Pour some water into the pail (glass, cup, bowl). *2.* Drink some water from the glass that's half-full. *3.* Write the chemical formula for water. *4.* Draw some flowers on the chalkboard, pick up the watering can, and water them.

watermelon Draw a slice of watermelon, cut it out, put it on the tray, and serve it to Maria.

wave *1.* Wave to a student who has long (short, curly, wavy) hair. *2.* Wave the handkerchief (flag). *3.* Draw a picture of a boat in a sea with big (tall, small) waves.

wavy Draw a wavy (crooked, straight, curved, diagonal, horizontal, vertical) line.

wax *1.* Light the candle and drip some wax onto the saucer (floor). Now pick up the knife and scrape it off. *2.* Touch (show me) an object made of wax.

way *1.* Do something in a strange way. *2.* Draw a street on the floor. Look both ways before you cross it. *3.* Write the name of a city that is (isn't) a long way from here. *4.* Draw a cat on the chalkboard and stand out of the way so that everybody can see it.

weak *1.* Speak in a weak (strong) voice. *2.* Pretend you're weak and can't pick up the chair. *3.* Draw a weak man next to a strong man.

wealthy *1.* Pull the nose (hair, ears) of the wealthy (rich, poor) student *(cc-9)*. *2.* Write the name of a famous wealthy person who is (isn't) alive today.

weapon *1.* Pick up a weapon and threaten Pedro. *2.* Draw a weapon that kills by cutting (shooting).

wear *1.* Smile (laugh) at a student who's wearing something blue. *2.* Draw a man (woman) wearing a hat (tie, necklace, watch, beard, mustache, wide belt). *3.* Rub the paper with the eraser until you wear a hole in it.

wedding *1.* We're going to have a wedding. Pedro is going to marry Maria. When they walk down the aisle, everybody will hum "Here Comes the Bride." *2.* Write the date and the place where your wedding took place.

wedding band *1.* Show your wedding band to the class. *2.* Shake hands with (pinch the nose of) a student who's wearing a wedding band (an engagement ring).

week Write (circle, underline) the day of the week that comes before (after) Monday.

weigh *1.* Pick up an object and estimate (guess) how much it weighs. *2.* Draw a picture of an object that usually weighs less than two pounds. *3.* Write the name of something that weighs more than a car.

weight *1.* Write your weight on the chalkboard. *2.* Pick up (hold up, touch, show the class) two objects that are about (nearly) the same weight.

welcome *1.* Welcome the next student to arrive with a smile (song, handshake). *2.* Maria is going to step out of the room. When she comes back in, give her a big welcome. *3.* Everybody, welcome the new student.

well *1.* You don't feel (aren't feeling) well today. Go to the doctor *(pc)*. *2.* Write the name of an actor (singer, author) who acts (sings, writes) well.

west *1.* Face west (east, north, south). *2.* Go to the map and touch a country that's to the west of Hungary. *3.* Write the name of a city that's on the West Coast.

wet *1.* Splash some water on the chalkboard and then touch the wet (dry) part. *2.* Wet the handkerchief

250

(cloth, towel) and wipe your forehead (cheeks, chin). *3.* Pour some water on one of your hands and shake hands with me with your wet (dry) hand.

whale Draw a whale with a boat (small fish, big shark) in back of it.

what *1.* Do what I say (do, ask you to do, tell you to do). *2.* Write what you said (heard) on the chalkboard. *3.* Perform some actions showing what you do when you wake up in the morning. *4.* Tell the class what time it is.

whatever *1.* Do whatever I do. *2.* Take whatever is on the teacher's desk and put it on the floor (in the wastebasket).

wheel *1.* Spin the wheels (tires) of the toy car. *2.* Draw an object that has two (four) wheels. *3.* Face the chalkboard, suddenly wheel around, point to a student, and shout his name.

when *1.* When I point to the desk (ceiling, door, window, floor), you will stand up (cry, laugh, sneeze, faint). *2.* Sing (stamp your feet, clap) when the next student walks in the class. *3.* Write the year when you were born.

whenever Whenever I touch my nose, I want you to clap (point to the floor, groan, sigh).

where *1.* Pedro, stand up and hop (run) to the door (window). Maria, sit where Pedro was sitting. *2.* Write the name of the country (state, city) where you were born. *3.* Touch a student who's from a country where the people speak Spanish *(cc-4)*.

251

wherever I'm going to walk around the class. Follow me and go wherever I go.

which *1.* Write a number which is greater than ten but less than twenty. *2.* Draw a triangle under a heart. Now draw a triangle over a car. Erase the triangle which is over the car. *3.* Write the name of a book which you have just finished reading.

whichever Shake a hand (foot). It doesn't matter which one. Shake whichever one you want.

while *1.* Clap (sing, hum) while Maria erases the chalkboard (walks around the class). *2.* Laugh (cry) while I'm pulling your nose. *3.* I'm going to step out of the class. While I'm gone, hide the eraser. *4.* Stand in the corner for a little while.

whisper *1.* Whisper (sing, say, shout) hello to the teacher. *2.* Read the commands on the chalkboard in a whisper (loud voice).

whistle *1.* Whistle (sing, hum) a song by the Beatles. *2.* When I blow the whistle, you will jump up and down (put your hands on your head, stop what you're doing, freeze like a statue).

who *1.* Swim (hop, skip, run) to the student who's sitting (standing, kneeling) next to (in back of, in front of) the chair. *2.* Touch the left (right) ear (knee, hand, elbow, foot) of the student who's from Mexico *(cc-4).*

whole *1.* When I count to three, I want the whole class (this row) to stand up and cry (dance, point to the floor, turn around three times). *2.* Recite the whole alphabet.

whose *1.* Smile (laugh, look, frown, stare) at a student whose first (last) name begins (ends) with the letter "m." *2.* Shake hands with a student whose birthday is in December *(student-made cc)*.

wide *1.* Put on the wide (narrow) tie. *2.* Draw a fat man wearing a wide (narrow) belt. *3.* Draw a narrow street intersecting a wide one. *4.* Open the door (window; your eyes, mouth) wide.

widen *1.* Draw a narrow street (tie). Now erase it and widen it. *2.* Stand in front of Pedro. Now widen (shorten) the distance between you.

width *1.* Draw a rectangle whose length is twice (three times) its width. *2.* Measure the width and the length of the table (rectangle you drew).

wife *1.* Stand on the feet of a student who has (doesn't have) a wife (husband). *2.* Write your wife's (husband's) name and put (insert) a vertical line between the last (first) two letters.

wig Put on (take off) the wig (hat, tie, scarf, glove, belt).

wiggle Wiggle your nose (fingers).

wild Imitate (pretend you are, draw a picture of) a wild (tame) animal.

will *1.* When I sit down, you will put your left foot in the wastebasket (run around the class, touch your toes). *2.* Will you please erase the chalkboard (clear off your desks, pass out the test booklets).

win *1.* Applaud the team that's winning the contest

(game) so far. 2. Pat the back of (shake hands with) the student who you think will win the race.

wind *1.* Wind the string (yarn, thread) around the pencil (spool, candle, ruler). *2.* Wind your watch. *3.* Pretend Pedro is a toy robot and wind him up. *4.* Draw a long winding (straight) road.

wind Make a noise like the wind.

window *1.* Throw (toss) the paper ball out the window. *2.* Open (close, shut) the window (door) slowly (quickly). *3.* Draw a house with round (square, rectangular) windows. *4.* Walk (run, swim, jump, skip, limp) to the window.

wing *1.* Draw a bird (bee; an airplane) with four wings. *2.* Pretend you're a bird and flap your wings.

wink Wink at the student who's standing in front of (in back of, next to) the teacher (chair, desk, student wearing green tennis shoes).

winner *1.* Serve (give, offer) the candy bar (raisin, apple, banana) to the winner of the race. *2.* Write the name of the team that was the winner of the soccer match (basketball game) last night.

winter *1.* Pretend you're participating in a typical winter sport. *2.* Walk to a student who has a card with a winter month written on it *(cc-2)*.

wipe *1.* Wipe your face on the napkin (towel, handkerchief). *2.* Wipe (clean) your glasses on your shirt. *3.* Spill some water on the table and wipe (soak) it up with the sponge (paper towel).

wire *1.* Bend the wire into a **C (J, U, W, V).** *2.* Touch an electrical wire.

wish *1.* Draw a picture of something you wish you could buy. *2.* Run to a country you wish to visit *(cc-4).* *3.* Maria is going to race Pedro to the door. Wish her good luck. *4.* Today's Pedro's birthday. Give him a present and wish him a happy birthday.

witch *1.* Draw a witch. *2.* Write the name of a story that has a witch in it. *3.* Laugh like a witch. *4.* Pretend you're a witch and ride the broom around the class.

with *1.* Hit me on the head with the book (notebook). *2.* Pretend you're fighting with Pedro. *3.* Sing a song (jump around the class) with Maria. *4.* Write your name with your left hand. *5.* Jump to the door with your eyes closed (your hands on your head).

within *1.* Draw as many circles (squares, stars) as you can within thirty seconds. *2.* Write the name of a building (hotel, restaurant, coffee shop, shopping center) that is (isn't) within walking distance.

without *1.* Walk (swim) to the door without your glasses. *2.* Leave the class without saying good-bye. *3.* Draw a girl without a head (nose, mouth, leg). *4.* Remain standing for two minutes without smiling while the class tries to make you laugh.

wolf *1.* Howl like a wolf. *2.* Give a wolf whistle.

woman *1.* Draw a woman wearing a hat (long dress, skirt, wide belt). *2.* Write the name of a famous woman. *3.* Show the class a picture of a woman (man).

women *1.* Draw a group of three women. *2.* I want all the women (men) in the class to stand up and sing hello to the teacher.

wood Touch an object made of wood (glass, metal, plastic, leather).

wool *1.* Touch something made of wool (cotton, leather, glass, metal). *2.* Imitate (draw, pretend you are) an animal that gives us wool.

word *1.* Write a command that has ten words. *2.* Underline (cross out, circle, draw a rectangle around) the third word in the sentence Maria wrote (put) on the chalkboard. *3.* Write a word that has five letters (begins with the letter "c").

work *1.* Swim (hop, run, jump) to the student who works as a barber *(pc)*. *2.* Work the exercises with your partner. *3.* Write where you work on the chalkboard.

world *1.* Open the almanac and find the longest river (tallest building, hottest city) in the world. *2.* Show the class a map (globe) of the world.

worm *1.* Draw a fish (bird) about to eat a worm. *2.* Draw a worm stuck on a fishhook.

worse *1.* I'm going to write the names of two movies (singers, tv programs). Circle (underline, put a check next to) the one you think is worse (better). *2.* Pedro and Maria are going to sing a song. Point to the worse (better) singer.

worst *1.* Write the name of the worst movie you ever saw (worst book you ever read). *2.* Pedro, Carlos, and Maria are going to draw a picture of the teacher. When they finish, we will vote for the worst (best) drawing.

would   *1.* Would you please open the door (close the window, erase the chalkboard, collect the papers, pass out the booklets). *2.* Hop (jump, swim) to a city you would like to visit *(cc-11)*. *3.* Draw a picture of something you would like to buy.

wrap *1.* Wrap the string (yarn, thread) around the pencil (spool, candle; your finger). *2.* Wrap the box with the wrapping paper and tie the ribbon around it.

wrench *1.* Draw a wrench, cut it out, and take it to the mechanic *(pc)*. *2.* Pick up the wrench and pretend you're fixing the car (tightening my nose). *3.* Wrench the book (ball) from Pedro's hands (grip).

wring out Spill (sprinkle) some water on the table (floor), soak it up with the rag, and then wring out the rag over the pail.

wrinkle Wrinkle your shirt (forehead).

wrist *1.* Measure the circumference of my wrist with the tape measure. *2.* Tie the string (ribbon, yarn) around Maria's right (left) wrist.

write *1.* Write (print) your (my) first (last) name with your left hand. *2.* Write the name of the student sitting behind (in front of) the girl whose notebook is under her desk. *3.* Write a letter to Maria.

wrong *1.* I'm going to write some sentences on the chalkboard. Some will be right; others will be wrong. Correct the wrong ones. *2.* If you see something wrong with the sentence Pedro wrote on the chalkboard, raise your hand (snap your fingers).

yard *1.* Draw a house with a tall tree in the front yard and many flowers in the back yard. *2.* Measure one yard of string (thread).

yarn *1.* Cut off a piece of red yarn and tie it in a bow in Pedro's hair. *2.* Wrap the yarn around the spool (pencil; your finger). *3.* Cut a length of yarn the same length as the diagonal (vertical) line Maria drew.

yawn You're sleepy (bored). Yawn and cover your mouth with your hand.

year *1.* Write the year you were born. *2.* Show the class the event that happened (occurred) in the year 1964 *(cc-7)*. *3.* Hop to a student who has lived here for more (less) than ten years *(student-made cc)*. *4.* Swim to the fifth month of the year *(cc-2)*.

yell Yell (shout, sing, whisper, say) hello to Maria.

yesterday *1.* If yesterday was Sunday, walk around the desk (chair, teacher) three times. If it wasn't, touch your nose (chin, knee). *2.* Smile at (wave to) someone who's in class today but was absent yesterday.

yet *1.* Pull the hair (nose) of the student who hasn't finished drawing the circles (stars, hearts) yet. *2.* Write the name of someone who hasn't arrived yet.

young *1.* Touch (shake hands with) someone who is too young to vote (get married, drink beer, drive a car) *(cc-1)*. *2.* Change places with a student who is younger (older) than you.

yourself *1.* Touch (hit, point to, pinch) yourself. *2.* Look at yourself in the mirror.

zip Zip up the purse (your jacket).

Appendix A: Cardboard Cutouts

Below are a few suggestions for some simple props you can make from light cardboard or pasteboard.

1. geometric figures

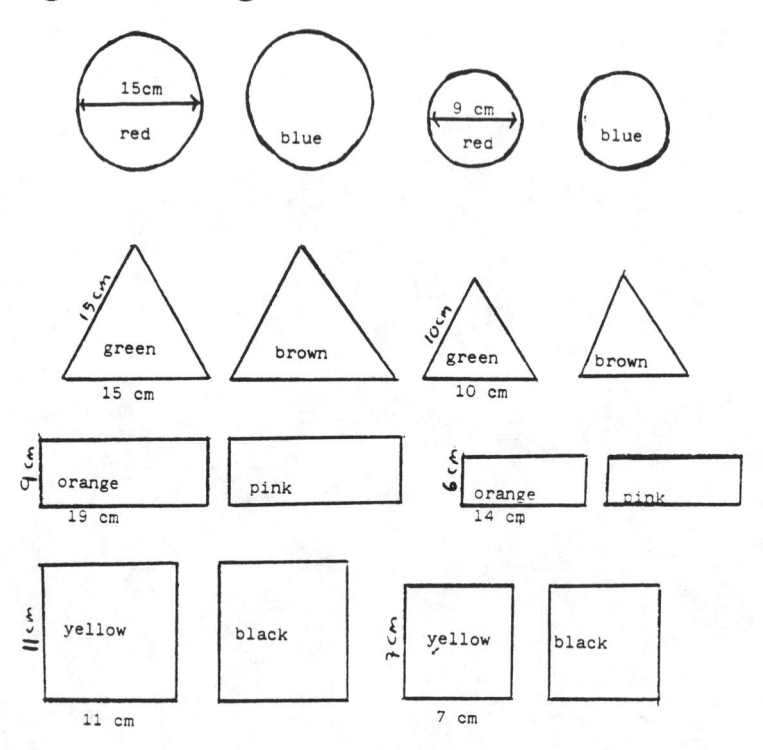

- 15cm red circle
- blue circle
- 9 cm red circle
- blue circle

- 15 cm green triangle (15 cm)
- brown triangle
- 10 cm green triangle (10 cm)
- brown triangle

- 9 cm × 19 cm orange rectangle
- pink rectangle
- 6 cm × 14 cm orange rectangle
- pink rectangle

- 11 cm yellow square
- black square
- 7 cm yellow square
- black square

2. cars

Make several cars, each one a different color. For some cars, make the wheels the same color as the car; for others, make them a different color.

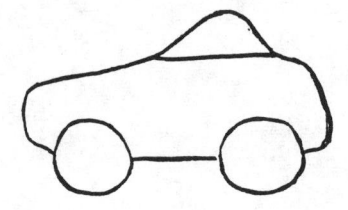

260

3. ties

Make several wide and several narrow ties. Use different types of decorations: plain, striped, checked, plaid; decorated with hearts, diamonds, etc.

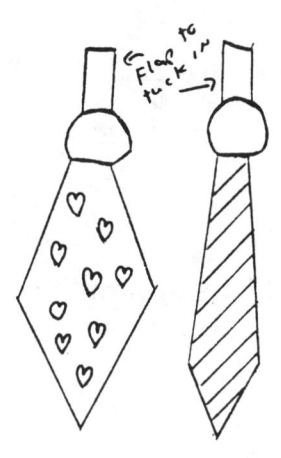

4. bow ties

Make several bow ties, each one decorated differently. You might make one yellow with back balls, another blue with red hearts, etc.

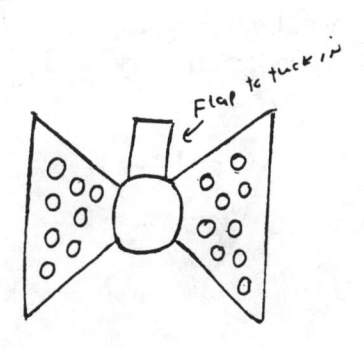

5. fish

Make eleven fish cards using the following colors: red, green, white, black, yellow, blue, brown, gray, orange, pink, purple.

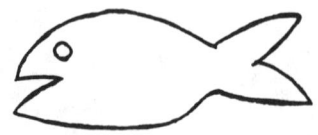

6. hats

Make several hats by forming construction paper into cones. Use different colors and decorations.

7. beards

Make several beards using the following colors: black, brown, yellow, red, and gray.

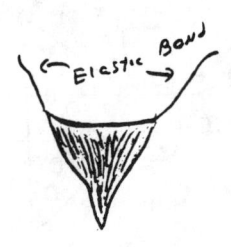

8. crowns

Make several of different colors.

9. masks

Make several of different colors.

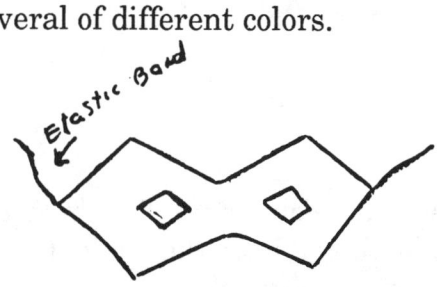

10. mustaches

The mustache is attached to the upper lip with a piece of tape doubled over on itself. Use the same colors as you did for the beards.

11. clock

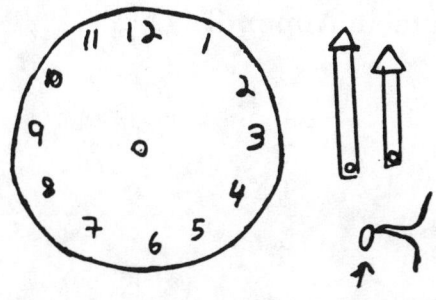

Appendix B: Picture Cards

Below you will find two sets of picture cards, one of occupations and the other of places, which you can enlarge and copy onto light cardboard or pasteboard. The pictures should be drawn with thick lines using a black marking pen, and the cards should be of a uniform size (about 20 by 20 cm). Note that the drawings are symbolic, not realistic. Thus a

is used to symbolize a carpenter.

To use the cards, you would distribute the ones you intend to work with and have the students hold them up. (Generally speaking, you would work with several cards at the same time so that the students are always selecting the correct one from among several options.) Then give a student who doesn't have a card a command related to one of the cards. Depending on the command, the action will be performed by (a) the student who has the card, or (b) the student to whom you gave the command:

Pedro, cut the barber's hair. (**Pedro cuts the hair of the student who has the barber card.**)

Pedro, go to the barber and get a haircut. (**The student with the barber card cuts Pedro's hair.**)

Following each set of pictures, there is a set of commands. Additional commands for use with the picture cards can be found in **Appendix D**.

Occupation Cards

actor

architect

actress

artist

angel

bank clerk

265

barber

carpenter

beggar

cashier

bus driver

clown

butcher

dentist

doctor

engineer

dressmaker

farmer

electrician

fireman

gardener

hairdresser

mechanic

king

nurse

maid

painter

mailman

photographer

pilot

sailor

policeman

salesman

priest

scientist

queen

secretary

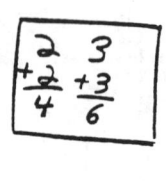

teacher

singer

waiter

soldier

waitress

sample commands

Walk to the ____ and _____.

1. actor — watch him dramatically pretend he's dying
2. actress — listen to her recite a poem
3. angel — say a prayer
4. architect — have her design a bridge
5. artist — ask him to paint your portrait
6. bank clerk — cash a check
7. barber — get a haircut
8. beggar — drop a few coins into his hand
9. bus driver — give him a bus pass
10. butcher — pretend you're a cow
11. carpenter — watch him saw the chair
12. cashier — hand her something you buy at a drugstore
13. clown — laugh loudly holding your belly
14. dentist — show him your teeth
15. doctor — let him feel your pulse
16. dressmaker — have her design a dress for you
17. electrician — tell him to turn on the lights
18. engineer — ask her to build a tower with the blocks
19. farmer — give him the corn cob
20. fireman — tell him to blow out the candle
21. gardener — give him the flower
22. hairdresser — let him comb your hair
23. king — kneel in front of him
24. maid — watch her sweep the floor
25. mailman — give him the envelope
26. mechanic — have him examine your car
27. nurse — let her feel your forehead
28. painter — draw a house for him to paint

29. photographer — pose for her
30. pilot — watch him fly the paper airplane
31. policeman — show him your driver's license
32. priest — go with him to the church Maria drew
33. queen — bow to her
34. sailor — give him the boat you drew
35. salesman — buy a radio with the play money
36. scientist — give him the test tube
37. secretary — hand her an eraser
38. singer — sing a song with her
39. soldier — salute him
40. teacher — give her a piece of chalk
41. waiter — drape the towel over his arm
42. waitress — have her serve you a cup of coffee

Place Cards

airport

barber shop

bedroom

apartment

bathroom

bookstore

bakery

beach

butcher shop

bank

beauty salon

castle

273

cemetery

drugstore

jail

church

garden

kitchen

clothing store

gas station

library

department store

hotel

living room

movie theater

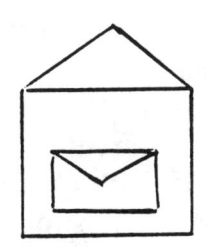

post office

supermarket

museum

restaurant

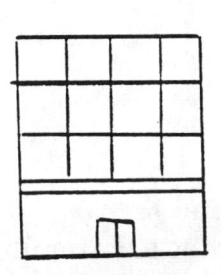

office building

school

park

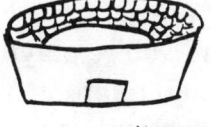

stadium

sample commands

Walk to the ____ and ____.
1. airport — fly the plane to the door
2. apartment — and ring the doorbell
3. bakery — buy a cookie
4. bank — deposit some money
5. barber shop — get a haircut
6. bathroom — pretend you're taking a shower
7. beach — pretend you're surfing
8. beauty salon — have your hair done
9. bedroom — pretend you're sleeping
10. bookstore — buy a book
11. butcher shop — buy some meat
12. castle — bow to the king
13. cemetery — put your face in your hands and cry
14. church — pray with the priest
15. clothing store — try on the ties
16. department store — buy a radio
17. drugstore — buy some cough medicine
18. garden — plant a flower
19. gas station — fill up the tank of your car
20. hotel — sign your name in the register
21. jail — put on the mask
22. kitchen — prepare a cup of coffee
23. library — read a book
24. living room — have a talk with a friend
25. movie theater — pretend you're watching a horror film
26. museum — write the name of a famous artist
27. office building — pretend you're typing a letter
28. park — pretend you're playing baseball
29. post office — mail a letter
30. restaurant — pretend you're eating
31. school — open your book and study
32. stadium — pretend you're playing soccer
33. supermarket — buy a can of soda pop

Appendix C: Cue Cards

Below you will find suggestions for thirteen sets of cue cards which you can make out of heavy construction paper or pasteboard. The cards should be 8-10 cm wide. The length will vary from set to set (but all of the cards within each set should be of the same length). Print the cues in thick letters using a different color for each card so that you can make commands related to the colors. Naturally you are free to modify the sets, substituting or adding new items as needed.

1. ages

Make cards with a wide variety of ages from very young to very old. So that you can use the expressions "the same age as" and "twice as old as," be sure to repeat some ages and to include some ages that are double other ages.

sample commands

Jump to the student who is—

> 10 years old
> older (younger) than Pedro
> the same age as Paula
> as old as (almost as old as) Maria
> twice (half) as old as Carlos

2. months

sample commands

Hop to—

> the month written in green letters

the month that comes before March
the first (last) month of the year
the month that begins (ends) with the letter "m"
the month that has 3 letters
a month that has 28 (30, 31) days

3. holidays and special occasions

Below are some U.S. holidays and special occasions. Make a separate card for each one, putting the month in which it occurs on the back.

April Fool's Day	April
Christmas	December
Easter	March/April
Fathers' Day	June
Halloween	October
Independence Day	July
Labor Day	September
Mother's Day	May
New Year's Day	January
Thanksgiving	November
Valentine's Day	February
Washington's Birthday	February

sample commands

Swim to the—

event celebrated (we celebrate) in May
card printed in red letters
holiday that begins with the letter "c"

4. countries

Below are 10 countries with the principal language(s) spoken there. Put the names of the countries on one side and the languages spoken on the other.

1. Brazil   Portuguese
2. Canada   English, French
3. Chile   Spanish
4. Egypt   Arabic
5. England   English
6. France   French
7. Israel   Hebrew
8. Japan   Japanese
9. Mexico   Spanish
10 Russia   Russian

sample commands

Pull the hair of the student who—

comes from Egypt
comes from a country located in Europe
plans to spend his vacation in Mexico
took a trip to Japan last year
lives in a country that begins with the letter "f"
lives in a country where the people speak French

5. languages

For these exercises you will use the reverse sides of the cards from Set 4 above.

sample commands

Hop to the student who—

279

speaks a language that begins with the letter "s"
has the card showing the language spoken in Mexico
understands (is studying) Japanese
speaks the same language as Pedro

6. courses of study

1. architecture
2. biology
3. business administration
4. economics
5. geology
6. history
7. journalism
8. law
9. medicine
10. nursing

sample commands

Run to the student who—

has a degree in law
studies medicine
is majoring in biology
is studying a subject that ends with the letter "h"

7. world events

1969   Neil Armstrong walks on the moon
1963   Kennedy assassinated
1945   World War II ends
1927   Lindbergh crosses the Atlantic
1865   Lincoln assassinated
1750   Industrial Revolution begins
1611   King James Bible published

    1521   Cortez conquers Mexico
    1492   Columbus discovers America
    1380   Bible translated into English

sample commands

Walk to the event that took place—

in 1969
about 25 years ago
in the 14th century
within the last 50 years

8. famous people

On the front of the cards write the names, dates of birth, and dates of death. Put their nationalities and what they were famous for on the back.

    1. Beethoven 1770 - 1827. (German composer)
    2. Cervantes 1547 - 1616. (Spanish novelist)
    3. Dante 1265 - 1321. (Italian poet)
    4. Darwin 1809 - 1882. (English naturalist)
    5. Edison 1847 - 1931. (American inventor)
    6. Einstein 1879 - 1955. (American/German-born physicist)
    7. Liszt 1811- 1886. (Hungarian composer)
    8. Napoleon 1769 - 1821. (French emperor)
    9. Picasso 1881 - 1973. (Spanish painter)
    10 Shakespeare 1564 - 1616. (English dramatist/poet)

sample commands

Jump to the person who—

was a famous Hungarian composer
was born in 1847
died in 1973
lived in the 19th century
had a short life
was an Italian poet

9. money

Make cards representing various denominations, from very low to very high. Be sure to repeat some values so that you can use the expression "the same amount as."

sample commands

Say hello to the student who—

doesn't have any money at all
has the least (most) money
has little (a lot of) money
has more (less) than $40
has just under (over) $94
has the same amount as Pedro

10. activities and times

For each activity make three separate cards (one for each of the times below). On each card write a student's name, the name of the activity, and the time. If you wish you can draw clocks to represent the times.

get up	4:30	6:25	7:20
have breakfast	5:00	7:00	7:25
leave the house	5:40	7:15	8:15
arrive at work	6:10	7:45	8:50
eat lunch	11:35	11:40	12:00

get home	5:05	6:55	6:10
have dinner	6:00	7:50	7:20
go to sleep	9:30	11:25	12:00

sample commands

Pull the nose of the student who—

> gets up the earliest
> has breakfast at 7:55
> goes to sleep at the same time as you do
> gets home earlier than Maria but later than Pedro

11. cities and when moved to

Below is a list of cities, each with a date representing the year the holder of the card moved to the city.

1. Amsterdam 1950
2. Athens 1975
3. Beirut 1985
4. Buenos Aires 1947
5. Lima 1981
6. Moscow 1965
7. Peking 1940
8. Quebec 1940
9. Rome 1951
10. Tokyo 1974

sample commands

Say hello to the student who—

> moved to Lima in 1981
> has been living in Peking for a long time

lives in a city in Europe
moved within the last ten years

12. numbers

Write the numbers 1-100 on cue cards, each one on a separate card. Then distribute the cards that have the numbers you want to work with. Note that for the more complicated math problems you will probably want to prepare the exact commands before hand.

sample commands

Touch the nose of the student who has a/the number—

under (over) 10
between 15 and 20
that's the sum of 15 and 30
that is two times 38
152 divided by 2

13. universities — when founded

1. Columbia 1754
2. Florida State 1857
3. Harvard 1636
4. Ohio State 1870
5. Stanford 1885
6. U.C.L.A. 1881
7. University of Chicago (the) 1891
8. University of Colorado (the) 1861
9. Washington State 1890
10. Yale 1701

sample commands

Point to the student who studies at a/the university—

that was founded in 1754
that was founded earlier than Yale
that was founded twenty years before U.C.L.A.
that has the shortest name

Appendix D: Operatives

This appendix consists of actions that one student can perform on or in relation to another student. For your convenience they have been grouped by syntactic patterns.

Group 1. Pattern: Jump to Pedro (the student who's singing).

1. Applaud
2. Attach the rope to
3. Award the trophy to
4. Back the car into
5. Bark at
6. Blindfold
7. Blow a kiss to
8. Borrow a pencil from
9. Bounce the ball to
10. Bow to
11. Bump into
12. Change places with
13. Choke
14. Clasp hands with
15. Collide with
16. Congratulate
17. Crash the car into
18. Creep up to
19. Crowd around
20. Dance with
21. Deal some cards to
22. Dictate a sentence to
23. Do a dance for
24. Drive the car to
25. Elbow
26. Embrace
27. Extend a hand to
28. Face
29. Fall down in front of
30. Fan
31. Feed a cookie to
32. Fly the airplane to
33. Frown at
34. Give the flower to
35. Glance at
36. Glare at
37. Go to
38. Grin at
39. Growl at
40. Hand a book to
41. Hide behind
42. Hold a book in front of
43. Hop to
44. Hug
45. Hum a song with
46. Hypnotize
47. Interrupt
48. Jab
49. Join hands with
50. Jump to
51. Kick
52. Kneel in front of
53. Laugh at
54. Lean against
55. Leap to
56. Lend a pencil to
57. Limp to
58. Line up in back of

59. Look at
60. Make a face at
61. March to
62. Mumble hello to
63. Nod to
64. Offer a raisin to
65. Paddle the canoe to
66. Park the car in front of
67. Pass the eraser to
68. Perform the dialogue with
69. Pinch
70. Play tic-tac-toe with
71. Point to
72. Poke
73. Pose for
74. Pray with
75. Propose to
76. Punch
77. Read a poem to
78. Roll the ball to
79. Row the boat to
80. Run around
81. Sail the boat to
82. Salute
83. Say hello to
84. Send a postcard to
85. Serve a cup of coffee to
86. Shake
87. Shake hands with
88. Share your book with
89. Shave
90. Shoot a rubber band at
91. Shout hello to
92. Shove
93. Show your drawing to
94. Sing a song with
95. Sit on
96. Skip to
97. Slap
98. Slide a coin to
99. Smile at
100. Speak to
101. Splash some water on
102. Sprinkle some water on
103. Stagger to
104. Stand in front of
105. Stare at
106. Stick out your tongue at
107. Stomp to
108. Stoop in back of
109. Surround
110. Swim to
111. Take a piece of chalk to
112. Take the book from
113. Throw the ball to
114. Tickle
115. Tie up
116. Tiptoe to
117. Toss the eraser to
118. Walk around
119. Waltz with
120. Wave to
121. Whisper hello to
122. Whistle at
123. Wink at

Group 2. Pattern: Carry Pedro around the class.

124. Carry _____ around the class
125. Cause _____ to laugh
126. Chase _____ around the class
127. Command _____ to jump
128. Drag _____ to the door
129. Follow _____ around the class
130. Greet _____ with a smile
131. Help _____ erase the chalkboard
132. Hit _____ on the head with the book
133. Introduce _____ to _____
134. Lead _____ to the door
135. Make _____ smile
136. Motion for _____ to sit down
137. Move _____ to the back of the class
138. Order _____ to close the door
139. Pat _____ on the head
140. Pull _____ up
141. Push _____ to the window
142. Race _____ to the chalkboard
143. Seize _____ by the wrist
144. Sock _____ on the arm
145. Spin _____ around
146. Tell _____ to stand up
147. Turn _____ around

Group 3. Patterns: (a) Close the book of the student who's singing.
(b) Close Pedro's Book

148. Bang on the desk of
149. Bend the arm of
150. Break the pencil of
151. Brush the hair of
152. Button the shirt of

153. Circle the name of
154. Clasp the wrist of
155. Clear off the desk of
156. Close the book of
157. Comb the hair of
158. Count the letters in the name of
159. Cover the head of
160. Cross out the name of
161. Cut the hair of
162. Dampen the forehead of
163. Deposit something on the desk of
164. Draw a picture of
165. Drip some water on the head of
166. Drop the sponge on the head of
167. Dry the hands of
168. Dump some books on the desk of
169. Dust the desk of
170. Erase the name of
171. Examine the eyes of
172. Fasten the rope to
173. Feel the forehead of
174. Grab the book of
175. Grasp the arm of
176. Grip the elbow of
177. Hang the hanger on the ear of
178. Heap some books on the desk of
179. Hide the notebook of
180. Insert a pencil in the notebook of
181. Inspect the documents of
182. Knock on the desk of
183. Lay your head on the desk of
184. Leave your book on the desk of
185. Lift the notebook of
186. Look over the shoulder of
187. Loosen the shoelaces of
188. Measure the nose of

189. Move the head of
190. Muss the hair of
191. Open the book of
192. Pick up the pencil of
193. Pile some books on the desk of
194. Place your purse on the foot of
195. Pour some water on the head of
196. Print the name of
197. Pull the hair of
198. Put your pencil under the desk of
199. Raise the left hand of
200. Remove something from the desk of
201. Rest your elbows on the head of
202. Roll up the sleeve of
203. Rub the back of
204. Saw the arm of
205. Scratch the back of
206. Scribble the name of
207. Set the can under the desk of
208. Shine the shoes of
209. Shut the book of
210. Squeeze the hand of
211. Step on the toes of
212. Take something from the desk of
213. Tape a circle to the forehead of
214. Tie the rope around the waist of
215. Touch the nose of
216. Tug on the sleeve of
217. Twist the arm of
218. Untie the shoes of
219. Wet the hand of
220. Wipe the face of
221. Wrap the string around the finger of
222. Wrinkle the shirt of
223. Write your name in the notebook of

Appendix E: Races and Contests

Below you will find a list of 30 races and contests involving physical actions. In the races the objective is, naturally, to be the first to do something. The contests are based not on speed but rather on doing something best. Here are some examples of the kinds of commands that you can use with them:

If you think Pedro will win, raise your hand.
This half of the class will cheer for Maria.
Congratulate the winner.
Console the loser.
Shake hands with the student who—

> came in first
> won the race
> built the tallest tower of blocks
> ran the fastest
> was able to roll the coin into the cup
> performed the best

Races

1. Blow up the balloon, knot it, and burst it by sitting on it
2. Blow a balloon to the door
3. Dribble the ball to the door
4. Get the correct answer to a mental math problem
5. Hop to the door backwards
6. Jump to the door holding a balloon between ankles
7. Light a candle and walk to the chalkboard without it going out
8. Run to the desk balancing a bottle cap on a ruler
9. Walk to the door carrying a tower of blocks
10. Walk to the desk balancing a paper cup on head

Contests

11. Blow out the candle from the greatest distance
12. Bounce the ball the most times
13. Build the tallest tower of blocks
14. Fly a paper airplane the farthest
15. Guess the object in the bag by feeling it
16. Jump the highest making a chalk mark on the wall
17. Jump the farthest
18. Jump rope the most times
19. Keep a serious face the longest
20. Make the tallest stack of coins
21. Open the book to the exact page the teacher calls out
22. Remain perfectly still like a statue the longest
23. Roll the ball and knock over the bottle
24. Roll a coin into a cup lying on its side
25. Shoot the rubber band and knock over the paper cup
26. Stand on tiptoes the longest
27. Throw the ball into the air and clap the most times before catching it
28. Throw the paper ball and knock the paper cup off of a student's head
29. Throw a raisin into the air and catch it in mouth
30. Toss a paper ball into the wastebasket

ORDER FORM FOR

TPR TRAINING MATERIALS

Your order **shipped promptly** within 48 hours

**SKY OAKS PRODUCTIONS, INC.
P.O. Box 1102
Los Gatos, CA 95031**

Phone (408) 395-7600

ORDER FORM FOR

	Quantity	Cost
Asher, James J. **Learning Another Language Through Actions: Complete Teacher's Guidebook** (Expanded 3rd Edition) ©1986		$12.95 ____
Asher, James J. **Brainswitching** ©1988		12.95 ____
Blair, Robert W. **Innovative Approaches to Language Teaching**	____	15.95 ____
Burling, Robbins, **Sounding Right.** ©1983. (For all age groups.)	____	12.95 ____
Cabello, Francisco. **Total Physical Response in 1st Year Spanish**	____	13.95 ____
Garcia, Ramiro. **Instructor's Notebook: How to Apply TPR for Best Results** ©1988 (Triple Expanded 2nd Edition, 288 pages illustrated)	____	14.95 ____
Garcia, Ramiro. **TPR Bingo** ©1988 (Specify which language you prefer).	____	25.00 ____
Klopp, Jody. **Actionlogues: Student Workbook in Spanish**	____	9.95 ____
Klopp, Jody. **Actionlogues: Audio Cassette in Spanish**	____	9.95 ____
Klopp, Jody. **Actionlogues: Student Workbook in French**	____	9.95 ____
Klopp, Jody. **Actionlogues: Audio Cassette in French**	____	9.95 ____
Márquez, Nancy. **Learning With Movements: Total Physical Response English** © (TPR English for beginning groups.)	____	7.95 ____
Márquez, Nancy. **Aprendiendo Con Movimientos: Método TPR Español** © (TPR Spanish for beginning Groups.)	____	7.95 ____
Márquez, Nancy. **L'Enseignement Par Le Mouvement** ©1984 (TPR French for beginning groups.)	____	7.95 ____
Moskowitz, Gertrude. **Caring and Sharing in the Foreign Language Class.** © (For intermediate and advanced groups.)	____	15.95 ____
Nelson, Gayle and Winters, Thomas, **ESL Operations.** © (For beginning and intermediate groups.)	____	7.50 ____
Romijn, Libby and Seely, Contee. **Live Action English**© (For intermediate groups.)	____	6.95 ____
Schessler, Eric J. **English Grammar Through Actions** ©1984 (For all age groups.)	____	8.95 ____
Schessler, Eric J. **French Grammar Through Actions** ©1986 (For all age groups.)	____	8.95 ____
Schessler, Eric J. **Spanish Grammar Through Actions** ©1985 (For all age groups.)	____	8.95 ____
Seely, Contee. **Español con Impacto: Texto Del Alumno** © (TPR Spanish for beginning and intermediate groups.)	____	7.95 ____
Silvers, Stephen M. **Listen and Perform: TPR Student Book** ©1985 (200 plus pages for beginning and intermediate ESL Students)	____	12.95 ____
Silvers, Stephen M. **Listen and Perform: Teacher's Guidebook**	____	4.95 ____
Silvers, Stephen M. **Listen and Perform: Audio Cassette** ©1985	____	12.95 ____
Silvers, Stephen M. **The Command Book** ©1988 (300 pages)	____	14.95 ____
USA Knowledge Game **(All About Us)**	____	25.00 ____
Woodruff, Margaret **Comprehension-Based Language Lessons; Level I** ©1986 (Prize-winning TPR Lessons)	____	9.95 ____

To: Sky Oaks Productions, Inc., P.O. Box 1102, Los Gatos, CA 95031

Please send to: Name _____

MY CHECK (OR PURCHASE ORDER) IS ENCLOSED

School _____
Address _____

City _____ State _____ Zip _____

VISA® MasterCard Visa/MC Card No. _____

Expiration Date _____ Authorized Signature _____

294

TPR TRAINING MATERIALS

Asher, James J. **TPR Student Kits**™: Quantity Cost
Please specify which language you prefer English Spanish French

Item	English	Spanish	French	Quantity	Cost
The Farm ©	☐	☐	☐	____	$5.50 ea. ____
The Harbor ©	☐	☐	☐	____	5.50 ea. ____
The Fire Station ©	☐	☐	☐	____	5.50 ea. ____
The Ski Resort ©	☐	☐	☐	____	5.50 ea. ____
The Hospital ©	☐	☐	☐	____	8.50 ea. ____
The Playground ©	☐	☐	☐	____	8.50 ea. ____
European Map ©	☐	☐	☐	____	8.50 ea. ____
United States Map ©	☐	☐	☐	____	8.50 ea. ____
The Sky Oaks Restaurant ©	☐	☐	☐	____	10.00 ea. ____
4 Kits in 1: Community, School, Work, Leisure ©	☐	☐	☐	____	21.00 ea. ____
The Gas Station ©	☐	☐	☐	____	6.50 ea. ____
The Home ©	☐	☐	☐	____	6.50 ea. ____
The Kitchen ©	☐	☐	☐	____	6.50 ea. ____
The Town ©	☐	☐	☐	____	6.50 ea. ____
The Airport ©	☐	☐	☐	____	6.50 ea. ____
The Department Store ©	☐	☐	☐	____	8.50 ea. ____
The Classroom ©	☐	☐	☐	____	8.50 ea. ____
The Supermarket ©	☐	☐	☐	____	8.50 ea. ____
The Beach ©	☐	☐	☐	____	8.50 ea. ____
The Picnic © .... NEW	☐	☐	☐	____	8.50 ea. ____
Mainstreet © .... NEW	☐	☐	☐	____	8.50 ea. ____
Country Garden © ...... NEW	☐	☐	☐	____	8.50 ea. ____
The Clock ©				____	14.50 ea. ____
The Calendar ©				____	14.50 ea. ____
The Alphabet ©				____	14.50 ea. ____

Asher, James J. **TPR Teacher Kits**™
(Includes transparencies for overhead projector).

Item				Quantity	Cost
The Home ©	☐	☐	☐	____	10.50 ea. ____
The Kitchen ©	☐	☐	☐	____	10.50 ea. ____
The Town ©	☐	☐	☐	____	10.50 ea. ____
The Airport ©	☐	☐	☐	____	10.50 ea. ____

Subtotal ____

LARGE QUANTITY DISCOUNTS
TPR BOOKS AND/OR KITS IN ANY ASSORTMENT
25 TO 49 5% ● 50 to 99 10% ● 100 or more 15%
ITEMS   ITEMS   ITEMS

Less **Large Quantity** Discount ____

Total ____

Winitz, Harris. **The Learnables: Self-Instructional Programs in English, French, German, Spanish, Russian, or Chinese (Mandarin).** (For beginning and intermediate groups.) (booklets and cassettes)
Lessons 1-40 **(Please specify which language)** .... ____ 148.00 ____
Lessons 41-80 **(English Only)** .... ____ 144.00 ____
Winitz, Harris. **Language Through Pictures** .... ____ 39.00

☐ USA: Add 5% for postage and handling. **(Gratis if prepaid)** .... ____
    California residents add sales tax. ....

☐ Outside the USA, for postage, insurance, and handling,
    add 10% for surface mail OR 40% for air mail ....
Prices subject to change without notice.   (U.S. Currency) **TOTAL** ____
Sky Oaks Productions, Inc. • P.O. Box 1102 • Los Gatos, CA 95031 • (408) 395-7600

TPR TEACHER KITS™

For any size class but especially **large** groups, use the **transparencies** in the **TPR Teacher Kits*** to flash the playboards on a large screen. Students listen to you utter a direction in the target language, **watch** you perform the action on the large screen, and then follow by performing the same action in their **TPR Student Kits.**

*****TPR Teacher Kits** are available only for the **Home, Kitchen, Town** and **Airport** (See the **TPR Order Form** on page 295).

DOCUMENTARY FILMS OF TPR INSTRUCTION

Sky Oaks Productions, Inc.
19544 Sky Oaks Way
Los Gatos, California 95030
(408) 395-7600

SERVICE POLICIES

Purchase

All 16 mm films in this brochure may be purchased for noncommercial in-house use only, and may not be copied, recast, transformed or adapted in any manner, in whole or part, or transmitted by television or other devices or processes without written consent of Sky Oaks Productions.

Rentals

To insure that a film will be available when you want to show it, please **place your order** at least **four weeks prior to show date.** To avoid late charges, films must be returned by **UPS** or **insured mail** not later than the next working day following the showing.

If you decide to buy a print, the cost of the first rental fee will be deducted from the sale price.

Prices quoted in this brochure are subject to change without notice.

> **A SPECIAL NOTE —**
> If you have developed new lessons, games or innovations using TPR training, please let us know. We are interested in publishing materials in any language and for any age group including adults. We are in touch with 60,000 language instructors who want additional TPR materials.

A **free catalog** of **TPR books** and **TPR Student Kits** will be sent upon request.

CHILDREN LEARNING ANOTHER LANGUAGE: AN INNOVATIVE APPROACH

Written, Directed and Produced by

James J. Asher

16mm • color • 26 minutes
• narrated in English

If you are searching for ways that motivate children to learn another language, don't miss this film. The **TPR ideas** you will see can be applied in your classroom for any **grade level** and for **any language** including **English as a second language**.

This film shows **children** from **kindergarten** through the **6th grade**
- enjoying immediate understanding of everything the instructor is saying in **Spanish** or **French**.
- **keenly motivated** day after day.
- spontaneously making the transition from **understanding to speaking**.
- assimilating the target language in **chunks** rather than word by word.

The keen motivation and genuine achievement of these children will inspire teachers at all levels. You'll want to see this film two or three times to pick up the subtle details.

> The astonishing results you will see have been documented in this research article: Asher, J.J. "Children Learning Another Language: A Developmental Hypothesis," 1977, **Child Development, 48, 1040-1048**. A **complimentary copy** of the research article will be sent upon request.

Purchase $599
Rental $49 for first day and $10 each additional day
Copyright© 1977
Prices in U.S. Currency—subject to change without notice.

A MOTIVATIONAL STRATEGY FOR LANGUAGE LEARNING

Written, Directed and Produced by
James J. Asher

16mm • color • 25 minutes • narrated in English

How can students be motivated to continue in a language program year after year?

In this film you will see the excitement as **college students** understand everything the instructor is saying in Spanish. The technique is to direct the students through commands, which is the essence of **TPR** training. As you watch, notice the rich grammatical structure which can be communicated through the imperative.

After several weeks in which the **students are silent,** but **responding rapidly to commands** in Spanish, there comes a time when the students are spontaneously **ready to talk.** You will see this interesting transition from **understanding to speaking.**

Next, you will see the **transfer-of-learning** to **reading** and **writing.** Once students could understand everything the instructor was saying in Spanish, **they could immediately read.**

Finally, you will **witness the creativity of students** as they invent and act out skits. All the student skits are superb, but the Santa Claus scene may be a classic in the genre of student inventions.

Everything you will see was filmed in the first year of an experimental **TPR** course, and carefully documented in this article published in **The Modern Language Journal:** Asher, J.J. Kusudo, J.A. and de la Torre, R. "Learning a Second Language Through Commands: The Second Field Test," 1974 (Jan.-Feb.), 58, (1-2), 24-32. **A complimentary copy** of the research article will be sent on request.

Purchase $599
Rental $49 for first day and $10 each additional day
Copyright© 1975

Prices in U.S. Currency—subject to change without notice.

STRATEGY FOR SECOND LANGUAGE LEARNING

Written, Directed and Produced by
James J. Asher

16mm • color • 19 min.
• narrated in English

Students can enjoy the thrill of achieving basic fluency in another language if they remain in a program long enough. The problem is that most students "give up" too soon.

This film presents one solution based on a **TPR** model of infants acquiring their first language. You will see **adults of all ages** from 17 to 60 **understanding German** when the instructor directs their behavior by uttering commands. You will be surprised at the **complexity** of **grammatical structure** that can be nested in the imperative.

Even when the class meets **only two nights a week** and **no homework is required**, the retention of spoken German is impressive. Then, after a few weeks in which the students **silently act out** directions in German, there is a **readiness to talk**. At this point, you will see **"role reversal"** in which the students enthusiastically utter directions in German to move the instructor about the room.

You will see the graceful transition from **understanding** to **reading and writing**. And, you will enjoy the creativity shown by students as they invent and act out problems.

Finally, with **time lapse photography**, you will see in **60 seconds**, one student's progress through the entire course from **zero understanding of German to conversational skill**.

This film has been used at the University of Texas at Austin to orient and **motivate hundreds of students** who enrolled in language programs.

Full documentation for what you will see in the film may be found in an article published in **The Modern Language Journal.** Asher, J.J. "Children's First Language as a Model for Second Language Learning," 1972, 56, (3), 133-139. A **complimentary copy** of the research article will be sent on request.

Purchase $450   Copyright © 1973
Rental $39 for first day and $10 each additional day
Prices in U.S. Currency — Subject to change without notice.

DEMONSTRATION OF A NEW STRATEGY IN LANGUAGE LEARNING

Written, Directed and Produced by
James J. Asher

16mm • B&W • 15 min.
• narrated in English

You will see the first demonstration of the **Total Physical Response** ever recorded on film when American children **rapidly internalize** a **complex sample of Japanese**. Step-by-step you will also see the **astonishing retention one year** after the experiment.

This classic film has been seen by thousands of language teachers, linguists, and psychologists in the U.S.A. and other countries.

As a follow-up to the experience you will see in the film, we will send, upon request, these research articles:

> Kunihira, S., and Asher, J.J. "The Strategy of the Total Physical Response: An Application to Learning Japanese." **International Review of Applied Linguistics,** 1965, 3, 277-289.
> Asher, J.J., "The Total Physical Response Technique of Learning." **The Journal of Special Education,** 1969, 3 (3), 253-262.

Purchase $350

Rental $35 for the first day and $10 each additional day

Copyright© 1964

Prices in U.S. Currency — subject to change without notice.

'TAN — GAU'
A COMPREHENSION APPROACH TO SECOND LANGUAGE LEARNING

16 mm • B&W • 30 Minutes
• Narrated in English

Dear Colleague:

In this **rare film footage** produced by the Canadian Broadcasting System you'll see the only demonstration of the **Tan Gau** method ever captured in a motion picture.

As you watch, notice that the instructor speaks to the children in French, but the children respond in their native language of English. Gradually, according to the **Tan Gau** theory, as understanding of French expands and expands, the students will **spontaneously begin** to **respond** in **French**.

This is "Must" viewing for those interested in different methods of comprehension instruction.

Sincerely,

James J. Asher

Rental — $49.00 for first day and $10 for each additional day.
Copyright© 1964
Prices in U.S. Currency — subject to change without notice.

WHERE THE ASHER TPR LANGUAGE

Abernathy Public Schools (Texas)
Acadia University (Nova Scotia)
Adult Education Center, Fort Smith, Ark.
Allan Hancock College
Alemany Community College Education Center (California)
Alief Independent School Dist. (Texas)
Alhambra City Schools (Calif.)
Andrews University
Arizona State University
Arlington Indep. School Dist. (Texas)
Atwater School Dist. (Calif.)
Augusta Public Schools, (Arkansas)
Baldwin Park Unified School Dist. (Calif.)
Ball State University
Baylor University
Beaver College
Bellevue Public Schools (Washington)
Bell Telephone Company (San Francisco)
Berkeley Adult School (Calif.)
Bilingual Educ. Center (Bethel, Alaska)
Bilingual Educ.Center (Salem, Oregon)
Bilingual Program (Downey, Calif.)
Boston University
Boston State College
Brea-Orlinda H.S. (Brea,Calif.)
Bridgewater State College
Brigham Young University (Hawaii)
Brigham Young University (Salt Lake City)
Cabrillo College
California Polytechnic State University
California State University, Chico
California State Dept. of Education
California State Unviersity, Fullerton
California State Univ.,Long Beach
California State University, Northridge
California State University, Sacramento
California State University, San Diego
California State University, Sonoma
Calvin College
Cambridge University, (England)
Canada College
Capitol Elem. School (Texas)
Cassiar Sch. Dist. (Cassiar, B.C.)
Central Intelligence Agency (Washington D. C.)
Central Michigan University
Chinatown Resources Development Center (San Francisco)
Cinnaminson High School (New Jersey)
Cincinnati Public Schools
Claremont Unified School Dist.
Cloverland School (Oakdale, Calif.)
Coast Comm. College Dist. (Calif.)
Commission Scolaire Baldwin-Cartier (Quebec)
Colegio Universitario del Turabo (Puerto Rico)
College of the Desert (Calif.)
College of Notre Dame
Colorado Women's College
Commission Scolaire de Varennes (Quebec)
Connecticut Adult Basic Ed.
Corona Norco Unified School District (California)
Corona Senior High School (Calif.)
CREE School Board (Quebec, Canada)
Dale Avenue School (New Jersey)
Downey Unified School District
Dissemination and Assessment Center For Bilingual Educ. (Austin ,Texas)
Earlham College
East Texas State University
Eckherd College Education Service Center Region 19 (Texas)
Education Service Center Region 16 (Texas)
Education Service Center Region 20 (Texas)

El Monte School Dist. (Calif.)
Emory University
Empire Elementary School (Calif.)
Escondido Elem. School (Calif.)
Family Tutorial Center (Calif.)
Foothill College
Fort Worth Independent School Dist. (Texas)
Fremont Unified School Dist. (Calif.)
Fresno County Supt. of Schools (Calif.)
Fresno Unified School Dist. (Calif.)
Fullerton Elementary School Dist. (Calif.)
Garden Grove Unified School Dist. (Calif.)
General Education Media Corp. (Osaka, Japan)
George Peabody College for Teachers
Georgetown University
Glendale Unified Sch. Dist. (Calif.)
Goethe Institute (San Francisco)
Goshen College (Indiana)
Greater Washington Association of Teachers of Foreign Languages
Great Lakes College Association (Indiana)
Hanford Staff Development Ctr. (Calif.)
Hartford Public Schools (Conn.)
Hickman High School (Missouri)
Highline High School (Washington)
Hilmar School Dist. (Calif.)
Hollister School District (Calif.)
Houston Baptist University
Houston Independent School District (Texas)
Hunter College
Illinois Dept. Correction (Joliet)
Inglewood Unified School Dist. (Calif.)
International Institute (Akron, Ohio)
Irving Unified School Dist. (Calif.)
Irving Public Schools (Texas)
Jesuit High School (Texas)
Jewish Community Center (Detroit)
Kings County Superintendent of Schools (Hanford, Calif.)
La Commission Scolaire de L'Asbestrie (Quebec)
Lennox School District (California)
Lindsay Staff Development Center (Calif.)
Los Angeles County Supt. of Schools
Lousiana Tech
Lucia Mar School Dist. (Calif.)
Mariano Castro School, Mt. View, (Calif.)
McCutcheon High School (Indiana)
McGill University (Canada)
Meadowbrook School (Illinois)
Metropolitan Adult Education (Calif.)
Metropolitan Public School (Tennessee)
Metropolitan State College
Michigan State University
Michigan Teachers of English to Speakers of Other Languages
Middle Tennessee State University
Middlebury Colleges
Migrant Education, Region III (Calif.)
Missouri State Department of Adult Education
Montebellow Union School Dist. (Calif.)
Monterey County Superintendent of Schools (Calif.)
Moorhead State University
Moorpark Union School District (Calif.)
Mount Holyoke College
Mount Wachusett Community College (Mass.)
Milwaukee Public Schools (Wisconsin)
Mt. Hood State University
Nashoba Regional School Dist. (Mass.)
Nellie Muir Elementary School (Oregon)
New City School (Missouri)
New Mexico State University
New York City, Board of Education

FILMS HAVE BEEN SHOWN

New York State Association of Foreign Language Teachers
New York University
North Carolina State University
Northern Nevada Community College
Northside Independent School Dist. (Texas)
Northwest Regional Education Laboratory
Northwood Community School (Calif.)
North York Board of Education (Ontario, Canada)
Oak Grove School District (Calif.)
Oakland Public Schools (Calif.)
Oakton Community College (Illionis)
Ocean View School Dist. (Huntington Beach, Calif.)
Office of Naval Research
Office of Santa Clara County Superintendent of Schools (Calif.)
Oglethorpe University
Ohio University
Ohio Wesleyan University
Old Dominion University
Ontario-Montclair School Dist. (Calif.)
Orange Unified Schools (Calif.)
Otterbein College
Palomar Community College (San Marcos, Calif.)
Parkway School System (Missouri)
Pennsylvania State University
Philadelphia School District (Pennsylvania)
Phoenix Union High School System (Arizona)
Pima College
Plano College (Texas)
Plano Senior High School (Texas)
Point Loma College (Calif.)
Portland Community College (Oregon)
Potrero School (El Monte, Calif.)
Prince George's County Public Schools (Maryland)
Purdue University
Queens College of the City University of New York
Refugee Workshop (Independence, Mo)
Riverside County Supt. of Schools (Calif.)
Rollins College
Roschbach, West Germany
Ruhr-Universitat Bochum, West Germany
Saddleback Comm. College Dist. (Calif.)
St. Cloud State University
St. Michael's College
Sakura no Seibo Junior College (Japan)
Salinas Adult School (California)
Salisbury State College
San Bernardino Bilingual Ed. (Calif.)
San Diego City School (Calif.)
San Diego Community College District
San Francisco Community College District
San Francisco Unified School Dist.
San Jose Area Bilingual Consortium (Calif.)
San Jose State University
San Jose Unified School Dist. (Calif.)
San Leandro Unified School Dist. (Calif.)
San Lorenzo School Dist. (Calif.)
San Mateo Union School Dist. (Calif.)
Santa Ana College
Saratoga School Dist. (Calif.)
School of International Training (Vermont)
Seattle Public Schools (Washington)
Selma Olender Elem. School (Calif.)
Seneca Nation of Indians, Bilingual Program
Southeast Missouri State University
Southern Illinois University
Southwest Texas State University
Southwest Educational Development Lab. (Texas)
Squires Elementary School (Las Vegas, Nevada)
Stanford University
Stanislaus State College
Stratford High School (Connecticut)

Temple University
Tennessee Technological University
TESOL Conference (New Oreleans, LA)
Texas City High School (Texas)
Texas Southern University
Texas Tech University
Tippecanoe School Corp. (Indiana)
Trinity University
Tulare County Dept. of Educ.
Tuolumne County Supt. of Schools (Calif.)
Tustin Unified School Dist. (Calif.)
University City Workshop (Missouri)
University of Alberta (Canada)
University of Arizona
University of Arkansas, Fayetteville
University of Arkansas, Little Rock
University of Austin
University of California, Berkeley
University of California, Irvine
University of California, San Diego
U.C.L.A.
University of California, Riverside
University of Central Arkansas
University of Colorado
University of Delaware
University of Detroit
University City School of Continuing Education (Missouri)
University of Hawaii, East-West Center
University Laval (Quebec)
University of Laverne (Calif.)
University of Massachusetts
University of Minnesota
University of Missouri
University of Nebraska
University of New Hampshire
University of Northern Colorado
University of Pennsylvania
University of Rochester
University of Rhode Island
University of San Diego
University of Tennessee, Knoxville
University of Tennessee, Martin
University of Texas, Arlington
University of Texas, Austin
University of Texas, El Paso
University of Texas, San Antonio
University of Vermont
University of Washington
University of Wisconsin
Vancouver Community College (British Columbia)
Ventura College
Ventura County Supt. of Schools (Calif.)
Virginia State Dept. of Education
Visalia Unified School District (Calif.)
Washington University, Saint Louis
Waukesha County Technical Inst. (Wisconsin)
Webster College, (Missouri)
West Chester State College
West Hartford Public Schools (Conn.)
Western Amids (Oregon)
Western Psychological Association
Western Washington State College
West Junior High School (Missouri)
Westminister Elementary School (Calif.)
West Texas Education Center
West Valley College (California)
Whisman School District (California)
Whittier School Dist. (Calif.)
Wichita State University
Wilbur Wright College
And many more places

ORDER FORM
DOCUMENTARY FILMS of TPR INSTRUCTION

(All 16mm, written, directed and produced by **James J. Asher** and narrated in English)

Children Learning Another Language: An Innovative Approach.©
Color, 26 minutes, shows children from K through 6th grades acquiring **Spanish** and **French**.
Rental $49 for first day and $10 for each additional day. (Purchase $599, U.S. Currency).
Preferred showing dates: 1st _____ 2nd _____

A Motivational Strategy for Language Learning.©
Color, 25 minutes, shows students from 17 to 60 acquiring Spanish.
Rental $49 for first day and $10 for each additional day. (Purchase $599, U.S. Currency).
Preferred showing dates: 1st _____ 2nd _____

Strategy for Second Language Learning.©
Color, 19 minutes, shows students from 17 to 60 acquiring German.
Rental $39 for first day and $10 for each additional day. (Purchase $450, U.S. Currency).
Preferred showing dates: 1st _____ 2nd _____

Demonstration of a New Strategy in Language Learning.©
B&W, 15 minutes, shows American children acquiring Japanese.
Rental $35 for first day and $10 for each additional day. (Purchase $350, U.S. Currency).
Preferred showing dates: 1st _____ 2nd _____

Tan — Gau. A Comprehension approach to second language learning.©
B&W, 30 minutes, shows children acquiring French with the Tan — Gau technique of comprehension training.
Rental $49 for first day and $10 for each additional day.
Preferred showing dates: 1st _____ 2nd _____

* * * NOTE * * *
As a follow-up to each film, **complimentary updated information** is available for distribution to each person in the audience.
Please send **updated information** for _____ people.

To: **Sky Oaks Productions, Inc., P. O. Box 1102, Los Gatos, California 95031**

Please send to: **Name** _____

MY CHECK (OR PURCHASE ORDER) IS ENCLOSED

School _____
Address _____

VISA® MasterCard

City _____ State _____ Zip _____
Visa/MC Card No. _____
Expiration Date _____ **Authorized Signature** _____

Dr. James J. Asher, creator of the unusually successful **Total Physical Response** approach to acquiring another language without stress, has just completed the book, **Brainswitching**.

Brainswitching is a brand-new skill for moving from one side of the brain to the other to **accelerate** the **mastery** of "**difficult**" **subjects** such as **foreign languages, mathematics,** and **science.** Also, Dr. Asher illustrates how **brainswitching** works in a fascinating range of phenomena including **illusions, hypnosis, work, play,** the **selection interview, counseling,** and **problem solving.**

> **BRAINSWITCHING**
> A NEW BOOK BY
> **DR. JAMES J. ASHER**
>
> PUBLISHED BY
> SKY OAKS PRODUCTIONS, INC.
> P.O. BOX 1102
> LOS GATOS, CA 95031

As we understand how **brainswitching** works, we can direct the flow of messages from one side of the brain to the other which opens up the potential for **acquiring complex skills** on the **first exposure to information** — a vital breakthrough for solving intricate problems coming at us in the 21st century.

The present slow-motion procedure for learning any skill — especially complex skills, is tolerable in the 20th century, but will be a museum-curiosity in the 21st century where large quantities of information must be assimilated in "gulps on the very first swallow."

Brainswitching expands human potential to **prepare instructors at all levels to work successfully** in the **super-schools** of the **21st century** where excellence is achievable by students who are perceived as average in today's educational institutions. The exciting ideas in Asher's book can be **applied now** to **stretch the limits** of **all children** and **adults.**

To order **Brainswitching,** see the **TPR Order Form** on page A-64

BEST-SELLER!

For 20 years, Ramiro Garcia has successfully applied the **Total Physical Response** in his high school and adult language classes.

Four **NEW** chapters in the Triple-Expanded Second Edition (288 pages):

- **Speaking, Reading, and Writing**

- **How To Create Your Own TPR Lessons.**

More than **200 TPR scenarios** for **beginning** and **advanced students.**

- **TPR Games** for **all age groups**

- **TPR Testing** for **all skills** including **oral proficiency.**

In this illustrated book, Ramiro shares the tips and tricks that he has discovered in using TPR with hundreds of students. No matter what language you teach, including **ESL** and the **sign language of the deaf,** you will enjoy this insightful and humorous book.

To order **Instructor's Notebook,** see the **TPR Order Form** on page 294.

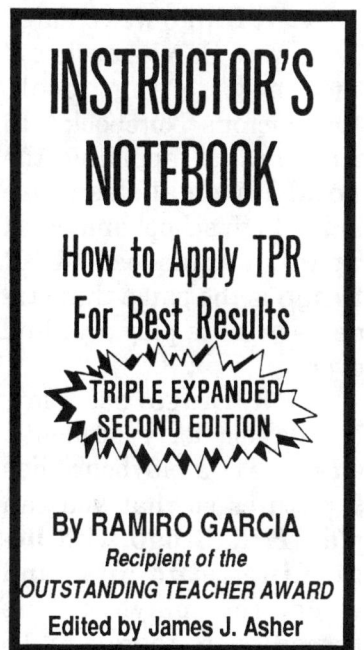

INSTRUCTOR'S NOTEBOOK

How to Apply TPR For Best Results

TRIPLE EXPANDED SECOND EDITION

By RAMIRO GARCIA
Recipient of the OUTSTANDING TEACHER AWARD
Edited by James J. Asher

TPR Bingo was created by Ramiro Garcia, author of the best-selling book, "Instructor's Notebook." In 20 years of applying the **Total Physical Response** in his high school and adult Spanish classes, **TPR Bingo** is the game that students want to play over and over.

TPR Bingo has playboards for forty students. One side of a playboard has 9 pictures so that you can play **TPR Bingo** with **beginning students** and when the playboard is turned over, there are 16 pictures for bingo with **advanced students.**

TPR BINGO©

SKY OAKS PRODUCTIONS, INC.
P.O. BOX 1102
LOS GATOS, CA 95031

Here's how **TPR Bingo** works: **You call out a direction in the target language** such as "The man turns off the light." Students listen to the utterance, search for a matching picture and if it is on their playboard, cover it with a chip. You may order the game in **English, Spanish, French or German.**

When students listen to the instructor utter directions in the target language they are **internalizing comprehension.** But, as they advance in understanding, individual students will ask to play the role of the caller which gives students valuable practice in **reading and speaking.** Incidentally, as students play **TPR Bingo,** they **internalize numbers** in the target language from 1 through 100.

TPR Bingo comes with complete **step-by-step directions for playing** the game, **rules for winning, 40 playboards** (one side for **beginners** and the reverse side for **advanced students**), a **master caller's board** with **100 pictures, chips,** and **caller-cards** in your choice of **English, Spanish, French** or **German.** As Ramiro says, "Try this game with your students. You will love it!"

To order **TPR Bingo,** see the **TPR Order Form** on page 294.

NEW TPR GAME

- (J) Who was the blind, deaf, and mute student who became a noted author and lecturer?
- (S) On whose gravestone would you find the words, "Free at last"?
- (E) Who was the first black U.S. Supreme Court Justice?

All About US is an exciting way for **all students** to learn more about the **history, geography** and **social studies** of the United States.

All About US may be played by **two or more players or teams.** Each team rolls a **color-coded die** that indicates which of five categories (**States, Cities, People, Events,** or **Potpourri**) a question will be asked.

The **questions** on each of **1,000 cards** are graded for **Junior, Senior,** or **Expert level. 50 score sheets** and **rules for winning** are also included with each game.

To order **All About US,** see the **TPR Order Form** on page 294.

NEW!

This exciting 200 plus page **TPR Student Workbook** in English has

- TPR exercises that students can perform **alone at their desks** or **at home**,
- TPR exercises in **reading** and **writing**,
- TPR exercises in **speaking** and in **pronunciation**,
- TPR exercises in **asking** and **answering** questions.

LISTEN AND PERFORM

THE TPR STUDENT WORKBOOK

By
STEPHEN MARK SILVERS
Edited by James J. Asher

Also, students expand their **comprehension of English** with "quiet" commands that can be performed individually or in pairs at their seats with stimulative right brain input such as

- drawing
- coloring
- touching
- pointing, and
- manipulating objects.

The TPR Student Workbook can be adapted for children or adults learning any language.

The **TPR Student Workbook** is ideal for **multi-level classes** and as a **self-study book** for students who have some skill in English but don't have time to study in a formal language class.

To: **Sky Oaks Productions, Inc., P.O. Box 1102, Los Gatos, CA 95031**

Please send me ____ copies of **Listen and Perform: TPR Student Workbook.**
($12.95 each)

Please send me ____ copies of **Listen and Perform: TPR Teacher's Guidebook.**
($4.95 each)

Please send me ____ copies of **Listen and Perform: Audio Cassette.**
($12.95 each)

☐ **USA:** If prepaid, no additional cost for postage and handling. (Calif. residents please add sales tax).

☐ **Outside the USA,** for postage, insurance, and handling, **add 10%** for surface mail **OR 40% for air mail** (U.S. Currency).

To order **Listen and Perform** materials, see the **TPR Order Form** on page 294.

BEST-SELLER

The expanded **third edition of James J. Asher's** book is now off the press with these features:

- **Easy to understand** summary of 20 years of research with his **Total Physical Response** approach to language acquisition.

- **Demonstrates** step-by-step **how to apply TPR** to help children and adults acquire another language **without stress.**

- **Explains why TPR** works.

LEARNING ANOTHER LANGUAGE THROUGH ACTIONS: THE COMPLETE TEACHER'S GUIDEBOOK

James J. Asher, Ph.D.

Originator of the stress-free Total Physical Response (TPR) Approach

Published by
Sky Oaks Productions, Inc.
P.O. Box 1102
Los Gatos, CA 95031

- More than **150 hours** of **classroom-tested TPR lessons** that **can be adapted to teaching any language** including Arabic, English, French, German, Hebrew, Japanese, Russian, Spanish, and the Sign Language of the Deaf.

- **Answers 175** of the **most often asked questions** about **TPR.**

- **New chapter** — "TPR: A personal story" is a behind-the-scenes story of how **TPR** was developed.

To order **Learning Another Language Through Actions: The Complete Teacher's Guidebook,** see the **TPR Order Form** on page 294.

For a FREE CATALOG
OF
TOTAL PHYSICAL RESPONSE

Books • Student • Kits • Films
WRITE OR CALL

SKY OAKS PRODUCTIONS, INC.
P.O. BOX 1102
LOS GATOS, CALIFORNIA 95031

PHONE (408) 395-7600

**ALSO SEE THE TPR ORDER FORM
ON PAGES 294, 295, and 305**